ideals
Treasury of Country Cooking

We've combined three of our best-selling cookbooks, featuring kitchen-tested recipes for hearty, home-style dishes sure to become family favorites.

Book I   Country Kitchen Cookbook
                  by Darlene Kronschnabel

Book II   From Mama's Kitchen Cookbook
                  by Catharine P. Smith

Book III   Farmhouse Cookbook
                  by Clarice L. Moon

Bonanza Books
New York, N.Y.

CONTENTS

Book I Country Kitchen Cookbook

Book II From Mama's Kitchen Cookbook

Book III Farmhouse Cookbook

ISBN: 0-517-332485
COUNTRY KITCHEN COOKBOOK
Copyright © MCMLXXV BY IDEALS PUBLISHING CORPORATION
FROM MAMA'S KITCHEN
Copyright © MCMLXXVI BY CATHARINE P. SMITH
FARMHOUSE COOKBOOK
Copyright © MCMLXXVIII BY IDEALS PUBLISHING CORPORATION
ALL RIGHTS RESERVED.

THIS EDITION IS PUBLISHED BY BONANZA BOOKS,
A DIVISION OF CROWN PUBLISHERS, INC.,
BY ARRANGEMENT WITH IDEALS PUBLISHING CORPORATION.
a b c d e f g h
BONANZA 1980 EDITION
MANUFACTURED IN THE UNITED STATES OF AMERICA

Book I
Country Kitchen
COOKBOOK

by Darlene Kronschnabel

BREADS

> Corn bread is as popular in country kitchens as apple pie. And it is a native American dish. Bread made from Indian corn helped the colonists survive the critical winters in their new land.
>
> Corn bread, as popular as ever, goes by many different names. In some areas it is called hoecake, ashcake, johnnycake, or journeycake.

GRANNY'S APPLE CORN BREAD

2 c. yellow cornmeal	2 T. butter, melted
¼ c. sugar	2 eggs, beaten
1½ t. salt	1 t. soda
2 c. sour milk	1 T. cold water
⅞ c. raw chopped apple	

In the top of a double boiler, mix the cornmeal, sugar, salt, milk and butter. Set over hot water and cook about 10 minutes. Cool, and add eggs, soda dissolved in water, and apples. Bake in greased 8 x 8 x 2-inch pan at 400° about 25 minutes or until done. Makes 8 large squares.

PINEAPPLE CORN BREAD

2 c. flour	1 egg, slightly beaten
5 t. baking powder	1 c. milk
¼ t. baking soda	¾ c. crushed pineapple, well-drained
1½ t. salt	
½ c. sugar	
1 c. yellow cornmeal	¼ c. butter, melted

Sift flour, baking powder, soda, salt and sugar; sift again and add cornmeal; mix thoroughly. Combine egg, milk, crushed pineapple and melted butter (slightly cooled); pour into flour mixture and stir just enough to moisten the dry ingredients. Do not beat. Turn into a greased square pan (8 x 8 x 2 inches) and bake in a 350° oven about 50 minutes. Cut into squares and serve hot.

CORNMEAL SPOON BREAD

¾ c. yellow cornmeal	
1 T. sugar	
½ t. salt	
2 c. milk	
¼ c. butter	
4 eggs, separated	

Preheat oven to 375°. Lightly grease a 1½ quart casserole. Mix cornmeal, sugar and salt in three-quart saucepan. Add milk and butter and heat mixture to boiling point. Stir constantly until thickened. Remove from heat. Beat egg yolks in small bowl. Gradually stir about ⅓ cup of hot cornmeal mixture into yolks, a tablespoon at a time. Stir egg yolk mixture into remaining cornmeal mixture; mix thoroughly. Cool to lukewarm. Beat egg whites in large bowl with clean eggbeater until stiff peaks form; gradually fold in cornmeal mixture. Pour into prepared casserole. Bake 40 minutes. Serve immediately. Makes 6 to 8 servings.

SWEET CORN BREAD

1 c. coarsely ground cornmeal	1½ c. sugar
	4 large eggs, separated
2 c. white flour	1 c. rich milk or half-and-half
1 T. baking powder	1 t. vanilla extract
½ t. salt	
¾ c. butter, melted	

Combine the cornmeal, flour, baking powder, salt and sugar. Combine the egg yolks, milk, vanilla and melted butter. Stir into the dry ingredients until they are thoroughly moistened. Beat the egg whites until stiff and fold into the batter carefully. Pour into a 3-quart shallow baking pan that has been buttered well. Bake at 350° for 30 minutes, or until it tests done. If desired, 2 8-inch square pans may be used.

Sally Lunn is a delicious old-time bread brought to the American Colonies by early English settlers. Some recipes that have been popular for several hundred years call Sally Lunn a bread, a bun, and even a bread cake.

According to tradition, Sally Lunn originated in Bath, England and was named for a young lady who made it popular. It is said she sold buns on the streets crying, "Solet Lune," to advertise her bread. In time the name became Sally Lunn.

By the time the great English recipe reached America, the popular English buns became a bread baked in a Turk's head mold. Another Americanization of the recipe turned Sally Lunn into a sweet bread cake using cornmeal–delicious with fresh fruits and whipped cream.

SALLY LUNN
(Baking Powder)

2¼ c. flour
1 t. salt
2 T. sugar
4 t. baking powder
⅓ c. butter
3 eggs, separated
1 c. milk

Sift the dry ingredients three times. Cut the butter into the dry ingredients as for pastry. Beat the egg yolks thoroughly and add the milk. Stir into the dry ingredients. Beat egg whites until stiff and fold into mixture. Pour batter into buttered muffin tins. Bake at 400° for 30 minutes or until done.

CORN SALLY LUNN

1 c. yellow cornmeal
2 c. white flour
1 T. baking powder
1 t. salt
¾ c. butter, melted
1¼ c. sugar
4 eggs, separated
1 c. top milk or half-and-half
1 t. vanilla extract

Sift together the cornmeal, flour, baking powder, sugar and salt. Blend the egg yolks, milk, vanilla and melted butter. Stir this mixture into the dry ingredients until they are well mixed. Beat the egg whites until stiff and fold carefully into the batter. Pour into a well-buttered, shallow, 3-quart pan. Bake at 350° for 30 minutes or until the cake tests done. Serve warm with fresh fruit and whipped cream.

CORN STICKS

1 c. flour
1 c. cornmeal
½ t. baking soda
1 t. salt
1 egg, beaten
1 c. sour milk or buttermilk
1 T. butter, melted

Mix and sift flour, cornmeal, soda and salt. Combine egg and milk. Add to flour mixture, stirring until well mixed. Stir in butter. Turn into greased breadstick pans and bake in 425° oven 15 to 20 minutes. Makes 12 corn sticks. To use sweet instead of sour milk, substitute 3 teaspoons baking powder for soda. For corn bread, bake in greased, shallow pan in 400° oven about 30 minutes.

SALLY LUNN
(Yeast)

⅓ c. sugar
½ c. butter
2 t. salt
1 c. rich milk, scalded and cooled
1½ pkgs. active dry yeast
¼ c. lukewarm water
3 medium eggs, beaten
4 c. flour

Cream the butter, sugar and salt. Add the cooled milk. Dissolve the yeast in the water and add to the creamed mixture along with the beaten eggs. Add the flour a little at a time, beating well after each addition. Cover and let rise until doubled. Then punch down and pour into a well-greased bundt, loaf or 10-inch angel food cake pan. Cover and let rise again. Bake in a 350° oven for about 40 minutes or until the bread is golden brown and tests done.

The traditional American breakfast of steaming pancakes with melted butter, dripping with maple syrup is a country kitchen favorite, but did not originate in this country.

Settlers brought the unique but widely popular bread to the New World. These tasty pancakes are known across the country as hot cakes, griddle cakes and flapjacks, and as flannel cakes in logging camps.

Pancakes are popular in most parts of the world where grain is a major crop. No one knows who invented pancakes. They predate leavened bread and no doubt are evidence of early man's mixing of pounded grain and water. The combination was not fried but spread on a flat rock in the hot sun to dry.

Pancakes became so popular that they even have a special day set aside for them. "Shrove Tuesday," the day before the start of Lent, is traditionally a day to serve pancakes. It was the day to use up all the milk, eggs and fat, which were not allowed during the strict days of Lent.

The pancake is still at home at all meals, from country kitchens to elegant dining rooms.

TASTY MAPLE SAUCE

2 T. cornstarch
¼ t. salt
2 c. maple blended syrup
4 T. butter

Combine all ingredients in a 1 quart saucepan. Bring to boil over medium heat. Simmer 3 minutes, stirring constantly. Serve hot over buckwheat pancakes. Makes 2 cups.

BUTTERMILK PANCAKES

2 eggs, beaten	2 t. baking powder
2½ c. buttermilk	1 t. salt
2½ c. flour	2 T. sugar
1 t. baking soda	¼ c. butter, melted

Combine well-beaten eggs and buttermilk in large bowl. Sift together flour, baking soda, baking powder, salt and sugar. Stir into egg mixture. Blend until smooth. Add melted butter. Drop by ladle or tablespoon on hot, lightly greased griddle. Brown on both sides until done. Makes 20 to 24 medium-sized pancakes.

APPLE CORN CAKES

1 egg, slightly beaten	½ t. baking soda
	½ t. salt
2 T. lard, melted	1 T. sugar
1 c. buttermilk	1½ c. apples
1 c. cornmeal	peeled, chopped

Stir together liquid ingredients; blend into sifted dry ingredients. Add chopped apples. Bake on pre-heated lightly greased griddle. Makes about 20 2-inch cakes. Serve with cinnamon applesauce.

NORWEGIAN PANCAKES

4 eggs	¼ t. salt
2 c. milk	Butter
1 c. flour	

Beat eggs at high speed, then lower speed and add milk, flour and salt. Beat until smooth. Mixture should be the consistency of thick cream. Heat 2 or 3 heavy iron skillets (No. 8 is an excellent size) and butter them lightly. Pour ¼ cup batter into each, tilting the pans to cover the entire surface. When bubbles form on top, turn quickly and brown the other side. Fold pancakes in half, then in quarters to serve. Serve with jelly or maple syrup.

DESSERT PANCAKES

¼ c. butter, softened	¼ c. flour
¼ c. sugar	½ c. milk
¼ t. salt	¼ t. vanilla
5 medium eggs, separated	Sugar
	Cinnamon

Cream together the butter, sugar and salt; add the egg yolks and beat well. Stir in the flour and then the milk. Beat the egg whites until stiff but not dry, add the vanilla, and fold into the batter. Grease a cast-iron griddle with unsalted butter and pour less than ¼ cup of batter onto it. Do not tip or spread. These pancakes will be 5 or 6 inches across and about ¼ inch thick while baking. Brown lightly on one side only, lift gently onto a flat ovenproof dish and set in a 250° oven. Sprinkle a little sugar and cinnamon on the uncooked surface of each pancake before placing the next one on top of it. Continue until there are 5 layers, then start another stack. Bake for 15 to 20 minutes or until the top is delicately brown. Cut pie-fashion. Serve at once. Makes 6 servings.

Coffee and fresh doughnuts are old-fashioned country kitchen treats, thanks to early Dutch settlers. They brought the "olykoeks" or oily cakes with them to the New World. But it took an ingenious Yankee mother to spread their fame around the world.

One interesting account claims that by 1803, fried pastries were popular in the New England states. About that time a sea captain's mother made up a dough recipe for deep frying that contained nutmeg, cinnamon and lemon rind.

Her idea was to prepare a pastry using lemon that could be taken to sea to help prevent scurvy and colds. The pastries were intended to be eaten by dunking in hot black coffee or tea.

She inserted hazelnuts in the center of the pastries to be sure the centers cooked all the way through and named her invention doughnuts.

It is said her son's ship sailed with 1500 doughnuts. By the time he returned home, doughnuts were popular in all ports of call. The doughnuts' popularity then spread across America.

POTATO DOUGHNUTS

- 1 c. sieved cooked potatoes (warm or cold)
- 1 c. liquid (reserved from cooking potatoes)
- ¾ c. vegetable shortening
- ½ c. sugar
- 1 T. salt
- 1 pkg. active dry yeast
- ¾ c. warm water (105° to 115°)
- 2 eggs, beaten
- 5 to 6 c. flour
- Shortening

Mix potatoes, potato liquid, shortening, sugar and salt. Dissolve yeast in warm water; stir into potato mixture. Stir in eggs and enough flour to make dough easy to handle. Turn dough onto lightly floured surface; knead until smooth and elastic, 5 to 8 minutes. Place in greased bowl; turn greased side up. (Don't punch down.) Cover; let rise until double, 1 to 1½ hours. Pat out dough on lightly-floured surface to ¾-inch thickness. Cut doughnuts with floured 2½-inch cutter. Let rise until double, about 1 hour. Heat 3 to 4 inches of shortening to 375° in heavy pan. Fry doughnuts 2 to 3 minutes on each side, or until golden. Drain on paper toweling. If desired, glaze or roll in sugar. Makes about 3 dozen.

OLD-FASHIONED DOUGHNUTS

- 2¼ c. flour
- ½ t. salt
- 3 t. baking powder
- ½ t. ground cinnamon
- ¼ t. ground nutmeg
- ½ c. sugar
- 1 egg
- ½ c. milk
- 1 t. grated lemon rind
- 2 T. butter, melted
- Shortening or pure vegetable oil
- Confectioners' sugar

Sift together flour, salt, baking powder, spices and sugar. Beat egg; stir in milk, lemon rind and melted butter. Blend into flour mixture, stirring until all flour is moistened. Chill 15 minutes. Roll dough out to ½-inch thickness on well-floured board. Cut with 3-inch floured doughnut cutter, dipping cutter into flour each time it is used. Heat shortening (it should be 1½ to 2 inches deep) in a heavy saucepan or electric skillet to 375° on deep-frying thermometer. Drop doughnuts gently into fat, 3 or 4 at a time. As they rise to surface, turn with fork or slotted spoon to brown other side. It will take about 3 minutes. Lift doughnuts from fat with slotted spoon. Drain well on paper towels. Serve plain or dusted with confectioners' sugar. Makes about 1 dozen.

HOLY POKES

Form bread dough, which has risen once, into balls the size of large marbles. Let rise again until it has doubled in volume. Slip dough balls into a kettle of fat that has been heated to 360° and fry until golden brown. Drain and serve with plenty of butter.

PEACHY PLUM FRITTERS

1½ c. flour
¼ c. sugar
2 t. baking powder
½ t. salt
½ to ¾ c. milk
1 egg, beaten
1 t. vanilla extract
1 c. chopped fresh peaches
½ c. chopped fresh plums
¼ c. chopped nuts
   Lard for deep frying
   Granulated or confectioners' sugar
   (optional)

Stir together dry ingredients. Combine ½ cup milk, egg, vanilla, fruits and nuts; add all at once to flour mixture, stirring until well blended. If necessary, stir in more milk to make a medium-thick batter. Drop by rounded tablespoonfuls into 2 to 3 inches of preheated 375° lard. Fry until golden brown, 3 to 4 minutes, turning once. Drain on absorbent paper. Serve warm coated with granulated or confectioners' sugar, if desired. Makes 18 fritters.

HONEY DOUGHNUTS

1 pkg. active dry yeast
¼ c. warm water (110° - 115°)
9 c. sifted flour
3 c. milk, scalded and cooled to lukewarm
½ c. butter
4 T. honey
2 eggs, beaten
1½ t. salt

Soften yeast in warm water. Let stand 5 to 10 minutes. Add 4 cups flour gradually to the milk, beating until smooth. Stir in the yeast. Cover; let rise in a warm place until doubled. Cream the butter until softened. Blend in the honey. Add the eggs, one at a time, beating well after each addition. Beat this mixture gradually into yeast mixture. Stir in salt and remaining flour. Cover; let rise until doubled. Punch down dough; divide into four portions. On a floured surface, roll out each portion about ½-inch thick. Cut with floured doughnut cutter. Cover; let rise until doubled. Fry in deep fat heated to 370° 3 to 4 minutes, turning doughnuts to brown evenly. Remove from fat; drain on absorbent paper. Makes about 3½ dozen doughnuts.

RAISED DOUGHNUTS

1 c. milk
1 pkg. active dry yeast
¼ c. lukewarm water
1 c. brown sugar, firmly packed
6 c. flour
1 t. salt
1 t. cinnamon or nutmeg
2 eggs, beaten
1 c. softened butter
   Fat for deep frying

Scald milk, then cool to lukewarm. Sprinkle yeast over lukewarm water to dissolve. Sift together sugar, flour, salt and cinnamon or nutmeg. Combine milk and yeast in a large bowl. Work in the flour with your hands (dough will be very heavy). Then stir in beaten eggs. Cover and let rise in a warm place until double in size. Punch down the dough, then work in the butter with your hands until dough is smooth and well blended. Roll about ½-inch thick on a lightly floured board and cut with a doughnut cutter. Place doughnuts on a tray lined with wax paper, cover again and let rise in a warm place until light and puffy. Drop several at a time into deep fat preheated to 375° on a deep fat thermometer or until a 1-inch cube of bread browns in 60 seconds. Fry until nicely browned on both sides. Lift from fat, drain on paper towels, and sprinkle with confectioners' sugar, granulated sugar or a mixture of sugar and cinnamon. Makes about 40.

ORANGE GLAZE

Add 1 teaspoon grated orange peel and 3 tablespoons orange juice or apple cider to 2 cups sifted confectioners' sugar. Glaze doughnuts while they are still warm.

MAPLE GLAZE

Combine 1 pound sifted confectioners' sugar with 6 tablespoons boiling water and ½ teaspoon maple extract to make a thin, smooth glaze. Add a few drops more water if glaze is too thick to coat doughnuts lightly.

Once again, the tantalizing aroma of home-baked breads steaming hot from the oven drifts from the back door of country kitchens. Bread-baking, once almost a lost art, is making a comeback.

Bakers were important tradesmen in Europe during the early American settling. However, villages in the New World were too small and far apart to support community bakers. Each homemaker, out of necessity, developed her baking talents. She used the only material on hand–corn, dried and pounded into coarse meal.

It was to be many years before the colonists tasted breads made from wheat flours. In fact, the development of bread-wheats came slowly and only with the westward migration.

WHITE BREAD

2 c. milk, scalded and cooled to lukewarm
2 c. lukewarm water
2 T. salt
5 T. sugar
5 T. butter, melted and slightly cooled
2 cakes compressed yeast
12 to 12½ c. flour

Put lukewarm liquids into mixing bowl. Crumble yeast into liquids and stir until dissolved. Measure salt and sugar and stir into yeast solution. Let stand 5 minutes. Add butter and stir well. Sift and measure flour. Add 6 cups of flour and beat until smooth. Add most of remaining flour. Stir to mix thoroughly. Turn out onto lightly floured board. Knead lightly, but thoroughly for 10 minutes. Round up dough and place in a large greased bowl and turn once to bring greased side up. Cover with cloth and set in a warm place until double in size. Knead down and let rise until almost double in size. Cut dough into 4 equal portions. Shape into loaves and place in well-greased bread pans. Cover lightly and set in warm place. Allow to rise until sides of dough have reached top of pan and corners are filled. Bake in 400° oven for 10 minutes. Reduce heat to 350° and bake 25 to 30 minutes or until bread is golden brown and sounds hollow when tapped. Turn out of pans and allow to cool before storing. Makes 4 loaves.

CINNAMON BREAD

2 pkgs. active dry yeast	1 t. salt
½ c. warm water	1 egg, slightly beaten
1 c. milk, scalded	5 to 5½ c. flour
½ c. butter	¾ c. wheat germ
⅓ c. honey	

Dissolve yeast in warm water. Let stand. Pour scalded milk over butter. Stir to melt butter. Add honey and salt. Add beaten egg. Mix well. Combine yeast, milk and egg mixtures. Blend well. Add 2½ cups flour and beat until smooth. Add the wheat germ and beat until smooth again. Add additional flour to make a soft dough. Knead gently for a few minutes to make a smooth but soft dough. Cover and let rise until double. Divide in half; roll each half to 7 x 12-inch rectangle. Brush with slightly beaten egg white and sprinkle with mixture of ½ cup sugar, 1 tablespoon cinnamon and ½ cup finely chopped nuts. Roll like jelly roll, put in greased loaf pan 9 x 5 x 3. Bake 35-40 minutes at 375°.

RYE BREAD

1 c. milk	1 T. caraway seeds
2 T. honey	2½ c. unsifted rye flour
1 T. sugar	
1 T. salt	2½ c. unsifted white flour (about)
1 T. butter	
¾ c. warm water	¼ c. cornmeal
1 pkg. active dry yeast	1 egg white
	2 T. water

Scald milk; add honey, sugar, salt and butter. Cool to lukewarm. Measure warm water into large warm bowl. Sprinkle in yeast; stir until dissolved. Add lukewarm milk mixture. Add caraway seeds and rye flour; beat well. Add enough white flour to make a soft dough. Turn dough out onto lightly floured board; knead until smooth and elastic, about 7 minutes. Place in greased bowl, turning to grease top. Cover; let rise in warm place, until doubled in bulk, about 1½ hours. Turn out onto lightly floured board. Divide dough in half; form each piece into a smooth ball. Flatten each piece slightly. Roll lightly on board to form loaves. Sprinkle two greased baking sheets with cornmeal. Place breads on baking sheets. Combine egg white and water; brush breads. Let rise, uncovered, in warm place, for 35 minutes. Bake in 400° oven 25 minutes. Cool on wire racks. Makes 2 loaves.

BUCKWHEAT BREAD

1 pkg. active dry yeast	1 T. salt
	3 T. brown sugar
1 T. brown sugar	3 T. butter
¼ c. lukewarm water	2 c. whole wheat flour
1 c. milk	1½ c. buckwheat flour
¼ c. water	

Dissolve the yeast with 1 tablespoon of sugar in lukewarm water until frothy. Scald the milk and water and add the salt, remaining sugar and butter. Mix the flours in a large mixing bowl. When the milk mixture is lukewarm mix it with the yeast and add to the flour. Beat very hard for 3 minutes with a rubber spatula. A little more warm water or flour may be needed to make a spongy dough that is not too soft. Put the bowl in a dishpan of hot water, cover with a towel and let the dough rise an hour or more until it is light. Beat again 2 or 3 minutes; put the dough in a greased bread pan. Set it in warm water again to rise an hour. Put the pan in a cold oven. Set at 400° and bake 15 minutes; turn heat to 350° and continue baking about 35 minutes more. Makes 1 loaf.

POTATO BREAD

2 c. milk, scalded
3 c. potato water
2 cakes compressed yeast
2 T. butter
4 t. salt
2 T. sugar
12 to 12½ c. flour

Scald milk, stir in butter, salt and sugar. Add potato water. Cool to lukewarm. Crumble in yeast. Stir until dissolved. Add 4 cups flour; beat until smooth. Add enough additional flour to make a soft dough. Turn out onto lightly floured board. Knead until smooth and elastic, about 8-10 minutes. Form into smooth ball. Place in greased bowl, turning to grease top. Cover; let rise in warm place until doubled in bulk, about 1 hour. Punch down. Divide dough in quarters. Shape each into a loaf. Place each loaf in a greased 9 x 5 x 3-inch bread pan. Cover; let rise in warm place, free from draft, until doubled in bulk, about 1 hour. Bake in 400° oven about 30 minutes. Remove from pans and cool.

BROWN BREAD

1½ c. all-purpose flour
1½ c. rye flour
1 c. yellow cornmeal
1 t. baking soda
1 t. salt
½ c. seedless raisins
½ c. walnuts
2 c. buttermilk
½ c. dark molasses
Butter

Mix together flour, rye flour, cornmeal, baking soda and salt. Add raisins and nuts. Slowly add buttermilk and molasses alternately to dry ingredients; beat after each addition. Pour batter into greased 9 x 5 x 3-inch loaf pan. Bake at 375° for 50 minutes or until done. Remove from oven and let stand in pan 5 minutes. Loosen sides with knife and turn out on wire rack. Brush with butter while still warm. Makes 1 loaf.

STEAMED BROWN BREAD

1 c. white flour
1 c. whole wheat flour
1 c. cornmeal
1½ t. salt
½ c. sugar
1 t. baking soda
½ c. molasses
1½ c. buttermilk
2 T. melted shortening

Sift flour, whole wheat flour, cornmeal, salt and sugar together. Mix soda and molasses. Add buttermilk and molasses to the dry mixture. Add shortening. Mix well. Fill a greased 2½-quart pudding mold ¾ full and steam 3 hours. Remove cover from pan and allow to cool 20 minutes. Remove to wire rack and finish cooling.

APPLESAUCE BROWN BREAD

2 c. whole wheat flour
1 c. cornmeal
¾ t. salt
1 t. baking soda
1 c. buttermilk
1 c. dark molasses
¾ c. sweetened applesauce
¾ c. raisins

Combine dry ingredients in large mixing bowl. Add buttermilk and molasses and beat until smooth. Mixture will be thick. Fold in applesauce and raisins. Turn into greased 9-inch square baking pan and bake in 350° oven 35 minutes or until done. Cool 10 minutes in pan, then remove from pan and cool on wire rack. Cut into squares. Makes 16 squares.

APRICOT BRAN BREAD

1 c. finely cut, dried apricots
¾ c. sugar
1½ c. cereal bran
1 c. milk
2 eggs, slightly beaten
⅓ c. vegetable oil
1½ c. flour
3 t. baking powder
1 t. salt
1 T. sugar

Pour enough boiling water over apricots to cover; let stand 10 minutes. Drain well; combine apricots and ¾ cup sugar. Set aside. Measure cereal bran and milk into large mixing bowl; stir until combined. Let stand 1-2 minutes or until most of the liquid is absorbed. Add eggs and oil to cereal mixture; beat well. Sift together flour, baking powder and salt. Add sifted dry ingredients to cereal mixture; stir only until combined. Gently fold in apricot mixture. Spread batter evenly in well-greased, waxed paper-lined 9 x 5 x 3-inch loaf pan. Sprinkle top with the one tablespoon sugar. Bake at 350° for about one hour or until toothpick inserted near center comes out clean. Let stand until thoroughly cooled before slicing. Makes one loaf.

tried

Tender, homemade coffee cakes spreading their delightful aroma through the country kitchen add a special touch to the invitation, "Come in, my friend, and share a cup of coffee with me."

Coffee cakes are simple, wonderful, unusual breads from many lands. Rich throughout, most are Americanized from old family favorites. Homemade coffee cakes add a simple, sweet touch to any meal you share with a friend.

BLUEBERRY BUCKLE

½ c. sugar	2 t. baking
¼ c. butter,	powder
softened	½ t. salt
1 egg	2½ c. fresh
½ c. milk	blueberries
2 c. flour	

Mix together sugar, butter and egg. Stir in milk. Sift together flour, baking powder and salt. Stir into batter. Mix well. Carefully blend in blueberries. Spread batter into greased and floured 9-inch square pan.

In separate bowl, blend together ½ cup sugar, ⅓ cup flour, ½ teaspoon cinnamon and ¼ cup soft butter. Sprinkle over top of batter. Bake 45 to 50 minutes or until wooden pick inserted in center comes out clean. Serve warm, plain or with ice cream.

CINNAMON COFFEE CAKE

3 c. flour	1 t. salt
1 c. brown sugar,	1 t. vanilla
firmly packed	1 t. baking soda
1 c. granulated sugar	2 eggs
1 T. cinnamon	1 c. buttermilk
1 c. butter	

In large bowl, cut butter into flour, sugars and cinnamon as for pie crust. Reserve ¾ cup of this mixture to use as a topping. To the remaining mixture add the salt, baking soda, vanilla and eggs. Stir until mixed. Add the buttermilk and blend the ingredients until smooth. Do not overbeat. Pour the mixture into a greased and floured angel food pan (spring form). Sprinkle the reserved topping lightly over the top. Bake in 350° oven for 45 minutes or until cake tests done. Cool before removing from the pan. Makes one large coffee cake.

ORANGE COFFEE CAKE

¼ c. butter	2 t. grated
½ c. sugar	orange peel
1 egg	½ c. rolled oats
1¼ c. flour	¼ c. brown sugar
1 t. baking	½ t. cinnamon
powder	2 T. melted butter
1 t. salt	½ c. chopped
½ t. soda	walnuts
½ c. orange juice	½ c. raisins

Cream butter and sugar till light and fluffy. Add egg; beat well. Sift together dry ingredients and add to creamed mixture alternately with orange juice. Stir in orange peel. Turn into greased 8 x 8 x 2-inch baking pan. Combine remaining ingredients and sprinkle over top of batter. Bake in 375° oven 25 minutes or till done.

CARROT COFFEE CAKE

1½ c. flour
2 t. baking powder
½ t. salt
1 t. cinnamon
⅔ c. butter
1 c. sugar
2 large eggs
1 c. raw carrots, pared and coarsely grated, packed firmly (2 very large)
½ c. raisins, rinsed in hot water and drained
½ c. walnuts, chopped (medium fine)

On wax paper sift together the flour, baking powder, salt and cinnamon. Cream butter and sugar; thoroughly beat in eggs, one at a time. Gradually stir in sifted ingredients; add carrots, raisins and walnuts and stir to distribute evenly.

Turn into a 9 x 5 x 3-inch loaf pan (bottom greased, then lined with buttered wax paper). Bake in a 350° oven for 1 hour or until cake tester inserted in center comes out clean. Turn out on wire rack; turn right side up; cool completely. Wrap tightly in plastic wrap and refrigerate overnight. Slice after chilling; wrap slices (piled one on top of the other) and reheat briefly in moderate or hot oven. Serve at once.

Among the many holiday breads popular in country kitchens are hot cross buns.

The cross on hot cross buns dates back to pre-Christian cultures when breads imprinted with various symbols were offered to different gods as sacrifices. The design represented both sun and fire. The sun symbol was a circle divided into quarters by a cross. The four sections represented the seasons.

In England the hot cross bun is associated with the traditions of Good Friday, and until recently was available only on that day. In America, hot cross buns are available throughout the Lenten season.

HOT CROSS BUNS

2 c. milk, scalded	8 c. flour
1 c. butter	½ t. salt
1 c. sugar	1½ c. raisins
2 cakes yeast	½ c. candied
dissolved in ⅓ c.	fruit peels
lukewarm water	½ t. cinnamon
2 eggs	or nutmeg

Pour the scalded milk over the butter and sugar and stir to dissolve. Let cool to lukewarm. Add the yeast mixture and eggs and mix well. Gradually add the flour and salt, reserving a small amount of flour to dust the fruits. Add the spice and floured fruits to the dough and knead in thoroughly. Place in a buttered bowl, cover and let rise until doubled. Punch the dough down and turn it out onto a floured board. Shape dough into 30 buns and place on buttered cookie sheets.

Cover and let rise for 30 minutes, then very carefully press the shape of a cross into each bun, using a spatula or the back of a knife. Bake in a 375° oven for 10 minutes, then reduce heat to 350° and continue baking until buns are browned and done, about 10 to 15 minutes longer. Frost either the entire bun or just the shape of the cross.

WHITE FROSTING

Beat one egg white until stiff, adding powdered sugar gradually until mixture is thick. Flavor with one teaspoon lemon juice or vanilla extract, or ¼ teaspoon almond extract. If the frosting thins, add more powdered sugar.

CHRISTMAS STOLLEN

1 pkg. active dry yeast
¼ c. very warm water (110 to 115°)
¼ c. lukewarm milk, scalded and cooled
¼ c. sugar
½ t. salt
1 egg
¼ c. butter, softened
2¼ to 2½ c. flour
½ c. walnuts
¼ c. citron chopped
¼ c. candied cherries, chopped
1 c. raisins
1 T. grated lemon rind

In mixing bowl, dissolve yeast in very warm water. Stir in milk, sugar, salt, soft butter and egg. Combine ½ of the flour with nuts, citron, candied cherries, raisins and lemon rind and add to yeast mixture. Mix with spoon until smooth. Add enough remaining flour to handle easily; mix with hand or spoon. Turn onto lightly floured board; knead until smooth and elastic (about 5 minutes). Place in greased bowl, bring greased side up. Cover and let rise in warm place until double. Punch down and let rise again until almost double, about 30 minutes. Turn onto lightly floured board after dough rises a second time. Spread with soft butter. Fold in half lengthwise. Form into a crescent. Press folded edge firmly so it won't spring open. Place on greased baking sheet. Brush top with butter. Let rise until double, 35 to 45 minutes. Bake in 375° oven for 30 to 35 minutes, or until golden brown. Frost while warm with quick white icing. Decorate with nut halves, pieces of citron and halves of candied cherries to simulate poinsettias. Makes 1 stollen.

QUICK WHITE FROSTING

Sift 1 cup confectioners' sugar. Moisten with 1½ tablespoons cream to spread. Add ½ teaspoon vanilla.

CHRISTMAS LOAF

1 pkg. active dry yeast
½ c. warm water
1 c. milk, scalded
⅓ c. butter
¼ c. sugar
2 t. salt
4 to 4½ c. flour
1 beaten egg
1 c. rolled oats
1 c. candied mixed fruit
½ c. chopped nuts

Soften yeast in water. Combine milk, butter, sugar and salt; cool to lukewarm. Beat in 1½ cups flour. Add egg and softened yeast; stir in oats, fruit, and nuts. Stir in enough additional flour to make soft dough. Turn out on lightly floured surface and knead till satiny, about 10 minutes. Place dough in greased bowl, turning once to grease surface. Cover and let rise in warm place till doubled, about 1¾ hours. Punch down; cover and let rest 10 minutes. Shape dough into 2 round loaves; place on greased baking sheets. Cover and let rise till doubled, about 1 hour. Bake in 375° oven 30 minutes. Cool and frost with confectioners' sugar frosting. Decorate with candied fruits and nuts. Makes 2 round loaves.

CRANBERRY NUT BREAD

1 c. fresh cranberries
1 c. sugar
2 c. flour
1½ t. baking powder
½ t. soda
1 t. salt
¼ c. shortening
¾ c. orange juice
1 t. grated orange rind
1 egg, well beaten
½ c. chopped nuts

Sift together flour, sugar, baking powder, soda and salt. Cut in shortening until mixture resembles coarse cornmeal. Combine orange juice and grated rind with well-beaten egg. Pour into dry ingredients and mix just enough to dampen. Fold in chopped nuts and coarsely chopped cranberries. Spoon into greased loaf pan, 9 x 5 x 3. Spread corners and sides a little higher than center. Bake in 350° oven about one hour or until crust is golden brown and toothpick inserted comes out clean. Remove from pan and cool. Store overnight for easy slicing. Makes one loaf.

SOUPS

HAM AND PEA SOUP WITH DUMPLINGS

1 1-lb. pkg. dried split peas
2 qts. boiling water
1 hambone or 2-3 ham hocks
1 c. diced onions
1 c. thinly-sliced celery
½ c. thinly-sliced carrots
　Salt and pepper to taste
　Dumplings

Rinse peas; drain and add to water with hambone or hocks, onion, celery and carrots. Cover and simmer gently for 2 hours. Stir occasionally. About 30 minutes before serving, remove hambone or hocks. Cut off meat and add to soup. Season to taste. Drop dumplings into soup 15 minutes before serving.

Sift together 2 cups flour, 3 teaspoons baking powder and 1 teaspoon salt. Cut in 3 tablespoons shortening. Add 1 cup milk and 1 beaten egg. Mix lightly. Drop from tablespoon into boiling soup to make 8 dumplings. Dip spoon in hot soup before spooning each dumpling so batter will not stick. Cover and cook 15 minutes. Makes 8 servings.

CHICKEN BOOYAH

1 stewing chicken
2 qts. water
1 T. salt
1½ c. potatoes, diced
1½ c. carrots, diced
1 c. celery, diced
1 medium onion, diced
2 c. tomato juice
2 c. canned peas

Cook one stewing chicken in 2 quarts water and 1 tablespoon salt until meat is very tender and can be easily removed from the bones. While chicken is cooking, prepare the diced vegetables. When chicken is tender, remove from broth and add diced vegetables (not peas). Cook until tender. Remove chicken meat from bones and cut into small pieces. When vegetables are tender, add the diced chicken, the tomato juice and the peas. Heat and season to taste. Makes 8 generous servings.

OLD-FASHIONED VEGETABLE SOUP

4 lbs. beef soupbones with generous
　amount of meat
4 qts. water
4 c. tomato juice or stewed tomatoes
1 c. celery stalks and leaves, diced
1 c. chopped onion
¼ c. chopped parsley
2 c. raw carrots, sliced
1 c. diced rutabaga
1 c. diced potatoes
2 c. green peas
2 c. green beans
2 c. shredded cabbage
　Salt and pepper to taste

Place meat and water in a large soup kettle. Bring to boil. Skim surface occasionally. When broth is clear, add tomatoes or juice, celery, onions and parsley. Cover and simmer gently for 2½ hours. Add carrots, rutabaga and potatoes. Simmer ½ hour. Remove soupbone from kettle and cut meat from the bone. Return all to kettle. Add peas, green beans and cabbage. Season to taste. Simmer another ½ hour or until all vegetables are tender. Makes 8 to 10 servings.

OXTAIL SOUP

1 lg. oxtail	1 bay leaf
Flour	6 peppercorns
3 T. fat	3 whole cloves
1 lg. onion, sliced	Salt
2 stalks celery with	4 pts. water
leaves, chopped	1½ T. cornstarch
2 carrots, sliced	

Have the oxtail cut into joints. Wash well and dry, then roll in flour and brown in the hot fat in a large saucepan. When browned evenly, add onions, celery and carrots and brown in the fat for a few minutes. Add water, bay leaf and seasonings, cover and bring slowly to boil, then simmer gently for 3 to 3½ hours, or until meat is tender. Strain the soup and cool quickly until fat sets on top, then skim. Heat soup and add cornstarch, then simmer for 20 minutes or until cornstarch is cooked. Addition of a tablespoon of claret or sherry is good with this soup.

SWEDISH MEATBALLS

4 T. butter	½ t. allspice
⅓ c. minced onion	¼ t. nutmeg
1 egg	1 lb. chuck, ground
½ c. milk	3 T. flour
½ c. fresh bread crumbs	⅛ t. pepper
2½ t. salt	1 c. water
3 t. sugar	¾ c. light cream

Sauté onion until golden brown in 2 tablespoons hot butter in large skillet. Meanwhile, in large mixing bowl, beat egg; add milk and crumbs. Let stand 5 minutes. Add 1¼ teaspoons salt, 2 teaspoons sugar, allspice, nutmeg, meat and onion. Blend well with fork. In same skillet, heat 2 tablespoons butter. Using 2 teaspoons, shape meat mixture into small balls, about ½- to ¾-inch in diameter. Drop some balls into skillet; brown well on all sides; remove to warm casserole. Repeat until all meatballs are browned.

Into the fat left in skillet, stir flour, 1 teaspoon sugar, 1¼ teaspoons salt and pepper; slowly add water and cream; stir until thickened. If desired, return meatballs to gravy and heat well; or serve meatballs in covered casserole; pass gravy. Makes 6 servings.

PARMESAN FRIED CHICKEN

- 2 broiler-fryer chickens (2½ lbs. each), cut into pieces
- 1 c. flour
- 2 t. salt
- ¼ t. pepper
- 2 t. paprika
- 2 eggs, slightly beaten
- 3 T. milk
- 1⅜ c. grated parmesan cheese
- ⅝ c. dry bread crumbs
- 2 T. butter
- 2 T. shortening
- ¼ c. butter, melted

Heat oven to 400°. Do not use chicken wings (refrigerate or freeze for another meal); remove skin from remaining pieces. Coat chicken with a mixture of flour, salt, pepper and paprika. Combine eggs and milk; dip chicken into egg mixture. Roll in mixture of cheese and bread crumbs. In oven melt the 2 tablespoons of butter and the shortening in jelly roll pan, 15½ x 10½ x 1-inch. Place chicken bone side down in pan. Drizzle with the ¼ cup melted butter. Bake one hour. Cool; cover and chill. Makes six servings.

CORN-CRISPED CHICKEN

- 1 broiler-fryer chicken, cut in serving pieces
- 1 c. cornflake crumbs
- 1 t. salt
- ⅛ t. pepper
- ½ c. evaporated milk

Mix cornflake crumbs with salt and pepper. Line shallow baking pan with aluminum foil. Dip chicken pieces in evaporated milk, then roll immediately in seasoned cornflake crumbs. Place chicken pieces, skin side up, in foil-lined pan; do not crowd. Bake in 350° oven for one hour or until tender. No need to cover or turn chicken while cooking. Makes 4 servings.

CHICKEN PAPRIKA CASSEROLE

- 8 oz. egg noodles
- 1 small onion, chopped
- ¼ c. butter
- 2 chickens, about 2 lbs. each, quartered
- ¼ c. flour
- 1 t. salt
- ½ t. pepper
- 1 T. sweet paprika
- 2 c. chicken broth
- 2 T. tomato sauce
- 2 t. Worcestershire sauce
- 2 c. sour cream

Cook noodles until barely tender, drain and put in 5-quart casserole. Sauté onion in the butter. Remove onion and, in same skillet, sauté chicken a few pieces at a time until lightly browned on both sides. Add more butter if necessary. Arrange chicken on noodles. Blend flour into drippings in skillet. Add salt, pepper and paprika. Cook, stirring, 1 or 2 minutes. Add chicken broth and cook until slightly reduced and thickened. Remove from heat, add tomato sauce, Worcestershire sauce and sour cream and pour over chicken. Bake in 350° oven about 1½ hours. Makes 6 to 8 servings.

CREAMED TURKEY

1 T. butter
3 T. minced onion
1 T. chopped parsley
2 c. leftover turkey, diced
2 c. frozen peas
2 T. leftover turkey gravy
  Pinch nutmeg
  Salt and pepper to taste

Melt butter in a skillet and lightly sauté onion and parsley. Stir in turkey, peas, gravy, nutmeg, salt and pepper. Keep warm while preparing the following cream sauce.

Add turkey mixture to cream sauce and blend well. Serve at once over hot, fluffy rice, buttered noodles or hot corn bread, split and generously buttered. Serves 5 to 6.

CREAM SAUCE

1½ T. butter
1½ T. flour
1½ c. top milk or ¾ c. each milk and cream
  2 eggs, beaten

Combine butter, flour and milk in saucepan. Cook, stirring constantly, until smooth and thickened. Season to taste. Quickly stir in eggs.

MUSHROOM & WILD RICE STUFFING

½ c. butter
1 lb. fresh mushrooms, sliced
½ c. onions, chopped
½ c. parsley, minced
1 c. celery, chopped
⅔ c. water
4 c. cooked wild rice
1½ t. salt
⅛ t. pepper

Melt butter in heavy skillet. Add mushrooms and cook over low heat for 5 minutes. Remove mushrooms. Add onion, parsley, and celery to skillet. Cook until onions turn yellow. Add ⅓ cup water along with wild rice and seasonings. Mix well. Add remaining water and the cooked mushrooms. Mix well. Simmer for 15 minutes. Makes 8 servings.

CHICKEN AND DUMPLINGS

1 4- to 5-lb. stewing hen, cut up
3 to 4 sprigs parsley
4 celery stalks with leaves, chopped
1 carrot, diced
½ c. chopped onion
2 t. salt
¼ t. pepper
  Cold water

DUMPLINGS

1½ c. flour
3 t. baking powder
½ t. salt
¾ c. milk
1 t. minced parsley

Fit pieces of prepared chicken into large, heavy kettle. Add vegetables and seasonings. Barely cover with cold water. Cover and heat to boiling. Remove any scum. Reduce heat to simmering and cook until tender —2½ to 3 hours. Fifteen minutes before chicken is done (make sure there is enough water to barely cover chicken), add dumplings prepared as follows:

Combine flour, baking powder and salt. Add milk and stir just until dry ingredients are moistened. Add parsley and stir in. Dip a teaspoon into hot chicken broth, then into dumpling batter; drop a spoonful of batter into chicken broth. Drop all dumplings in quickly. Replace cover and boil gently for 12 minutes. Remove dumplings to platter and arrange pieces of chicken around them. Makes 6 to 8 servings.

APPLE & PRUNE STUFFING

¼ c. butter
2 qts. tart firm apples, diced
¼ c. brown sugar
¾ t. cinnamon
1 T. grated lemon rind
2 c. dry bread cubes
1 lb. prunes, stewed and pitted

Heat butter in a large heavy skillet; add diced apples, brown sugar, cinnamon and lemon rind. Stir over low heat until apples are just tender but not mushy. Add bread cubes and prunes, tossing together lightly. Makes enough for a 10- to 12-pound goose.

CORNISH PASTIES

2 medium potatoes
1 small onion, finely chopped
½ lb. lean thick pork steak
2 medium carrots
½ lb. lean thick round steak
   Salt and pepper to taste

For two good-sized pasties, make enough regular pie crust for a two-crust pie. Divide in half. Roll dough in circle, place ingredients near front edge of crust, dot with butter, and fold other half of crust over ingredients. Pinch together firmly. Pierce with fork to let out excess steam. Bake at 450° for 45 minutes or until tested with toothpick for doneness.

DUTCH "POCKETBOOKS"

Pastry for two double-crust pies
½ lb. finely diced beef chuck
   (other meat, such as pork,
   lamb or liver may be substituted)
2 small potatoes, pared and thinly sliced
2 T. chopped onion
2 small carrots, thinly sliced
2 small turnips, thinly sliced
   Salt and pepper to taste
   Butter

Prepare pastry and divide into two portions. Roll each portion into a round about 9 inches in diameter and about ¼-inch thick. Using one-half of the meat and vegetables for each pasty and lightly sprinkling each layer with salt and pepper, put a layer of meat and vegetables onto one half of each round. Dot with butter. Fold pastry over filling to form a "pocketbook" and seal edges with the tines of a fork. Slit top of pastry to allow steam to escape while baking. Place pasties on a baking sheet. Bake at 450° for 15 minutes. Reduce heat to 350° and bake 40 minutes longer, or until golden brown. Makes 2 large pasties.

PORK STEAKS

4 pork blade steaks,
   ½ to ¾ inch thick
2 T. lard
1½ t. salt
¼ t. pepper
4 slices onion, ¼-inch thick
4 slices tomato, ½-inch thick
4 green pepper rings,
   ¼-inch thick

Brown steaks in lard. Remove steaks from pan and arrange in shallow casserole or baking pan. Season with salt and pepper. Cover and bake in a 350° oven for 30 minutes. Remove from oven and place a slice of onion, a slice of tomato and a slice of green pepper on each steak. Cover and return to oven for another 15 minutes.

SAUSAGE PASTIES

Pastry for double-crust pie
½ lb. bulk pork sausage
¼ c. onion, finely chopped
2½ c. mashed turnips
1 c. mashed potatoes
1 t. salt
⅛ t. pepper

In a large skillet, brown sausage, crumbling meat with a fork as it cooks. Remove with a slotted spoon and place in a large bowl; set aside. Add onion to skillet and sauté until transparent, about 5 minutes. Remove with a slotted spoon and add to sausage. Add turnips, potatoes, salt and pepper. Blend well.

Divide dough in half. Roll each half into a 12-inch square. Cut into four 6-inch squares. Place about ½ cup filling in the center of each square and moisten 2 adjacent sides with water. Fold remaining 2 sides across filling to form a triangle. Pinch edges to seal. Place on greased baking sheets. Slash tops of triangles to allow steam to escape. Bake in 350° oven for about 30 minutes or until done. Makes 8 small pasties.

HOT DOGS IN BLANKETS

1 lb. hot dogs	8 fresh bread slices
Pickle relish	8 slices bacon

Slit hot dogs lengthwise and fill with pickle relish. Cut crusts from bread and wrap a slice around each hot dog. Roll bacon around bread. Put on baking sheet and bake in 400° oven about 15 minutes. Makes 4 servings.

PIZZA DOGS

¼ c. onion, chopped
  Dash garlic salt (optional)
2 T. vegetable oil
1 can condensed tomato soup
2 T. chopped parsley
¼ t. crushed dried oregano
8 hot dogs, slit lengthwise
8 rolls, split
6 oz. sliced mozzarella cheese

Sauté onion in oil until golden. Add ¼ cup water, soup, parsley and oregano. Bring to boil and simmer, stirring frequently, 15 minutes. Put a hot dog on each roll and arrange in large shallow baking pan. Cover hot dogs with tomato sauce and top with cheese. Put under broiler 1 minute, or until cheese is melted. Makes 8.

HOT DOGS WITH SAUERKRAUT

8 long thin hot dogs, partially split
  lengthwise
3 T. prepared mustard
8 T. butter, softened
8 rolls, partially split
¾ c. green pepper, slivered
¾ c. onion, chopped
1 lb. sauerkraut, undrained

Sauté hot dogs lightly until curled. Mix mustard with 6 tablespoons butter, spread on rolls and toast under broiler. Sauté next 2 ingredients lightly in remaining butter. Add sauerkraut and heat. Put a hot dog on each roll and top with sauerkraut. Makes 8.

CHEESE-TOPPED HOT DOGS IN ROLLS

6 hot dog rolls, split
  Prepared mustard
¼ c. soft butter
1 c. shredded sharp cheddar
2 egg whites, stiffly beaten
6 hot dogs

Spread inside of rolls with mustard. Cream butter and cheese until blended. Fold in egg whites. Split hot dogs lengthwise almost all the way through; put one into each roll and top with cheese mixture. Bake in 425° oven about 15 minutes. Makes 6.

HOT DOGS WITH ONION-CHILI SAUCE

1 c. onion, minced
2 cloves garlic, minced
¼ c. butter
½ t. salt
⅛ t. pepper
1½ T. Worcestershire
1½ T. prepared mustard
1½ t. sugar
½ c. chili sauce
1 lb. hot dogs
  Thick slices of Italian bread, toasted

Cook onion and garlic in the butter until golden. Add remaining ingredients except hot dogs and bread; heat. Split hot dogs lengthwise, put split side up in shallow pan and spoon sauce over them. Heat under broiler and serve between toasted bread slices topped with remaining sauce. Serves 4.

HOT DOGS IN BEER

1 lb. hot dogs	1 lg. carrot,
About 1½ c. beer	thinly sliced
1 lg. onion, sliced	½ t. Worcestershire

Put hot dogs in large saucepan and add enough beer to cover. Add remaining ingredients, bring to boil, lower heat and simmer 5 minutes. Remove hot dogs and serve on warm rolls. Makes 4 servings.

BEEF LOAF

2 lbs. ground beef
1 c. tomato sauce
1 egg
1 T. Worcestershire sauce
⅓ c. chopped green pepper
2 medium onions, chopped
¾ c. cracker crumbs, finely crushed
1 t. salt
¼ t. pepper
¼ c. catsup

Combine ground beef, tomato sauce, egg, Worcestershire sauce, green pepper, onions, cracker crumbs, salt and pepper. Mix lightly but thoroughly. Shape meat mixture into a 9 x 4 x 3-inch loaf and place on a rack in an open roasting pan. Bake in a 350° oven for 1 hour and 15 minutes. Pour catsup over top of beef loaf and continue baking 10 to 15 minutes or until done. Makes 6 to 8 servings.

SHEPHERD'S PIE (WITH ROAST)

2 c. mashed potatoes
2 c. cut up cooked roast beef, lamb, veal or pork
1 T. flour
2 T. fat or salad oil
Leftover gravy
6 small onions, cooked and drained
1 c. carrots, cooked and quartered
1 c. cooked or canned peas, drained
1 egg, beaten

Grease 1½-quart casserole. Prepare mashed potatoes. In bowl lightly roll meat in flour until coated. In hot fat in skillet, brown meat lightly on all sides. Add 2½ cups leftover gravy (or as much as you have with hot water added to make 2½ cups.) Season to taste; thicken if necessary. Add onions, carrots, peas. Heat. Then pour into casserole. Fold egg into potatoes; arrange in ring on top of meat. Bake in a 425° oven for 10 to 15 minutes, until gravy bubbles and potato ring is light golden brown. Makes four servings.

You can also use lamb taken from a cold joint and put through a blender. Season well with herbs, onions, salt and pepper, and a few drops of Worcestershire sauce. Mix in a little good jellied stock—sufficient to moisten the meat throughout. Top with mashed potatoes beaten up with a little hot milk, butter, pepper and salt. Spread the potato crust evenly, and score with a knife. Bake in a hot oven until the surface is nicely browned and serve with stewed tomatoes.

BEEF CUBED STEAKS-TASTY TOPPING

4 beef cubed steaks
2 T. cooking fat
½ t. salt
¼ c. catsup
2 T. chopped green onion
¼ c. shredded cheddar cheese

Brown steaks on both sides in fat for 7 to 10 minutes. Pour off drippings. Top each steak with ⅛ teaspoon salt, 1 tablespoon catsup, 1½ teaspoons onion and 1 tablespoon shredded cheese. Cover and cook over low heat 2 to 3 minutes or until cheese melts. Makes 4 servings.

ALL-IN-A-POT LAMB ROAST

1 lamb leg, shank half (about 4 pounds)
2 onions, sliced thin
1 c. dry white wine
1 c. water
2 t. salt
1 t. rosemary
½ t. pepper
6 large carrots, quartered
1½ c. fresh mushrooms, sliced

Place lamb in small roasting pan that has a lid to fit. Add onion, wine, water, salt, rosemary and pepper. Cover roaster and bake at 325° for about one hour. Add carrots and mushrooms; cover and return to oven for another hour or until lamb and vegetables are tender. Remove lamb from oven and allow it to "rest" for about 10 minutes before carving. Cooking liquid may be skimmed of fat, strained and served with lamb and vegetables if desired. Makes 4 servings.

BARBECUED BEEF STRIPS

2 lbs. round steak (cut ½- to ¾-inch thick)
2 T. cooking fat
2 c. tomato sauce
⅓ c. water
2 T. brown sugar
1 T. prepared mustard
1 T. Worcestershire sauce
1 medium onion

Slice round steak in strips ⅛-inch thick or thinner and 3 to 4 inches long. Brown strips in fat. Pour off drippings. Combine tomato sauce, water, brown sugar, mustard and Worcestershire sauce. Add sauce and onion, thinly sliced. Stir to combine. Cover and cook slowly, stirring occasionally for 30 minutes or until meat is tender. Makes 6 to 8 servings.

BEEF KABOBS

1 steak, filet or sirloin, 1-inch thick
   (2 to 3 lbs.)
½ c. red wine
1 T. wine vinegar
¼ c. olive oil
1 t. Worcestershire sauce
1 T. chopped fresh tarragon
1 clove garlic, crushed
½ t. salt
¼ t. pepper
4 onions, quartered
2 green peppers, cut lengthwise
   in eighths
4 tomatoes, quartered

Prepare 8 long skewers. Cut steak into 1-inch cubes. Mix wine, wine vinegar, oil, Worcestershire sauce, tarragon, garlic, salt and pepper in a bowl. Stir meat into marinade and marinate for 1 to 24 hours. Place meat on skewers, alternating with vegetables. Pour marinade into a large flat baking pan (jelly roll pan). Place skewers in marinade so that vegetables and meat will rest in seasoning. This may be prepared well in advance. Skewers should be grilled over a hot fire about 3 to 4 inches over coals so that vegetables have a chance to cook without charring. Turn skewers frequently. Kabobs should take no more than 10 minutes. Serves 4.

SHEPHERD'S PIE

1 lb. ground beef chuck
¼ c. chopped green pepper
¼ c. chopped onion
1 T. shortening
1 T. flour
1 t. salt
½ t. chili powder
   Dash pepper
½ c. tomato ketchup
1 c. water
1½ to 2 c. mixed vegetables, cooked and
   drained
3 c. seasoned hot mashed potatoes
   Paprika

Sauté ground beef, green pepper and onion in shortening until meat is browned and green pepper is tender. Drain off any excess fat. Sprinkle in four next ingredients; stir in ketchup, water and cooked vegetables. Combine well and cook until mixture thickens. Divide mixture into six 10-ounce baking dishes or one 2-quart casserole. Top with potatoes and sprinkle with paprika. Place under broiler to brown; or bake in preheated 425° oven for 15 minutes. Makes six servings.

Sausage, so familiar in country kitchens, was popular over a thousand years B.C. Sausage-eating was a popular pastime in ancient Rome. In fact, many of their feasts centered around sausage. The Romans called it "salus," meaning salted or preserved meat.

Early American settlers found the Indians making sausage. They preserved a combination of chopped, dried meat with dried berries. Sausage-making skills came to the New World with each ethnic group. Old family recipes once shared freely in country kitchens became closely guarded secrets. Old World specialties blended with new taste preferences.

In all likelihood, no two sausage makers will agree on ingredients. Still, regional sausage recipes make outstanding country kitchen dishes.

SAUSAGE-CORN BREAD PIE

  1 lb. fresh pork sausage
  1 c. yellow cornmeal
  1 c. flour
 ¼ c. sugar
  4 t. baking powder
  1 egg
  1 c. milk

Brown pork sausage, separating it into pieces. Pour off drippings, reserving ¼ cup. Sift together cornmeal, flour, sugar and baking powder. Add egg, milk and ¼ cup pork sausage drippings. Mix to combine thoroughly. Fold in sausage. Turn batter into a greased 9-inch pie plate. Bake in a 425° oven for 25 minutes or until done. Makes 6 servings.

SAUSAGEBURGERS

 2 lbs. pork sausage
 3 T. water
 2 large tomatoes, each cut into 4 slices
 1 medium-sized onion, cut into 8 slices and separated into rings
 8 hamburger buns, warmed

Shape sausage into 8 patties, ½- to ¾-inch thick and 3 to 4 inches in diameter. Place in a cold frying pan, add water, cover and cook over low heat for 5 minutes. Pour off drippings. Cook patties slowly on both sides until well-done. Place patties, tomato slices and onion rings between halves of warmed hamburger buns. Makes 8 sandwiches.

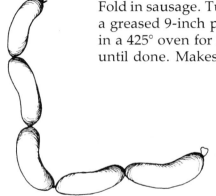

SAUSAGE-MACARONI GOULASH

   1 lb. pork sausage links
   1 c. chopped green pepper
   1 c. chopped onion
 3½ c. stewed tomatoes, undrained
   1 c. elbow macaroni, uncooked
   1 t. salt
  ¼ t. pepper
   1 T. thick steak sauce
   1 c. dairy sour cream
    Chopped parsley

Halve sausages crosswise. Sauté in large skillet until nicely browned. Remove. Drain off all but 3 tablespoons fat from skillet. In hot fat, sauté green pepper and onion, stirring, about 5 minutes. Add sausages, tomatoes, macaroni, salt, pepper and steak sauce; bring to boiling. Reduce heat; simmer, covered, 30 minutes, stirring occasionally. Remove from heat. Stir in sour cream, mixing well. Sprinkle with parsley. Makes 4 servings.

SURPRISE SAUSAGE 'N EGGS

 1 lb. bulk pork sausage meat
½ c. oatmeal (quick or old-fashioned, uncooked)
 1 egg
¼ c. milk
 4 hard-cooked eggs

Combine sausage, oats, egg and milk. Mix thoroughly. Divide meat mixture into four parts and shape each part around a hard-cooked egg. Place eggs on a rack in a shallow baking pan. Bake in a preheated 375° oven about 35 minutes or until sausage is cooked. Makes 4 servings.

Casseroles are the convenience food of country kitchens. The wonderful thing about them is that country cooks can combine an amazing variety of meats, vegetables and seasonings to make hot and bubbly one-dish meals.

Each ethnic group has its own favorite casserole. Many times the gourmet-sounding names are actually simple everyday fare.

Generally speaking, the main ingredient in casseroles is usually rice, potatoes or pasta with meat, fish or vegetables.

BEEF CASSEROLE

2 lbs. round steak, cut in ½-inch cubes
3 T. fat
1 large onion, chopped
1 clove garlic, finely chopped
2 T. flour
¾ c. canned mushrooms and broth
½ c. chopped celery
1 c. thick sour cream
1 c. tomato sauce
1 t. salt
⅛ t. pepper
1 T. Worcestershire sauce

Brown meat in hot fat. Add onion and garlic and cook until golden. Stir in flour slowly. Add remaining ingredients and mix well. Turn into greased 3-quart casserole. Bake, uncovered, in 325° oven until meat is tender, about 1½ hours. Serves 6.

SPANISH RICE

1 lb. ground beef
4 t. butter
1 c. chopped onion
1 green pepper, chopped
¼ c. diced celery
2 c. stewed tomatoes
2 t. salt
⅛ t. black pepper
3 c. hot cooked rice
Chopped parsley

Brown ground beef in butter. Add onions, green pepper and celery and simmer on range top until almost tender. Pour into ovenproof casserole (4 quarts or larger). Mix in tomatoes, salt, pepper and rice. Blend well. Garnish top with chopped parsley. Bake in 350° oven for 30 minutes. Serves eight.

PORK AND TOMATO SCALLOP

2 pork blade steaks, cut ¾- to 1-inch thick
1 large onion, chopped
3½ c. stewed tomatoes
1 T. sugar
1½ t. salt
⅛ t. pepper
⅛ t. thyme
8 slices bread, toasted
4 oz. sliced cheese, if desired

Cut pork steaks into strips ½-inch wide and 3 inches long. Cook pork strips and onion slowly in large frying pan, stirring until lightly browned. Add tomatoes, sugar, salt, pepper and thyme and stir to combine, breaking up tomatoes. Cut slices of toast into 1-inch squares and place in 13 x 9-inch baking dish. Pour meat mixture over toast squares, distributing evenly. Cut cheese slices into 1-inch squares and place on top. Cover securely and bake in a 350° oven for 35 minutes. Remove cover and bake 10 minutes longer. Makes 6 servings.

MACARONI AND CHEESE BAKE

1 c. uncooked elbow macaroni
2 c. corn flakes
¼ c. butter, melted
3 T. finely chopped onion
1 10¾-oz. can (1¼ cups) condensed cream of mushroom soup
⅓ c. milk
1¼ c. (5 oz.) grated sharp cheddar cheese

Cook macaroni according to package directions. Drain, rinse and set aside. Measure corn flakes; crush into fine crumbs. Mix crumbs with 2 tablespoons of the melted butter. Set crumb mixture aside for topping. Place remaining melted butter and onion in medium-sized saucepan; cook over low heat until tender. Stir in soup, milk and cheese; cook just until cheese is melted, stirring occasionally. Remove from heat. Place cooked macaroni in buttered 8 x 8 x 2-inch (1-quart) baking dish; pour hot cheese sauce over top. Stir to combine. Sprinkle evenly with crumb mixture. Bake in 350° oven about 30 minutes or until thoroughly heated. Makes 4 servings.

APPLE-GINGER RELISH

1 c. apples, cored and chopped
1 c. crushed pineapple, drained
¼ c. broken walnut meats
2 T. finely minced, candied ginger
Few grains of salt

Combine all ingredients. Let flavors blend for 2 hours. Serve as relish with meats. Makes about 2 cups.

ACCOMPANIMENTS

DILLY CARROTS

8 medium carrots,   1 t. tarragon
   cut into sticks   1 t. dill weed
½ c. water   1 t. seasoned salt
¼ c. cider vinegar

Place all ingredients in a saucepan. Bring to a boil; cover and reduce heat. Simmer 30 minutes or until tender-crisp. Chill several hours or overnight. Great as a snack, hors d'oeuvre, or salad.

CORN RELISH

8 c. corn, boiled and cut from cob
4 c. chopped cabbage
1 c. chopped sweet green pepper
1 c. chopped sweet red pepper
2 large onions, chopped
1 c. sugar
2 T. ground mustard
1 T. mustard seed
1 T. salt
1 T. celery seed
4 c. cider vinegar
1 c. water

Combine all ingredients in large, heavy kettle. Simmer 20 minutes. You may add more sugar and salt to taste. Pack, boiling hot, into sterilized jars, leaving ½-inch headspace. Adjust caps. Process 10 minutes in boiling water bath. Makes about 6 pints.

APPLE BUTTER

Wash and quarter enough apples to fill a 16-quart kettle. Add 2 cups of water. Cook slowly over very low heat and stir constantly. Use a heavy kettle with a broad, flat bottom to allow the apples to bubble freely. When they are thoroughly cooked, cool slightly. Run through a food mill. There should be about 8 quarts of pulp.

Measure 2 cups of sugar to 4 cups of apple pulp. Place mixture back in a heavy kettle. Here again the broad, flat kettle bottom is necessary to allow the sugar and pulp to mix and cook freely. Use a wooden spoon or a flat paddle to stir the mixture constantly while it is cooking over a very low heat. The stirring allows the steam to escape and prevents scorching. Add 10 2-inch sticks of cinnamon. Check for doneness by placing some apple butter on a cool saucer. If no rim of liquid forms around the edge of the butter, it is ready for the jar. Place in hot sterilized jars. Seal at once. Makes about 12 pints.

PEACH CHUTNEY

1 29-oz. can sliced   1 clove garlic,
   cling peaches   minced
1 c. sugar   ½ t. curry powder
¾ c. vinegar   ¼ t. cinnamon
1 c. pitted prunes   ¼ t. ground cloves
⅓ c. chopped candied   ⅓ c. chopped almonds
   ginger

Drain peaches, reserving syrup. In large saucepan, combine syrup with remaining ingredients except nuts and peaches. Bring to a boil; reduce heat and simmer, stirring frequently, for 45 minutes. Add nuts and peaches. Pour into sterilized jars and seal tightly. Cool and store in dark place. Makes 8 cups.

END-OF-THE-GARDEN PICKLES

1 c. sliced cucumbers
1 c. chopped sweet peppers
1 c. chopped cabbage
1 c. sliced onions
1 c. chopped green tomatoes
1 c. chopped carrots
1 c. green beans, cut in 1-inch pieces
1 c. chopped celery
2 T. mustard seed
1 T. celery seed
2 c. cider vinegar
2 c. sugar
2 T. turmeric

Combine cucumbers, peppers, cabbage, onions and tomatoes in large container. Soak in salt brine (½ cup salt to 2 quarts cold water) overnight. Drain well. Combine and cook the carrots and green beans until tender. Drain well. Mix all vegetables together with remaining ingredients. Boil 10 minutes. Pack into hot, sterilized jars. Adjust caps. Process 10 minutes in boiling water bath. Makes about 6 pints.

No picnic basket should leave a country kitchen without some pickled eggs. This old-fashioned method of preserving eggs offers a country cook a unique economical source of protein to serve with her picnic lunch.

Pickled eggs can be kept up to several months in the pickling solution at refrigerator temperatures. It is a good idea to check the refrigerated pickled eggs often as their spicy flavor becomes too pronounced for some tastes.

DEVILED EGGS

6 pickled eggs	2 t. lemon juice
1 t. Worcestershire	or vinegar
sauce	⅛ t. ground pepper
¾ t. salad mustard	3 T. mayonnaise
½ t. salt	or salad dressing

Cut eggs in half. Remove yolks and press through sieve. Combine yolks with remaining ingredients; beat until smooth. If desired add more seasoning and salad dressing. Refill whites with fork, spoon or pastry tube. Makes 12 stuffed halves.

RED BEET EGGS

1 t. dried mustard	1 1-lb. can
2 T. sugar	baby beets
1 t. salt	4 hard-boiled eggs
½ c. cider vinegar	

Mix together mustard, sugar, salt and vinegar and cook to the boiling point. Pour over well-drained beets and set aside to cool. When cool, add the shelled hard-boiled eggs and refrigerate overnight. Shake container occasionally so eggs will pick up the beet color all over. Serve beets as a salad on water cress. The pickled eggs may be used to garnish a salad or served separately. Makes four servings.

DARK AND SPICY EGGS

1½ c. cider vinegar
½ c. water
1 T. dark brown sugar
2 t. granulated sugar
1 t. mixed pickling spice
¼ t. liquid smoke or hickory smoke salt
2 t. salt
1 doz. hard-boiled eggs, peeled

Combine all ingredients except eggs, heat to near boiling and simmer for five minutes. Pour the solution over the hard-boiled eggs in a quart jar or other suitable container which can be sealed tightly. Seal and immediately store in the refrigerator to season.

DILLED EGGS

1½ c. white vinegar	¼ t. mustard seed
1 c. water	½ t. onion juice
¾ t. dill seed	½ t. minced garlic
¼ t. white pepper	1 doz. hard-boiled
3 t. salt	eggs, peeled

Combine all ingredients but eggs in saucepan. Bring to boiling over medium heat. Boil for five minutes. Pour the pickling solution over the hard-cooked eggs in a quart jar or larger container. Seal and refrigerate. Season for one week.

PICKLED EGGS WITH CARAWAY SEED

8 eggs	2 c. cider vinegar
2 T. sugar	8 black peppers
1 t. salt	3 to 4 whole cloves
1 bud garlic	2 t. caraway seed

Hard-boil eggs; remove shells and cool. Put eggs in jar with a tight cover. In a pan combine above ingredients and bring to boiling. Cook slowly 20 to 25 minutes. Strain and pour boiling mixture over cold eggs. Cover tightly. Store at least two days before using.

Some folks claim you can find a little bit of heaven when you step into a country kitchen when the catsup kettle is brewing. The tangy combination of tomatoes, onions and green peppers with a floating spice bag releases a heady draft of steam each time the wooden spoon makes its path through the thickening broth.

Call it what you will—catsup, catchup, or ketchup—this nippy condiment is a favorite with young and old alike.

Catsup or sauces may be made of either fruits or vegetables. The main difference between the two is that catsup is strained through a fine sieve, while the sauce is left unstrained. Both are boiled to a thick liquid stage.

Pioneer cooks made catsup from any number of ingredients including apples, grapes, walnuts, mushrooms, currants, cranberries and gooseberries. Still it is the classic tomato catsup we know best today.

TOMATO CATSUP

    1 peck (12½ lbs.) ripe tomatoes
    3 large onions
   ¼ t. cayenne pepper
    2 c. cider vinegar
 1½ T. broken stick cinnamon
    1 T. whole cloves
    3 cloves garlic (finely chopped)
    1 T. paprika
    1 c. sugar
 2½ t. salt

Wash and slice tomatoes and boil about 15 minutes or until soft. Slice the onions into another kettle. Cover with a small quantity of water and cook until tender. Run the cooked onions and tomatoes through a sieve. Mix the onion and tomato pulp. Add the cayenne pepper. Boil this mixture rapidly until it has been reduced to about ½ of its original volume.

Meanwhile place vinegar in an enamel pan; add a spice bag containing the cinnamon, cloves and garlic. Allow this to simmer for about 30 minutes. Then bring to boiling point. Place cover on pan and remove from heat. Allow this to stand in covered pan until ready to use.

When tomato mixture has cooked down to ½ original volume, add vinegar mixture, which should measure 1½ cups. Add the paprika, sugar and salt and boil rapidly for 10 minutes or until desired consistency is reached. Pour while boiling hot into sterilized jars and seal at once.

BEST-OF-ALL CHILI SAUCE

 1½ t. ground nutmeg
 1½ t. ground allspice
 1½ t. ground cloves
   ½ t. ginger
    1 dried hot red pepper
    7 lbs. peeled tomatoes
    3 c. onions
    2 large sweet green peppers
 1½ T. salt
    3 c. chopped celery
    2 c. cider vinegar
 1½ c. granulated sugar
 1½ sticks cinnamon

Combine first 5 ingredients in cheesecloth bag. Chop tomatoes, onions, celery and peppers fine. Add remaining ingredients. Bring to a boil on range top. Then place pan in a 350° oven for 2 to 3 hours, stirring occasionally during the last hour of cooking. When sauce reaches desired consistency, pour into sterilized jars and seal at once. Makes 5 to 6 pints.

BLENDER CATSUP

  48 medium tomatoes (about 8 lbs.)
    2 ripe sweet red peppers
    2 sweet green peppers
    4 onions
    3 T. salt
 1½ t. allspice
    3 t. dry mustard
    3 c. white vinegar
    3 c. sugar
 1½ t. cloves
 1½ t. cinnamon
   ½ t. hot red pepper

Quarter tomatoes; remove stem ends. Add peppers, seeded and cut in strips, and onions, peeled and quartered. Mix. Put vegetables in blender container, filling jar ¾ full. Blend at high speed 4 seconds; pour into large kettle. Repeat until all vegetables are blended. Add vinegar, sugar, salt and spices, tied loosely in thin muslin bag. Simmer, uncovered, in 325° oven or in electric saucepan until volume is reduced one-half. Remove spices. Seal immediately in hot sterilized jars. Makes five pints.

Legends say the cranberry, as traditional as apple pie, was served at the first Thanksgiving dinner. The Eastern Indians taught the Pilgrims how to use the "sassamanesh"—as they called the cranberry. The berries were the delightful condiment of the Indian world. They considered the bright, tangy, wild berry a symbol of peace.

Gradually, colonial settlers adopted ways to use the berry—its juice in sauce, jellies and in jams.

Henry Hall of Cape Cod was reportedly the first to commercialize cranberry raising about 1816. By the late 1800's, the growing industry spread to New Jersey, Wisconsin and Oregon.

Cranberries, once considered a fruit delicacy for use only at Thanksgiving, are now popular all year in country kitchens.

CRANBERRY RIBBON SALAD

1 1-lb. can whole cranberry sauce
2 T. lemon juice
½ pt. cream, whipped
¼ c. confectioners' sugar
1 t. vanilla
¾ c. chopped hickory nuts

Add lemon juice to cranberry sauce. Pour into freezing tray. Combine whipped cream, sugar, vanilla and nuts. Spoon whipped cream mixture over cranberry layer and freeze. When ready to serve, slice and place each piece on crisp lettuce.

TANGERINE-CRANBERRY RELISH

1 lb. fresh or frozen cranberries
4 medium tangerines
1½ to 2 c. sugar
2 c. seedless raisins or nuts, coarsely chopped

Wash cranberries (do not thaw frozen berries) and put through the medium blade of food chopper. Wash tangerines; remove peel. Put the peel through food chopper. Remove seeds from tangerines and cut sections into small pieces. Combine cranberries, tangerine peel and pieces, and sugar; stir until sugar is dissolved. Add raisins or nuts, blend well and turn into glass jars. Cover and refrigerate. Relish will keep for several weeks. Makes 2½ pints.

HOT CRANBERRY BUTTER

2 c. cranberries   ½ c. water
  (fresh or frozen)   ¼ c. brown sugar
1 c. granulated sugar   ¼ c. butter

Combine cranberries, granulated sugar and water in saucepan. Heat to boiling, stirring until sugar dissolves. Boil until berries pop (about 5 minutes). Add brown sugar and butter. Heat until dissolved. Serve hot with French toast, waffles or pancakes.

CRANBERRY-APPLE CIDER

1 lb. fresh or frozen cranberries
1 c. sweet cider
2 tart apples with skins, sliced
1 c. honey
  Grated rind of 1 lemon
  Pinch of ground mace

Simmer the cranberries, cider and apples gently until fruit is soft. Add honey, rind and mace. Simmer for 5 minutes. Cool. Serve with meat, fowl or fish. Makes 2 pints.

MOLASSES CRANBERRY SHERBET

1 envelope   2½ c. water
  unflavored gelatin   1½ c. sugar
½ c. cold water   ⅓ c. molasses
4 c. fresh or   ¼ c. lemon juice
  frozen cranberries

Soften gelatin in one-half cup water. Cook cranberries, covered, in the two and one-half cups water until skins break open. Put cranberries through sieve. Combine cranberries, sugar, molasses and gelatin. Cook over medium heat, stirring constantly, until sugar and gelatin dissolve. Remove from heat. Stir in lemon juice. Cool. Pour into an eight-inch square pan. Freeze until firm. Turn into chilled bowl and let stand until slightly softened. Beat until thick and mushy. Pour into pan and freeze until firm. Makes about one and one-half quarts.

CRANBERRY-ORANGE HONEY

1 1-lb. can whole cranberry sauce
¼ c. orange juice
2 to 3 T. honey

Mix cranberry sauce, orange juice and honey to suit your "sweet tooth." Delightful sauce with pancakes. Makes 2 cups.

CIDER SAUCE

2 T. quick-cooking	¼ t. salt
tapioca	1½ c. cider
¼ c. sugar	1 T. butter

Combine tapioca, sugar, salt and cider in saucepan. Let stand 5 minutes. Cook and stir over medium heat until mixture comes to boil; remove from heat; stir in butter. Cool 15 to 20 minutes; stir. Serve warm on plain cake, gingerbread or ice cream. Makes about 1⅔ cups sauce.

HOT MULLED CIDER

½ c. brown sugar	1 t. whole cloves
¼ t. salt	3-inch cinnamon
2 qts. cider	sticks
1 t. whole allspice	Dash nutmeg

Combine brown sugar, salt and cider. Tie spices in small cheesecloth bag; add to cider mixture. Slowly bring to boil; simmer, covered, about 20 minutes. Use cinnamon stick as muddlers. Makes 10 servings.

BOILED CIDER PIE

8-inch shallow pastry shell, baked
⅓ c. grated maple sugar (or brown sugar)
⅓ c. boiled cider
3 eggs, separated
½ t. nutmeg
1 t. butter
½ c. seeded raisins
⅓ c. granulated sugar

Dissolve maple sugar by heating with boiled cider. Add beaten egg yolks very slowly, stirring constantly; cook until thickened. Add nutmeg, butter and raisins. Pour into baked shell. Cover with meringue made from egg whites and granulated sugar. Bake in 325° oven about 15 minutes, or until meringue is a delicate, golden brown.

CIDER SAUCE FOR PUDDING

2 T. butter	1 c. cider
1 c. brown sugar,	¼ c. raisins
packed	Nutmeg
2 T. flour	

Melt butter in saucepan. Gradually add the combined brown sugar and flour, stirring constantly. Add cider; bring to boil, and let thicken just a little. Remove from heat. Add raisins. Pour into small pitcher or serving bowl and sprinkle with nutmeg. Serve hot with bread, cottage, or plain steamed pudding, or white cake. Note: If sauce becomes too thick, thin with cold cider.

SPICED CIDER

1 qt. cider	1 stick cinnamon
1 lemon, sliced	1 whole nutmeg,
thinly	crushed
Peel of 1 orange	6 cloves
and 1 lemon	1 T. sugar

In a large saucepan, mix cider, fruit and peels, spices, and sugar. Bring just to a boil. Immediately turn down heat and let cider simmer for 10 minutes. Strain and serve hot.

If you prefer, make this recipe a day ahead. Keep it chilled in the refrigerator and reheat just before serving. Garnish with lemon slices and cinnamon sticks.

CIDER GELATIN SALAD

1 T. unflavored	¼ c. sugar
gelatin	1¾ c. hot cider
2 T. cold water	1½ c. diced apple
2 T. lemon juice	½ c. diced celery

Soften gelatin in combined cold water and lemon juice. Dissolve sugar in hot cider. Add softened gelatin; stir until dissolved. Chill. When mixture begins to set, stir in apple and celery. Turn into 6 wet individual molds; chill. Unmold; serve on lettuce and top with mayonnaise and sprinkling of chopped nuts. Makes 6 servings.

VEGETABLES

Asparagus can rightly be called nature's gift to the country cook. Its tender green shoots, hidden beneath last year's dried fernlike stalks, dot fence lines, roadways and country gardens.

We can directly thank our third president, Thomas Jefferson, for importing asparagus seed to America. During his term of office, he introduced the simple but elegant gift of nature at state dinners.

ASPARAGUS WITH WATER CHESTNUT SAUCE

- ¼ c. butter
- 5 T. flour
- 2 t. salt
- ¼ t. pepper
- 2¼ c. milk
- 3 T. lemon juice
- 2 T. cubed sharp cheddar cheese
- ½ c. thinly sliced water chestnuts
- 2 lbs. fresh asparagus spears, cooked

Melt butter in saucepan. Stir in flour and seasonings. Gradually add milk and lemon juice. Cook over low heat, stirring constantly, until mixture thickens. Stir in cheddar cheese and water chestnuts. Arrange asparagus on platter. Spoon sauce over asparagus. Garnish with strips of lemon rind. Makes 6 to 8 servings.

CREAM OF ASPARAGUS SOUP

- ¾ c. water
- ¾ t. salt
- 1 lb. fresh asparagus, cut in pieces (about 2½ c.)
- 1 c. light cream
- 2 T. butter

In saucepan, heat water and salt to boiling. Add asparagus; cover and simmer 8 to 10 minutes, till asparagus is just tender. Put asparagus and cooking water into blender container; cover and blend on low speed till asparagus is finely chopped. Add cream and blend on high speed till smooth. Return soup to saucepan; add butter and heat through. If desired, dot each serving with additional butter. Makes 4 servings.

ASPARAGUS CASSEROLE

- 1 lb. fresh asparagus, cooked and drained
- ½ lb. fresh mushrooms, sliced and lightly sautéed
- 2 T. butter
- 2 T. regular flour
- ¾ t. seasoned salt
- ¼ t. freshly ground pepper
  Few grains paprika
- 1 c. cream
- ½ c. shredded Swiss cheese
- ½ c. very finely cut celery
  Round scalloped crackers, crushed

Heat butter in a saucepan. Stir in flour and seasonings; cook until mixture bubbles. Add cream gradually, stirring until blended. Bring rapidly to boiling; cook and stir 1 to 2 minutes. Remove from heat; add cheese and stir until cheese is melted. Mix in mushrooms and celery. Line the bottom of a greased shallow 1½-quart casserole with half the asparagus. Pour sauce over asparagus and arrange the remaining asparagus on top. Sprinkle with cracker crumbs. Bake at 350° for 25 minutes or until thoroughly heated. If desired, place under broiler until crumbs are browned. Makes 6 servings.

SWEET 'N SOUR ASPARAGUS SALAD

- 1 lb. fresh asparagus spears
- 6 slices bacon
- ¼ c. wine vinegar
- 2 t. sugar
  Dash salt
  Dash pepper
- 2 green onions, finely chopped (about 2 t.)
  Shredded lettuce
- 2 hard-boiled eggs, sliced

Cook asparagus in boiling salted water 8 to 10 minutes or until tender; drain. Meanwhile, cook bacon in skillet till crisp. Remove bacon, drain and crumble and set aside. Add vinegar, sugar, salt, pepper and onion to bacon drippings in skillet. Add asparagus; heat through. Arrange a bed of lettuce in each of 6 salad bowls. Remove asparagus from skillet; arrange on lettuce. Top with egg slices. Pour hot bacon dressing over each salad. Sprinkle with bacon. Makes 6 servings.

BAKED BEANS WITH TOMATOES

2½ c. dried navy beans
1 medium onion, sliced
3 oz. salt pork, sliced
2 c. canned tomatoes, sieved
2 c. water
1 t. salt
⅛ t. dry mustard
   Few grains cayenne
⅓ c. brown sugar, packed

Wash beans thoroughly and put them into a 3-quart bowl. Add enough water to come 2 inches above beans and soak overnight. Next morning drain and combine with the next 7 ingredients in a saucepan; bring to boil, reduce heat, cover and simmer 1 hour or until beans are soft enough to break open. Turn into a buttered casserole or baking dish and add brown sugar. Pull slices of salt pork to the top, cover and bake 2 hours in a 250° oven. Remove cover and bake another hour. Serve hot. Makes 5 servings.

LIMA BAKE

1½ c. dried lima beans
½ c. chopped onion
½ t. salt
1 c. chopped celery
¼ c. chopped green pepper
2 c. stewed tomatoes
¼ t. hot pepper sauce
4 slices bacon

Soak beans in cold water for 8 hours or overnight. Drain well. Place limas in large kettle; cover with water and bring to boil. Add onion and salt. Lower heat and let simmer slowly until beans are tender, about 30 minutes. Drain beans well, reserving ¼ cup liquid. Combine limas, celery, green pepper, tomatoes, hot pepper sauce and reserved lima liquid in 2½-quart casserole. Bake uncovered at 350° about 1 hour or until vegetables are tender. Meanwhile, fry bacon to desired doneness. Arrange bacon as desired on top of casserole before serving. Makes 4 to 6 servings.

COUNTRY BAKED BEANS

2 c. dried Great Northern Beans
6 slices bacon or salt pork
2 T. chopped onion
1 t. salt
⅛ t. pepper
4 T. molasses
3 T. brown sugar
1 t. dry mustard
2 c. hot water
3 T. tomato soup
2 T. catsup

Soak beans overnight. Drain. Brown meat in heavy skillet until golden brown. Put into bean pot. Add chopped onion and stir. Add beans, salt, pepper, molasses, sugar, mustard and water. Stir. Add tomato soup, catsup and enough additional water to cover the beans. Cover the bean pot. Bake 6 to 8 hours at 250°. Add water as needed to keep the beans moist. Uncover the last hour of baking so that the beans brown. Serves 4 or 5.

BOSTON BAKED BEANS

4 c. navy beans
½ lb. fat salt pork
2 t. salt
1½ T. brown sugar
¼ c. molasses
½ t. dry mustard

Wash and pick over beans. Soak overnight in cold water. In the morning, drain, cover with fresh water and simmer until skins break; turn into bean pot. Score pork and press into beans, leaving ¼ inch above the beans. Add salt, sugar, molasses and mustard. Add boiling water to cover. Cover and bake in 250° oven for about 8 hours without stirring, adding water as necessary to keep beans covered. Uncover during last half hour to brown. Serves 8.

HOME-BAKED BEANS

2 c. navy beans
½ lb. fat bacon, sliced
1½ t. salt
½ t. pepper
¼ c. brown sugar
1½ t. dry mustard
1 medium onion, quartered

Wash beans, cover with water and soak overnight. Cook slowly until skins burst or until just tender. Drain, reserving liquid. Place half the beans in bean pot. Bury part of bacon in beans and add half of combined remaining ingredients. Add remaining beans and seasonings. Place remaining bacon over top. Cover with bean liquid. Cover and bake at 250° to 300° for 6 to 8 hours. If necessary, add more liquid. Serves 6 to 8.

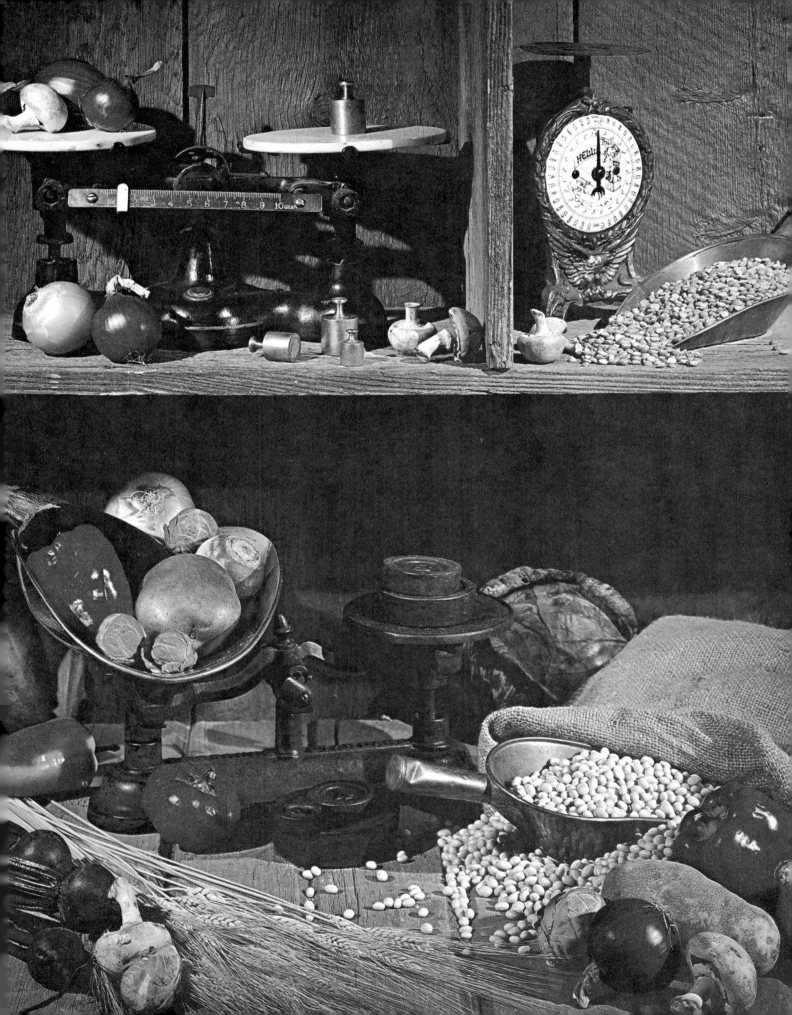

Tomatoes have an interesting history. Intrigued by the bright South American fruit, Spanish explorers took seeds back to Europe. But Europeans soon developed superstitions about the member of the deadly nightshade family.

Some thought them poisonous or a powerful drug. Others grew the plants as curiosities. Rumors that the tomato stimulated love earned it the name "love apple."

This superstition traveled to the colonies, where it was said that Thomas Jefferson was one of the first to try the fruit.

While some folks take the tomato for granted, country cooks know it is a food for all seasons. You will find it in everything from sauces, soups, stews, casseroles, baked dishes and salads to preserves, cakes, dinner drinks and country kitchen snacks.

TOMATO AND CUCUMBER SALAD

    5 tomatoes, sliced
    ¼ c. salad oil
    ¼ c. cider vinegar
    1 T. chopped parsley
       Fresh dill, minced
    3 fresh green onions,
       finely chopped
    1 small head of lettuce
    3 cucumbers, peeled
       and sliced
       Salt and pepper

Combine the tomatoes, oil, vinegar, parsley, dill and green onions in a large bowl. Refrigerate 2 hours. To serve: Shred lettuce in large salad bowl. Arrange tomato mixture and cucumbers on top of lettuce. Season with salt and pepper to taste. Toss lightly to blend. Serve. Makes 6 to 8 servings.

STUFFED TOMATO SALAD

    5 large tomatoes, chilled
       Crisp lettuce
    2 c. creamed cottage cheese
    1 T. chopped chives
       Paprika

Wash tomatoes and remove core from stem ends. Cut into 6 sections, leaving bottom attached; then open sections out like petals. Place on salad plates in nests of lettuce. Mix cottage cheese with chives. Pile into centers of tomatoes and sprinkle tops lightly with paprika. Makes 5 servings.

TOMATO AND ZUCCHINI CASSEROLE

    2 c. sliced zucchini (about ½ lb.)
    1 c. (1 medium) onion, thinly sliced
    2 small tomatoes, sliced
    ⅓ c. fine, dry bread crumbs
       Salt
       Pepper
    ½ c. cheddar cheese, grated
    1 tomato, cut in wedges

In a 1½-quart casserole, layer half each of the zucchini, onions, sliced tomatoes, and bread crumbs, sprinkling liberally with salt and pepper. Repeat layers. Top with tomato wedges. Cover and bake one hour in 375° oven. Uncover and sprinkle with cheese. Return to oven until cheese melts. Makes 6 servings.

MOLDED TOMATO RELISH

    2 c. canned stewed tomatoes
    1 3-oz. pkg. lemon gelatin
    ½ t. salt
    1 T. vinegar

Pour tomatoes into saucepan, saving can to use as a mold. Bring tomatoes to a boil. Reduce heat and simmer 2 minutes. Add gelatin, salt and vinegar; stir until gelatin is dissolved. Pour into can. Chill until firm, about 4 hours. To unmold, dip can in warm water and puncture bottom of can. Makes about 2 cups or 6 servings.

BAKED EGG AND TOMATO

    4 large slices tomato
       Salt and pepper to taste
    4 eggs

Put tomato slices in separate greased custard cups. Sprinkle with salt and pepper. Drop egg in each. Bake in 350° oven until eggs are set. Serve on buttered toast. Serves 4.

PENNSYLVANIA DUTCH SPINACH

    4 slices bacon, diced
    3 c. chopped raw spinach
    3 T. flour
1¼ c. hot water
    2 T. sugar
    1 T. cider vinegar
    1 t. salt
 ⅛ t. pepper
    2 hard-cooked eggs

Fry bacon until crisp; add bacon to spinach. Add flour to drippings and blend. Add hot water and cook over low heat until thick, stirring constantly. Add sugar, vinegar and seasonings. Pour over spinach. Stir well until wilted and garnish with sliced, hard-cooked eggs. Serves 6.

SPINACH SOUFFLÉ

    3 c. fresh chopped spinach
    3 T. butter
    3 T. flour
1½ c. milk or cream
 ½ t. sugar
    Salt to taste
    Pepper to taste
    Dash of nutmeg
    Garlic powder to taste
    Buttered bread crumbs

Cook spinach 5 minutes. Drain. Melt butter over low heat. Stir in flour until well mixed. Gradually add milk and continue stirring until thoroughly blended. Cook over low heat until thickened, stirring constantly. Season with sugar, salt, pepper, nutmeg and garlic powder. Add spinach and mix well. Turn into buttered casserole. Top with bread crumbs. Bake at 350° for about 25 minutes, or until bread crumbs are browned and casserole is bubbly.

WILTED SPINACH TOSS

    3 slices bacon
 ¼ c. vinegar
    1 T. salad oil
1½ t. sugar
 ¼ t. salt
 ⅛ t. dried tarragon leaves, crushed
    Dash freshly ground black pepper
 ¼ c. chopped celery
    1 T. sliced green onion
    6 c. torn fresh spinach (about ½ lb.)
    2 medium oranges, peeled and cut in bite-size pieces

In large skillet, cook bacon till crisp; drain, reserving 2 tablespoons drippings. Crumble bacon and set aside. Stir vinegar, oil, sugar, salt, tarragon and pepper into reserved drippings; bring to a boil. Add chopped celery and sliced green onion. Gradually add spinach, tossing just till leaves are coated and wilted slightly. Add oranges and crumbled bacon; toss lightly. Makes 6 to 8 servings.

CREAMED SPINACH

4 T. butter	1 c. milk
1 large onion, chopped	½ t. nutmeg
	¼ t. allspice
2 lbs. fresh spinach	1 t. salt
2 T. flour	¼ t. pepper

Melt 2 tablespoons butter in large saucepan. Sauté onion in butter until brown. Add washed, drained spinach to onion and cook, covered, for 3 to 5 minutes. Drain and chop. Return spinach to saucepan. While spinach is cooking, work remaining butter and flour together with a fork. When spinach is cooked, lower heat and add butter/flour mixture a little at a time until it is all smoothly incorporated. Add milk and seasonings. Reheat. Use as a garnish with other vegetables. Serves 6.

BOILED CORN ON THE COB

Place cleaned corn on the cob into a large kettle. Cover with cold water. Omit salt; it tends to toughen the corn. Bring just to a boil and then let the ears stand in boiling water for 1 minute. Eat at once with plenty of soft butter and salt to taste.

PARSLEY BUTTER

Mix ¼ cup softened butter, 2 tablespoons each chopped parsley and green onion, ½ teaspoon salt and a dash of pepper.

ROASTED CORN ON THE COB

Remove outer husks and silks, but leave a complete covering of inner husks. Soak in salted water for about 30 minutes. Wrap each ear tightly in foil and place on gray, glowing coals for about 15 minutes. Turn frequently. Remove the foil and husks. Serve with melted butter and pastry brushes.

CARROT-STUFFED BAKED POTATOES

    4 baking potatoes
    1 c. mashed cooked carrots
    2 T. grated onion
1½ t. salt
 ¼ t. dried dill weed
 ⅛ t. pepper
    3 T. milk
    2 T. butter
    1 egg

Scrub potatoes well. Dry potatoes and prick with fork. Bake in 425° oven 55 to 60 minutes or until soft. Immediately cut slice from top of each. Carefully scoop out potato without breaking skin. Place potato in a large bowl. Add remaining ingredients and beat until smooth. Pile potato mixture into shells. Bake in 350° oven for 25 to 30 minutes. Makes 4 servings.

RAW POTATO DUMPLINGS

6 raw potatoes   Flour
2 eggs   Butter
  Salt

Peel and grate potatoes and let drain until most of the water is drawn off. Add the eggs and salt and beat well. Add enough flour to make a stiff dough. Knead and shape into dumplings. Drop into boiling salted water and cook gently. When dumplings come to the top, remove them, brush with butter and brown in the oven, or cut in half and brush with melted butter.

COTTAGE FRIED POTATOES

    3 T. butter
    3 c. cubed potatoes, cooked with skins on
 ¼ c. chopped onion
 ½ t. salt
 ⅛ t. pepper

Heat butter in large cast-iron skillet. Sauté onions until tender and transparent. Add cooled, peeled and cubed potatoes. Fry until golden brown on one side; carefully turn and brown on second side. Season with salt and pepper. Makes 4 to 6 servings.

SCALLOPED POTATOES

    4 large potatoes   1½ t. salt
    3 T. butter   ⅛ t. pepper
 ⅓ c. chopped onion   2 c. milk
4½ t. flour

Pare potatoes and cut into ⅛-inch crosswise slices. Place in a buttered 1½-quart baking dish. In a medium saucepan melt butter; add onion and cook until tender. Remove from heat and blend in flour, salt and pepper. Stir in milk. Return to heat and cook, stirring constantly, until mixture thickens slightly and comes to a boil. Pour over potato slices. Bake, covered, in a 350° oven for 30 minutes. Uncover and bake 1 hour longer, or until potatoes are tender. Makes 4 to 6 servings.

DILL BUTTER

Mix ¼ cup softened butter, 1 teaspoon dillweed, ½ teaspoon salt and
a dash of pepper.

GLAZED BABY CARROTS

2 bunches baby carrots
6 T. butter
6 T. sugar
½ t. cinnamon or ginger

Wash carrots, scrape if necessary and leave whole. Cook in a small amount of boiling, salted water for 12 to 15 minutes or until tender when tested with a fork. Drain thoroughly. Combine butter, sugar and cinnamon or ginger in a large skillet. Cook, stirring constantly, until well blended. Add carrots and cook over low heat, shaking the pan frequently to glaze carrots on all sides until shiny and well glazed. Serves 6.

VINEGAR CARROTS

Wash and scrape 12 medium carrots. Boil until tender. Cut lengthwise in quarters and place in heated shallow serving dish. Season with salt, pepper, paprika and 2 tablespoons melted butter. Pour ⅓ cup hot cider vinegar over carrots. Serves 6 to 8.

CARROT-CELERY COMBO

1 bouillon cube
2¼ c. water, divided
½ t. salt
2 c. celery, sliced
2 c. carrots, sliced
2 T. cornstarch
Dash of Worcestershire, if desired

In a skillet dissolve bouillon cube in ¾ cup water, add salt, celery and carrots. Cook covered 8 to 10 minutes until tender. Moisten cornstarch with remaining 1½ cups water and thicken sauce slightly. Add dash of Worcestershire. Serves 6 to 8.

BAKED SQUASH

Wash 2 squash and cut them in half. Spoon out seeds and fibers from the cavity. Put 4 slices of bacon in a shallow baking pan and bake in a preheated 350° oven until crisp. Remove from oven, drain on paper towels and set aside. Sprinkle squash with salt and pepper and place, cut side down, in the bacon fat. Bake at 350° for about 1 hour or until tender when tested with a fork. Just before serving, sprinkle lightly with brown sugar, brush with some of the bacon fat, and drop the bacon, crumbled, into squash cavities. Serves 4.

GLAZED WINTER SQUASH

½ medium	¼ c. brown sugar
Hubbard squash	1 t. salt
⅓ c. butter	2 T. lemon juice

Cut squash in 1-inch cubes and peel. Melt butter; add brown sugar, salt and lemon juice. Pour over cubes of squash in a greased shallow baking pan. Cover and bake in a 400° oven about 45 minutes or until tender. Remove cover after 30 minutes of baking. Baste occasionally. Makes 4 to 6 servings.

TANGY STUFFED SQUASH

4 acorn squash
1 lb. chopped beef
¼ c. chopped onion
¼ c. bread crumbs
1½ t. salt
¼ t. dried tarragon
⅔ c. sour cream
½ t. hot pepper sauce

Cut squash in half. Scoop out seeds and fibers. Drop halves into boiling, salted water and cook about 10 minutes. Blend remaining ingredients. Mound meat filling into squash halves. Place halves in pan with 1 inch of hot water. Bake in a 350° oven for about 30 minutes or until squash is tender. Makes 4 to 6 servings.

Two generations ago, everyone raised rutabagas. Large piles of them were stored in cool, dark basements each fall, right alongside potatoes, cabbages, squash and pumpkins. Country cooks prepared them at least once a week and never failed to include at least part of one in their vegetable soup.

The rutabaga, a cross between a cabbage and a turnip, is a member of the mustard family. Its name comes from the Swedish word "Rotabagge." Most Europeans recognized the Swedish ability to prepare appealing "rutabagges" and in some areas rutabagas are called "Swedes" or "Swede turnips."

RUTABAGA-POTATO CASSEROLE

2 medium potatoes
2 medium rutabagas
½ c. flour
1 t. baking powder
1 t. salt
⅛ t. pepper, or to taste
4 eggs, well beaten
¼ c. milk
¼ c. melted butter

Peel potatoes and rutabagas; cover with cold water and let stand. Sift together flour, baking powder and seasonings. Blend half of dry ingredients with eggs, stir in milk and butter and mix well. Drain vegetables; run through blender or food grater. With a wooden spoon, mix remaining dry ingredients with vegetables. Work quickly so potatoes do not darken. Place mixture in greased 1-quart casserole. Set in pan of hot water with level at least ⅔ of the height of the casserole. Bake at 325° for one hour. Makes 6 servings.

RUTABAGA - ONION CASSEROLE

2 lbs. rutabaga, peeled and cut into
   ½-inch slices
3 c. thinly sliced onion
   Salt and pepper to taste
1 chicken bouillon cube
½ c. boiling water
2 T. butter

Arrange alternate layers of rutabaga and onions in a greased 2-quart casserole. Sprinkle layers lightly with salt and pepper. Dissolve bouillon in boiling water and pour over vegetables. Dot with butter. Cover and bake at 400° for 1¼ hours or until rutabagas are tender. Makes 6 servings.

RUTABAGAS IN SOUR CREAM

4 c. cubed rutabaga
¼ t. salt
   Dash pepper
1 medium onion,
   sliced
2 T. butter
1 c. sour cream
½ t. caraway or
   dill seed

Cook rutabaga in small amount of boiling salted water until tender, 15 - 20 minutes. Drain well. Sprinkle with salt and pepper. Sauté onion in butter until tender; add to sour cream. Pour over cubed rutabaga. Sprinkle with caraway or dill.

FRENCH FRIED RUTABAGAS

1 medium rutabaga
1 t. sugar
1 egg, beaten
½ c. cornmeal
1 t. salt
   Vegetable oil
   for frying

Cut rutabaga slices lengthwise into ¼-inch strips. If the strips are too long, cut crosswise once. Parboil strips for 5 minutes in a small amount of boiling water with 1 teaspoon sugar added. Drain well and cool. Beat egg slightly in shallow bowl; mix cornmeal and salt together on waxed paper. Preheat frying pan to 370°. Add ¼ inch of oil. Dip cooled rutabaga strips in egg and roll in seasoned cornmeal. Without crowding, fry strips to brown evenly. Remove strips from skillet and place on baking sheets lined with paper towels. Keep warm in 250° oven while the remaining strips are cooked. Serve hot. Makes 4 to 6 servings.

MASHED RUTABAGAS AND POTATOES

4 c. (2 lbs.) sliced, pared rutabagas
3 c. quartered, pared potatoes (3 medium)
2 t. salt
1 T. sugar
1 chicken bouillon cube
2 c. boiling water
¼ t. pepper
1 c. grated cheddar cheese
2 T. finely chopped onion

Place rutabagas, potatoes, salt and sugar in saucepan. Dissolve bouillon cube in boiling water and pour over vegetables. Quickly bring to a boil, reduce heat and continue cooking gently until vegetables are tender. Drain, mash and add pepper, grated cheese and onion. Beat until fluffy. Top with buttered crumbs and broil until golden brown if desired. Makes 6 servings.

Sauerkraut was probably the first food to travel around the world. It has come a long way since the days when chunks of wine-fermented cabbage were fed to hardworking Chinese coolies building the Great Wall of China.

German and Dutch settlers brought their kraut-making skills with them to the new colonies. Cabbage grew well in the New World.

In autumn, you could count on a trip to Grandmother's cellar to sample the tawny kraut working mysteriously in the big crock. Grandmother's tangy kraut had a wide variety of uses, from stuffing pork or poultry to baking a cake.

BEEF WITH SAUERKRAUT

2 T. vegetable oil
3 lbs. eye round or chuck beef,
   cut into 2-inch cubes
1½ c. sliced onions
1½ t. salt
½ t. freshly ground black pepper
1 t. paprika
1½ lbs. sauerkraut, rinsed and drained
1 bay leaf
1½ c. chopped canned tomatoes

Heat the oil in a casserole; brown the meat and onions. Sprinkle with salt, pepper and paprika. Cover and cook over low heat for 20 minutes; watch carefully and add a little water if necessary to keep from burning. Mix in the sauerkraut. Cook 10 minutes. Add the bay leaf and tomatoes. Cover and cook 1½ hours longer. Discard bay leaf. Serves 6 to 8.

BAKED SAUERKRAUT

½ c. chopped onion
½ c. green pepper strips
2 T. shortening
10 pineapple slices with liquid
2 T. cornstarch
1 c. beef bouillon
1 t. soy sauce
2 t. vinegar
¼ c. sugar
⅛ t. pepper
½ t. ground ginger
4 c. sauerkraut, drained
9 hot dogs, cut in half

Sauté onion and green pepper in shortening until tender. Drain pineapple, reserving liquid; mix half the pineapple liquid with cornstarch and add to onion and green pepper. Gradually blend in remaining pineapple liquid and bouillon. Stir in soy sauce, vinegar, sugar, pepper and ginger. Cook until thickened. Arrange half the sauerkraut and half the pineapple slices in the bottom of a 3½-quart casserole. Top with half the sauce mixture. Add remaining sauerkraut and pineapple. Pile hot dogs in center and pour remaining sauce over all. Bake at 350° for 30 minutes. Makes 6 to 8 servings.

SAUERKRAUT RELISH

3 c. sauerkraut, well drained
   and chopped
1 c. chopped onion
2 c. chopped celery
1 large green pepper, chopped
1½ c. sugar
1½ c. water
½ c. vinegar

Combine sauerkraut, onion, celery and green pepper. Set aside. In a medium saucepan, combine sugar, water and vinegar. Bring liquid mixture to a boil to dissolve sugar. Cool. Add liquid mixture to vegetable mixture and mix well. Let stand in refrigerator for 24 hours. Makes 6 to 8 servings.

CRISPY KRAUT SALAD

2 c. finely chopped sauerkraut
½ c. chopped onion
½ c. chopped celery
¼ c. chopped green pepper
1 c. chopped pimiento
½ c. cider vinegar
¼ c. salad oil
½ c. sugar

Drain kraut well. Chop onion, celery, green pepper and pimiento. Make a dressing from vinegar, oil and sugar. Blend all ingredients together and marinate for an hour or longer. Makes 6 servings.

SCALLOPED SAUERKRAUT AND TOMATOES

2½ c. whole stewed tomatoes
   Salt
   Pepper
2 T. butter
2 c. bread crumbs
2½ c. sauerkraut

Drain tomatoes, reserving liquid. Put tomato pieces in greased baking dish. Sprinkle with salt and pepper. Dot with butter. Cover with layer of crumbs. Add layer of sauerkraut. Alternate layers, seasoning and dotting each with butter, until all ingredients are used. Have layer of buttered crumbs on top. Add tomato liquid. Bake at 400° 20 minutes. Serves 6.

SALADS

WILTED LETTUCE TOSS

4 slices bacon
¼ c. sliced green onion
1 large tomato, chopped
4 c. torn leaf lettuce
2 T. vinegar
¼ t. salt
Dash pepper

Fry bacon in large skillet until crisp; drain, reserving 1 tablespoon drippings. Crumble bacon and set aside. Meanwhile, combine lettuce, tomato and onion. In skillet, heat reserved drippings, vinegar, salt and pepper to boiling. Gradually add lettuce mixture, tossing only until leaves are coated and wilted slightly. Turn into serving bowl. Top with crumbled bacon. Serve immediately. Makes 4 to 5 servings.

CREAMY CELERY SLAW

1 t. salt	¼ c. sour cream
1½ t. sugar	2 c. celery, thinly
⅛ t. pepper	sliced on diagonal
Dash paprika	1 pimiento, slivered
⅓ c. salad oil	2 T. wine vinegar

Combine salt, sugar, pepper, paprika, oil and vinegar; beat well with hand beater; then slowly beat in sour cream. Pour this dressing over celery. Marinate in refrigerator about 3 hours; then toss in pimiento. Makes 3 servings.

TOMATO FRENCH DRESSING

1 c. tomato juice	1 t. paprika
½ c. corn oil	1 t. salt
¼ c. vinegar	1 t. Worcestershire
2 T. sugar	sauce
1 t. dry mustard	1 clove garlic

Measure all ingredients into a bottle or jar. Cover tightly and shake well. Chill several hours, then remove garlic. Shake thoroughly before serving. Makes about 2 cups.

ORANGE SLAW

3 medium or 4 small oranges
1 small head cabbage
¼ small onion
¾ c. mayonnaise
1 T. fresh squeezed lemon juice
1 T. sugar
½ t. salt

Peel oranges and cut into bite-sized pieces. Shred cabbage using long blade of grater, or cut finely with sharp knife. Chop onion finely. Place oranges, cabbage and onion in large serving bowl. Mix together mayonnaise, lemon juice, sugar and salt. Pour over slaw and mix lightly. Cover and refrigerate for 20 to 30 minutes before serving. Makes 6 servings.

TUNA - BEAN SALAD

1 c. chunk light tuna, drained
¾ c. celery, chopped
¼ c. onion, chopped
¼ c. sweet pickle relish
¾ t. curry powder
½ c. mayonnaise
2 hard-cooked eggs, chopped
¼ t. salt
1 15-oz. can red kidney beans, drained and rinsed
¼ c. chopped nuts

Lightly mix all ingredients, except nuts. Line serving bowl with salad greens and fill with mixture. Top with chopped nuts. Makes 4 to 6 servings.

CREAMY COTTAGE - POTATO SALAD

Add 2 cups (16 ounces) creamed cottage cheese to each 3 cups of your favorite cold potato salad. Chill well. Makes 6 to 8 servings.

They called them the "meetin' seeds." Colonists grew fennel, dill and caraway seeds in their gardens and carried them to church to nibble during long Sabbath sermons.

From pickles to salads, delightful seeds accent country kitchen fare. Dill, perhaps the most familiar today, was also used medicinally and as a nerve-calming tea in medieval times. Some claim its name is derived from the Norse word "dilla," meaning to lull. The Greeks, however, reportedly chewed on dill seeds to keep them awake. Some cultures prescribed the seeds as a cure for insomnia. Others used it to hinder a witch's will.

The European native, with a parasol of yellow-green flowers on tall, flowing stems, is at home in backyard gardens. Country cooks have always prized dill seeds for their tasty pickle flavoring. Other country kitchen treats can be flavored by dropping a pinch or two in a green apple pie or scattering some across a summer salad.

DEVIL-DILLED EGGS

8 hard-boiled eggs
¼ c. mayonnaise
¼ t. chopped dillweed
Dash of pepper
Paprika (optional)

Cut eggs into halves. Remove yolks, mash and mix with remaining ingredients except paprika. Spoon yolk mixture into whites. Garnish with paprika, if desired. Chill before serving.

DILLY DRESSING

1 c. tomato juice
1 t. grated lemon rind
2 T. fresh lemon juice or wine vinegar
1 t. salt
½ t. fresh or dried dillweed
½ t. dry mustard
¼ t. liquid sugar substitute

Combine all ingredients in a jar. Shake to blend. Chill. Serve with tossed salad or over sliced tomatoes with onion rings. Makes about 1 cup.

CREAMY CELERY SEED DRESSING

½ c. dairy
   sour cream
2 T. milk
1 t. chopped chives
¾ t. celery seed
¼ t. salt
¼ t. pepper
1 T. vinegar

In a small bowl combine sour cream, milk, chives, celery seed, salt and pepper. Mix well. Blend in vinegar. Serve with molded vegetable salads, cucumbers, tomatoes, tossed salads, etc. Makes about ½ cup.

HERB DRESSING

¾ c. mayonnaise
1 hard-boiled egg, finely chopped
2 T. finely chopped parsley
1½ t. tarragon vinegar
½ t. prepared mustard
1 t. finely chopped chives

Blend all ingredients. Chill. Serve with mixed greens, vegetables or meat salads. Makes one cup.

COTTAGE CHEESE DRESSING

½ cup French dressing
½ cup mayonnaise
½ cup cottage cheese

Fold French dressing into mayonnaise. Lightly fold in cottage cheese. Chill. Serve with fruit, vegetable or mixed green salads. Makes 1¼ cups.

FRUIT SALAD DRESSING

½ c. mayonnaise
½ c. dairy sour cream
2½ T. confectioners' sugar
1½ T. lemon juice

Blend all ingredients. Chill about one hour. Serve with fruit salads. Makes about 1¼ cups.

FRUITS

STRAWBERRY SURPRISE

½ c. milk
1½ c. miniature marshmallows
1 c. whipping cream
½ c. sliced almonds
2½ c. fresh strawberries, cut in half

Heat milk to boiling, add marshmallows and stir at medium heat until marshmallows melt. Remove from heat and allow to cool thoroughly. Whip cream; fold berries and whipped cream into cooled marshmallow mixture. Pour into sherbet dishes and chill several hours. When ready to serve, sprinkle sliced almonds on top or garnish with fresh mint leaves. Serves 6.

STRAWBERRY-RHUBARB COBBLER

2 qts. drained stemmed fresh strawberries
2 qts. drained ½-inch pieces fresh rhubarb (about 2½ lbs.)
5 c. (2¼ lbs.) sugar
¾ c. quick-cooking tapioca
1 t. salt
1 T. butter
Unbaked biscuits (your favorite recipe)

To prepare and freeze filling: Combine fruits, sugar, tapioca and salt; mix well. Divide filling mixture evenly among four 1-quart aluminum foil baking pans, taking care that filling is at least ¾-inch below top of pans. Cover with aluminum foil, sealing close to surface of fruits. Freeze firmly. Filling may be stored in freezer up to six months.

To bake each cobbler: Bake covered pan of frozen filling at 425° for 50 minutes or until filling is bubbling. Then remove cover, dot filling with butter, and top with 8 unbaked biscuits. Return to oven and bake 20 minutes longer, covering biscuits loosely with aluminum foil during last 5 minutes to prevent overbrowning. Serve warm. Each cobbler makes 8 servings. Makes 4 cobblers.

STRAWBERRY SHORTCAKE

2 c. flour
4 t. baking powder
½ t. salt
1 T. sugar
⅓ c. shortening
¾ c. milk
Butter
Whipping cream
Whole strawberries

GARNISH
2 qts. fresh strawberries, mashed and sweetened to taste

Preheat oven to 450°. Sift flour, baking powder, salt and sugar together and cut in shortening. Gradually stir in milk to make a soft dough. On a floured board, knead dough 8 to 10 times, then roll to ½-inch thickness. Cut with large cookie cutter and place on greased cookie sheet or bake as one sheet on greased cookie sheet and cut into squares after baking. Bake 12 to 15 minutes. Remove shortcake from oven, split and butter immediately. Keep warm until ready to serve (wrap in foil) or serve immediately. Place warm shortcake (bottom halves) in individual bowls. Spoon strawberries over shortcake halves, place remaining half on top and spoon more berries on top. Garnish with whipping cream and whole strawberries. Serves 6 to 8.

Each spring, country cooks eagerly watch the rhubarb patch for the first sign of the ruddy, tinged knobs to make their appearance. They coax the large green leaves to unfold and the tender red stalks to grow tall enough for picking. When the rhubarb awakes in the warm soil, spring is here to stay.

Before the days of freezers and year-round fresh foods, country cooks looked forward to the first serving of "pie plant" as the annual spring tonic to awaken dull appetites.

Although the rhubarb plant has been grown as a cultivated crop for 3000 years, it was first introduced to England late in the sixteenth century. From here it was only a short time before the plants reached the shores of the New World.

Colonists found this member of the buckwheat family easy to grow in the rich new soil. Homemade rhubarb pies, sauces, cobblers and jams continue to be country kitchen classics.

RHUBARB COBBLER

1 c. sugar	1½ t. baking
2 T. cornstarch	powder
½ t. cinnamon	½ t. salt
4 c. rhubarb, cut	4 T. butter
in 1-inch pieces	⅓ c. milk
1 T. water	½ c. chopped
2 T. butter	pecans
1 c. flour	1 t. shredded
⅓ c. sugar	orange peel

Combine the 1 cup sugar, cornstarch and cinnamon. Add rhubarb and water. Cook and stir until mixture is boiling; cook 1 minute longer. Pour into 8 x 1½-inch round baking dish; dot with the 2 tablespoons butter. Place in 400° oven while preparing biscuits. Sift together flour, ⅓ cup sugar, baking powder and salt. Cut in 4 tablespoons butter. Stir in milk, pecans and orange peel. Drop spoonfuls of butter onto hot rhubarb mixture. Bake in 400° oven for about 25 minutes. Serve with light cream or milk. Makes 6 servings.

RHUBARB-CUSTARD KUCHEN

CRUST

½ c. butter	½ c. sugar
1 egg yolk	1¼ c. flour
½ t. salt	¼ c. water
2½ c. rhubarb	½ t. nutmeg

CUSTARD

2 eggs	¼ t. salt
1 egg white	¼ c. milk
¾ c. sugar	1 t. vanilla

Cream butter, sugar, salt and egg yolk together well. Then add flour. Moisten like pie crust, using milk. Pat into 10 x 12-inch pan. Bring rhubarb and water to boil in small pan, cooking only until rhubarb begins to soften. Cool slightly. Pour rhubarb into lined pan. Beat together eggs, egg white, sugar, salt, milk and vanilla. Pour over rhubarb. Sprinkle nutmeg over all. Bake at 350° for 45 minutes. Serve warm or cooled in 2½-inch squares topped with whipped cream.

RHUBARB CREAM PIE

1½ c. sugar	2 eggs, well-beaten
3 T. flour	3 c. cut rhubarb
1 t. nutmeg	Pastry for
1½ T. butter	double-crust pie

Blend sugar, flour, nutmeg and butter. Add eggs; beat until smooth; pour over rhubarb in 9-inch pastry-lined pie pan. Top with pastry. Bake at 450° for 10 minutes, then at 350° about 30 minutes. Serve warm or cooled.

RHUBARB BETTY

5 c. rhubarb, cut in ½-inch pieces
1¾ c. sugar
1 T. flour
½ t. salt
2 t. grated orange rind
1 orange, sectioned and cubed
4 c. small bread cubes
½ c. butter, melted
½ c. flaked coconut

Mix together rhubarb, sugar, flour, salt, 1 teaspoon of the orange rind and fruit. Add half of bread cubes and half of butter; mix. Put into greased 8 x 8 x 2-inch baking pan. Combine remaining bread cubes, butter, orange rind and coconut. Sprinkle over top of rhubarb. Bake at 375° for about 40 minutes or until browned. Serve warm. Makes 6 to 8 servings.

CHERRY CHIFFON PIE

    2 c. frozen cherries, thawed
    5 T. sugar
    ½ c. water
    1 T. lemon juice
    1 pkg. cherry flavored gelatin
    ¼ t. almond extract
    1 c. evaporated milk, chilled
    1 baked 9-inch pie shell

Drain cherries, saving juice. Cut cherries in half; combine with juice, sugar, water and lemon juice. Cook over low heat for 4 or 5 minutes. Pour mixture over gelatin, stir until dissolved and add almond extract; chill until slightly thickened. Whip evaporated milk until stiff peaks form; fold into cherry mixture and chill for 10 minutes. Pile lightly into baked pie shell. Chill at least 3 hours before serving. Makes 1 pie.

CHERRY SAUCE I

    2½ c. canned, pitted, sour red cherries
      2 T. lemon juice
      1 T. cornstarch
     ¾ c. sugar
     ½ t. almond extract
      1 qt. ice cream

Drain cherries, reserving one cup juice. Place cherries, lemon juice and reserved cherry juice in a saucepan. Combine cornstarch and sugar; add to cherry mixture. Cook over medium heat, stirring constantly until thickened and mixture comes to a boil. Cook slightly; stir in almond extract. Serve warm or cold over cherry or vanilla ice cream. Makes about 2¾ cups sauce, or 6 to 8 servings.

OLD-FASHIONED CHERRY PIE

    2½ T. tapioca
     ⅛ t. salt
      1 c. sugar
      3 c. drained tart cherries
     ½ c. cherry juice
     ¼ t. almond extract
      1 T. butter
        9-inch pie shell

Mix together all ingredients except butter and let stand 15 minutes. Pour into pie shell; dot with butter. Add top crust. Bake at 425° for about 45 minutes. Makes 6 to 8 servings.

CHERRY SPONGE PUDDING

    2 T. quick-cooking tapioca
    ½ c. sugar
    ⅛ t. salt
    2½ c. sour cherries and juice
    1 T. lemon juice
    1 T. butter
    ½ c. sifted flour
    2 eggs, unbeaten
    ¼ t. cream of tartar
    ⅛ t. salt
    ½ c. sugar

Combine tapioca, sugar, salt, cherries and juice in saucepan. Cook and stir over medium heat until mixture comes to a boil. Add lemon juice and butter; blend. Remove from heat. If desired, add a few drops of red coloring. Pour into a 2-quart baking dish and keep warm. Measure sifted flour and set aside. Combine eggs, cream of tartar and salt in bowl. Beat with eggbeater until foamy. Then add sugar gradually and continue beating until very fluffy, thick and light-colored. Gradually fold in flour. Pour the batter over warm fruit. Bake in 325° oven for 50 minutes or until cake is baked. Serve warm. Makes 8 servings.

CHERRY SAUCE II

    2½ c. tart red cherries
      1 c. cherry juice
      4 t. cornstarch
     ¼ c. sugar

In a 2-quart saucepan, combine cornstarch and sugar. Gradually stir in cherry juice. Cook, stirring constantly, till thick and clear. Add cherries. Heat through. Makes 2 cups.

49

DESSERTS

OLD-FASHIONED RICE PUDDING

2 large eggs	½ c. seedless raisins
½ c. sugar	½ c. chopped
½ t. salt	cooking apples
2 c. milk	1 t. vanilla
2 c. cooked rice	Dash nutmeg

Blend together eggs, sugar and salt. Scald milk. Slowly stir into egg mixture. Blend. Add rice, raisins, apples and vanilla. Mix well. Pour into a 3-quart casserole. Sprinkle top with nutmeg. Set casserole in a pan of water and bake in a 350° oven for 1 hour and 15 minutes. Bake until knife inserted into pudding comes out clean. Serve warm with cream or milk. Makes 6 servings.

BLUEBERRY TREASURE SQUARES

2 c. crisp rice cereal
½ c. chopped almonds, toasted
½ c. flaked coconut, toasted
½ c. brown sugar
⅓ c. butter, melted
1 qt. vanilla ice cream
½ c. blueberry ice-cream topping

Mix rice cereal which has been slightly crushed with almonds, coconut, brown sugar and butter. Press ½ of mixture in bottom of 9 x 9 x 2-inch pan. Chill. Stir vanilla ice cream to soften. Add topping and quickly swirl through ice cream to marble. Freeze. Makes 9 servings. Serve with topping, if desired.

FRESH BLUEBERRY TOPPING

Combine ¼ cup sugar, 2 teaspoons cornstarch, dash each salt, cinnamon and cloves. Stir in 2 cups fresh blueberries (slightly crushed) and ⅓ cup light corn syrup. Cook and stir till mixture boils; simmer 7 minutes. Cool; add 2 tablespoons lemon juice. Makes 1½ cups.

HONEY-GLAZED FRUITS

4 c. canned pear halves, drained
2 c. canned sliced pineapple, drained
⅓ c. honey
½ t. grated fresh orange rind
8 maraschino cherries with stems, drained

In shallow baking pan, place 1 pear half on top of each of 8 pineapple slices. Stir together honey and orange rind. Spoon over fruits. Broil 4 to 6 inches from heat until thoroughly heated, 3 to 4 minutes. Garnish with cherries. Makes 8 servings.

Hidden in the memories of long-past summer days, there is a hand-cranked ice-cream freezer on the back porch of our childhood home.

Ice cream became a socially acceptable dessert when Dolly Madison created a sensation at her husband's second inaugural ball serving "high on a silver platter a large shining dome of pink ice cream."

However, it wasn't until Nancy Johnson invented the hand-cranked ice-cream freezer in 1846 that homemade ice cream became common in country kitchens. Nancy, by the way, forgot to patent her machine, so William Young, who did, received all the credit.

VANILLA ICE CREAM (Custard Base)

1½ c. sugar
¼ c. flour
Dash salt
2 c. milk
4 eggs, slightly beaten
1 qt. (4 cups) heavy cream
1 T. vanilla

Combine sugar, flour and salt in a large saucepan; stir in milk. Cook over medium heat, stirring constantly, until mixture thickens and bubbles 1 minute. Stir half the hot mixture slowly into beaten eggs in a medium-size bowl; stir back into remaining mixture in saucepan. Cook, stirring, for 1 minute. Pour into a large bowl; stir in cream and vanilla. Chill at least 2 hours. Pour mixture into a 4- to 6-quart freezer can; freeze following directions of your freezer. Pack in plastic containers; freeze until firm. Makes about 2 quarts.

PUMPKIN CHIFFON PIE

2 envelopes unflavored gelatin
¼ c. cold water
2 eggs, separated
1½ c. canned pumpkin
1 c. milk
¾ c. brown sugar, firmly packed
2 t. pumpkin pie spice
½ t. salt
½ pt. (1 cup) whipping cream, whipped
9-inch graham cracker crumb crust

Soften gelatin in cold water. Beat egg yolks. Add pumpkin, milk, one-half cup brown sugar, spice and salt to yolks. Cook over low heat, stirring constantly, until thickened. Add gelatin; stir to dissolve. Chill until mixture thickens. Beat egg whites until they hold soft peaks. Add remaining one-fourth cup brown sugar and continue beating until egg whites are stiff. Fold into pumpkin mixture, then fold in whipped cream. Pour into crust. Chill until firm. Makes one 9-inch pie.

PUMPKIN-APPLE TARTS

2 c. canned pumpkin
2 c. applesauce
1 c. light brown sugar
1½ t. salt
3 t. cinnamon
2 t. nutmeg
½ t. ginger
1 t. cloves
8 eggs, beaten
1 c. heavy cream
½ c. milk
10 5-inch unbaked pastry shells

Combine pumpkin, applesauce, sugar, salt and spices. Add eggs. Scald cream and milk; add slowly to pumpkin mixture, mixing well. Pour into individual pastry shells. Bake in 400° oven for 40 minutes or until knife inserted near center of pie comes out clean. Cool. Garnish with whipped cream, candy shot, cheese wedges or walnut halves. Makes 10 servings.

PUMPKIN CAKE

2¼ c. flour
3 t. baking powder
½ t. salt
¼ t. baking soda
1½ t. cinnamon
½ t. ginger
½ t. allspice
½ c. butter
1 c. brown sugar, firmly packed
½ c. granulated sugar
2 eggs, unbeaten
¾ c. buttermilk or sour milk
¾ c. canned pumpkin
½ c. chopped nuts

Measure flour and add baking powder, salt, soda and spices. Mix together. Cream butter and add sugars gradually. Cream well. Add eggs, one at a time, beating until light. Add flour mixture alternately with buttermilk in small amounts. After each addition beat until smooth. Add pumpkin and nuts. Mix well. Bake in greased 9 x 13-inch pan in a 350° oven for 30 minutes or until done. Frost with a plain butter frosting.

PUMPKIN PIE

2 eggs, slightly beaten
½ c. brown sugar
½ c. granulated sugar
2 c. pumpkin
2 c. top milk
1 T. flour
½ t. ginger
½ t. salt
1½ t. cinnamon
½ t. nutmeg
Pastry for one-crust, 10-inch pie

Beat eggs and sugars; add pumpkin and milk. Add flour mixed with salt and spices. Beat well. Pour into 10-inch pastry-lined pie pan. Bake in 450° oven 10 minutes; reduce heat to 325° and bake 40 minutes longer, or until a knife inserted near center of pie comes out clean.

TOMATO SOUP CAKE

2 c. flour
1⅓ c. sugar
4 t. baking powder
1 t. baking soda
1½ t. allspice
1 t. cinnamon
½ t. ground cloves
1 10¾-oz. can condensed tomato soup
½ c. vegetable shortening
2 eggs
¼ c. water
1 c. raisins or chopped nuts

Measure dry ingredients into large bowl. Add soup and shortening. Beat for two minutes, scraping sides and bottom of bowl constantly. Add eggs and water. Beat two minutes more, scraping bowl frequently. Add raisins or nuts. Pour into either two round layers or a 13 x 9 x 2-inch pan that has been generously greased and floured. Bake at 350° for 35 to 40 minutes. Let stand in pans 10 minutes, remove and cool on rack. Frost with your favorite icing.

CARROT CAKE

½ c. shortening	2 c. flour
1 c. brown sugar	¼ t. baking soda
½ c. granulated sugar	3 t. baking powder
	1 t. salt
1 egg	1 t. cinnamon
¾ c. cooked, mashed carrots	⅔ c. chopped nuts
	⅓ c. sour milk

Cream shortening and sugars together. Add egg and mashed carrots. Sift flour, soda, baking powder, salt and cinnamon together. Add nuts and dry ingredients alternately with sour milk. Mix batter well. Pour into two 8-inch square pans with greased and floured paper in the bottoms. Bake 25 minutes at 350°. Cool. Put layers together with your favorite butter icing or whipped cream.

HOMEMADE MINCEMEAT

½ lb. fresh beef suet, chopped fine
4 c. seedless raisins
2 c. dried currants
1¼ c. chopped candied fruit
½ c. chopped dried figs
4 c. chopped, peeled cored apples
1 c. coarsely chopped nuts
1¼ c. sugar
1 t. ground nutmeg
1 t. ground allspice
1 t. ground cinnamon
½ t. ground cloves
2½ c. brandy
1 c. dry red wine

Combine the suet, fruit, nuts, sugar and spices in a large mixing bowl and stir together thoroughly. Pour in the brandy and wine, and mix with a large wooden spoon until all ingredients are well-moistened. Cover the bowl and set the mincemeat aside in a cool place (not in the refrigerator) for at least three weeks.

Check the mincemeat once a week. As the liquid is absorbed by the fruit, replenish it with wine and brandy, using about ¼ cup of each at a time. Mincemeat can be kept indefinitely in a covered container in the refrigerator. Makes 3 quarts.

To make pies with homemade mincemeat, prepare your favorite pastry for a two-crust pie. Line the pan with the bottom crust. Add undrained mincemeat. Add top crust. Bake in 425° oven 30 minutes or until done.

OLD-FASHIONED MINCEMEAT PIE

3 c. prepared mincemeat
1½ c. coarsely broken walnuts
½ c. brown sugar, packed
½ c. brandy
Pastry for two-crust pie
4 T. butter, softened
1 T. light cream
Pastry for two-crust, 9-inch pie

Combine walnuts, mincemeat, brown sugar and brandy; refrigerate to allow flavors to mingle. You can do this for several days. Roll out pastry for bottom crust, spread with two tablespoons butter; fold into thirds; refrigerate until well chilled; repeat with top crust. Heat oven to 425°. Roll out pastry crust. Fill with undrained mincemeat mixture. Adjust top crust; brush top with light cream. Bake 30 minutes or until nicely browned.

GROUND CHERRY PIE

Pastry for one-crust, 9-inch pie
1½ c. ground cherries, husked
2 eggs
¼ t. salt
¾ c. sugar
1⅓ T. flour
1 c. milk
1 t. vanilla

Line pie pan with pastry and fill with ground cherries. Beat eggs with salt and add sugar and flour. Add milk and vanilla and stir well. Pour over cherries and bake in 425° oven 10 minutes, then reduce temperature to 350° and bake 25 to 30 minutes longer or until a knife inserted in center comes out clean. Cover with whipped cream topping. Makes 1 9-inch pie.

SOUR CREAM RAISIN PIE

2 eggs, slightly beaten
¾ c. sugar
¼ t. salt
1 t. cinnamon
½ t. nutmeg
¼ t. cloves
1 c. sour cream
1 c. seeded raisins
Pastry for one-crust, 8-inch pie

Combine ingredients; pour into 8-inch pastry-lined pie pan. Bake in 450° oven 10 minutes, then in 350° oven about 30 minutes, or until mixture doesn't stick to knife. Serve warm or cold.

BLACKBERRY PIE

4 c. fresh blackberries
1 c. sugar
2 T. flour
2 T. lemon juice
¼ t. salt
Pastry for two-crust, 9-inch pie
1 T. butter

Combine berries, sugar, flour, lemon juice and salt. Line pie pan with pastry, add filling, dot with butter and cover with top crust. Bake in 450° oven 10 minutes; reduce temperature to 350° and bake 25 to 30 minutes longer. Makes 1 9-inch pie.

LEMON CREME PIE

1 c. sugar
¼ c. cornstarch
3 egg yolks, beaten
3 T. cold water
1¼ c. water
1 T. butter
6 T. lemon juice
1 T. grated lemon peel
1 9-inch baked pastry shell

Mix cornstarch with sugar. Beat egg yolks until lemon-colored. Add 3 tablespoons cold water. Stir into cornstarch-sugar mixture. Blend well. Bring 1¼ cups water to boil. Slowly add the above mixture to boiling water and cook until clear and thick, about 5 minutes. Add butter, lemon juice, and lemon peel. Return to heat and cook 2 additional minutes. Remove from heat. Cool. Pour into baked 9-inch pie shell.

MERINGUE

3 egg whites
4 T. confectioners' sugar

Beat egg whites until stiff but not dry; add sugar gradually; spread over cooled filling, sealing to edges of pastry. Brown in 350° oven 13 to 15 minutes.

GOLDEN APPLE-PECAN PIE

2 Golden Delicious apples, peeled and sliced
3 eggs
¾ c. brown sugar
⅛ t. salt
¾ c. light corn syrup
2 t. butter
⅔ c. coarsely chopped pecans
Pastry for single-crust pie

Line a 9-inch pie plate with pastry. Place apple slices in bottom of pie plate. Beat eggs; add remaining ingredients, reserving a few pecan halves or large pieces, and mix well. Bake at 425° for 10 minutes. Then reduce heat to 300° and bake for about one hour or until set. Garnish with whipped cream and a few pecan halves.

CAKES

KWIK KRAZY KAKE

1½ c. all-purpose flour
1 t. baking soda
½ t. salt
1 t. cinnamon
1 c. sugar
¼ c. cocoa
½ c. whole-bran cereal
1 c. cold strong coffee
¼ c. vegetable oil
1 T. vinegar
1 t. vanilla

Sift together flour, soda, salt, cinnamon, sugar and cocoa. Set aside. Measure whole bran cereal and coffee into ungreased 8 x 8 x 2-inch baking pan; stir to combine. Let stand 1 to 2 minutes or until most of liquid is absorbed. Mix in oil, vinegar and vanilla. Add sifted dry ingredients; stir until smooth. Bake in 350° oven about 40 minutes or until wooden pick inserted near center comes out clean. Serve with cinnamon-flavored whipped topping, orange or lemon sauce or ice cream. Sprinkle with nuts, if desired.

POOR MAN'S CAKE

1 c. light brown sugar, firmly packed
1 c. water
⅜ c. shortening
1 c. seeded raisins
1 t. cinnamon
½ t. nutmeg
½ t. salt
2¼ c. cake flour
1 t. baking soda
1¼ t. baking powder

Combine sugar, water, shortening, raisins, spices and salt in a medium saucepan. Bring to a boil over medium heat and boil for 3 minutes, stirring constantly. Cool. Measure sifted flour, add soda and baking powder and sift again. Gradually stir dry ingredients into raisin mixture. Then beat well. Pour into an 8 x 4 x 3-inch loaf pan, which has been greased generously on bottom and sides. Bake in a 325° oven for about one hour.

Spice cakes, always popular in country kitchens, can be as fancy as you want to make them. Or they can be moist, fresh-from-the-oven, after-school snacks for the children to help themselves.

Country cooks did not always have the handy baking spices so familiar today. They had to pound and pulverize the popular whole spices, such as cinnamon, cloves, nutmeg and allspice, before they could bake cakes. This extra detailed work truly can be termed making cakes "from scratch."

PRUNE SPICE CAKE

⅔ c. prune pulp   ¼ t. salt
1½ c. flour   ½ c. butter
½ t. cinnamon   1½ c. sugar
½ t. nutmeg   2 eggs
½ t. allspice   ⅔ c. buttermilk
½ t. baking soda   ½ c. chopped nuts

Chop unsweetened cooked prunes, measure correct amount and set aside. Sift together flour, spices, baking soda and salt. Set this aside, too. Cream butter until soft, then work in sugar, a little at a time, as thoroughly as possible. Add eggs and beat well, then stir in prune pulp. Stir in flour mixture and buttermilk alternately, beginning and ending with flour. Stir in nuts. Pour into a greased 10-inch tube pan and bake at 350° for 50 to 60 minutes or until cake pulls away from the sides of pan. Cool about 10 minutes before turning out of pan. Cool completely before covering with your favorite butter icing.

CHOCOLATE CHIP CAKE

1 c. dates,   1 c. sugar
   chopped fine   2 eggs
1 t. baking soda   1 t. baking powder
1¼ c. boiling water   ¾ t. salt
¾ c. shortening   1½ c. flour

TOPPING:

½ c. brown sugar
1 c. chocolate chips
½ c. chopped nuts

Chop dates into fine pieces and sprinkle with baking soda. Pour boiling water over the mixture. Set aside. Cream shortening and sugar. Blend in eggs. Add baking powder, salt and flour. Mix well; add date mixture. Beat until well blended. Pour into greased 9 x 13 x 2-inch pan. Sprinkle topping mixture over cake batter. Bake in 350° oven for 40 minutes.

HARVEST SPICE CAKE

¾ c. butter, softened
1½ c. light brown sugar, firmly packed
3 eggs
3 c. flour
1 T. baking powder
2 t. baking soda
1½ t. salt
½ t. ground allspice
½ t. ground nutmeg
½ t. ground cinnamon
1 c. apple cider
¾ c. milk

Cream together butter and sugar. Beat in eggs, one at a time. Stir together dry ingredients. Combine cider and milk. Thoroughly blend flour into creamed mixture alternately with cider mixture, beginning and ending with flour. Pour into three greased, wax-paper-lined, 8-inch round cake pans or into greased and floured 9 x 13-inch cake pan. Bake in preheated 350° oven 25 to 30 minutes or until cake tests done. Cool 10 minutes before removing from pans. Cool completely before frosting with your favorite icing or BUTTER RUM FROSTING. Decorate with walnuts if desired.

RAISIN-APPLE SPICE CAKE

2½ c. flour
1½ t. soda
1 t. salt
1 t. cinnamon
½ t. cloves
½ t. nutmeg
¾ c. butter
1¼ c. sugar
2 eggs
½ c. light molasses
2¼ c. thick applesauce
½ c. finely chopped nuts
Raisin Penuche Icing
English walnut halves

Sift flour with soda, salt and spices. Cream butter, add sugar gradually and beat until fluffy. Add eggs one at a time. Add molasses and beat thoroughly. Stir in applesauce and nuts. Gradually blend in sifted dry ingredients. Pour batter into two wax-paper-lined and greased 8- or 9-inch square baking pans, or three 8-inch round layer pans. Bake in a 350° oven for 20 to 25 minutes. Spread cooled layers with Raisin Penuche Icing and stack. Frost sides. Garnish with English walnut halves.

BUTTER RUM FROSTING

1 c. butter, softened
4 c. confectioners' sugar
⅓ c. dark corn syrup
2 t. rum extract

Cream butter. Add sugar and syrup alternately to butter, beating well after each addition. Beat in rum extract. If necessary add more sugar until proper spreading consistency is reached.

RAISIN PENUCHE ICING

⅓ c. butter
⅓ c. brown sugar, packed
⅓ c. light cream
3 to 3½ c. sifted confectioners' sugar
1 t. vanilla
¼ c. chopped nuts
1 c. coarsely chopped raisins

Combine butter, brown sugar and cream. Bring to a boil over medium heat. Remove from heat and gradually stir in confectioners' sugar until mixture is of a velvety spreading consistency. Add vanilla, nuts and raisins.

If you have difficulty removing a baked cake from the pan, place the hot pan on a damp cloth for a few seconds; steam helps release the cake.

For cakes, cookies and butter frostings, always cream the extract with the shortening to disperse flavor effectively.

SNACKS

Popcorn is a long-time Native American snack. In fact, it is claimed that the Indians brought a deer-skin bag of popped corn to the Pilgrims' first Thanksgiving feast.

Street corner vendors helped promote the popularity of popcorn. The ingenuity of the American farmer also aided its development. Some varieties will now explode roughly 44 times the original size with big, flaky kernels waiting to melt in your mouth. A far cry from the 15 times puff-up claim of a mere half-century ago.

"Goodness how delicious, eatin' goober peas" is a simple phrase from a Civil War Song that express-es our fascination with the lowly peanut. During the Civil War, when other foods were scarce, Confederate soldiers lived on peanuts, or "goobers" as they were known in Virginia and North Carolina. Even Union soldiers appreciated them. Their newly-acquired taste for peanuts led to a postwar demand for the nut.

Peanuts, rich in protein, are one of the most economical and enjoyed nuts found in country kitchens.

ROOT BEER POPCORN CRUNCH

8 c. popped corn
1 c. salted nuts
2 12-oz. containers root beer
1 c. sugar
½ c. light corn syrup
½ c. butter
¼ t. salt

Combine popcorn and nuts in a buttered bowl. Pour root beer slowly down side of heavy saucepan; add sugar, syrup, butter and salt; stir gently, but well. Bring to a boil, stirring until sugar melts. Cook to 290° (hard crack stage). Pour in a fine stream over popcorn and nuts; toss gently until popcorn is coated with syrup. Spread onto two buttered baking sheets and separate with a fork. Cool. Makes 12 cups.

HERB BUTTER FOR POPCORN

2 t. lemon juice   2 t. chives
1 t. parsley flakes   ½ c. soft butter
½ t. garlic salt   ½ t. salt

Measure lemon juice into small bowl. Add parsley flakes, garlic salt and chives. Add softened butter, stirring with a wooden spoon to thoroughly mix. Stir in salt. Mix well. Cover and store in refrigerator. Makes ½ cup herb butter.

To use with popcorn, allow 3 tablespoons per 3 quarts of popped corn to soften naturally to almost melted state. Toss with popped corn. Taste and add additional salt if needed.

RAISIN CLUSTERS

1 6-oz. pkg. chocolate chips
¼ c. light corn syrup
1½ t. vanilla
2 T. confectioners' sugar
2 c. seedless raisins

Combine chocolate chips and syrup in top of double boiler over hot water. Cook and stir over low heat until chocolate is melted. Remove from heat. Add vanilla, confectioners' sugar and raisins. Stir to coat raisins with chocolate. Drop from spoon onto buttered baking sheet. Chill. Store in cool place. Makes about 30 pieces.

UNBAKED PEANUT-CEREAL SQUARES

2½ c. sugar-coated crisp rice cereal
1½ c. flaked coconut
½ c. chopped salted peanuts
½ c. sugar
½ c. light corn syrup
½ c. heavy cream
½ t. vanilla extract

Mix first 3 ingredients in buttered large bowl; set aside. Mix next 3 ingredients in saucepan, put over low heat and stir until sugar is dissolved. Cook, stirring occasionally, to 236°F. on candy thermometer, or until small amount of mixture forms a soft ball when dropped in cold water. Remove from heat and add vanilla. Pour over cereal mixture in bowl and mix well. Press into greased 9-inch square pan. Cut in 36 squares; let stand until firm.

COOKIES

Cookie jars belong in country kitchens. They help make lasting friendships with hungry husbands, children and unexpected guests. In the words of an unknown author:

"Be sorry for people
Whoever they are,
Who live in a house
Where there's no cookie jar."

Every country has its own favorite "small sweet cakes." The English call them biscuits. However, the word cookie is strictly American. It comes from the Dutch "koefje," the diminutive of "koek" meaning cake.

America's most popular cookie must surely be the chocolate chip. This fantastic cookie swept the nation back in 1939. It was introduced to homemakers on a radio series called "Famous Foods From Famous Places." The cookie from the New England Toll House, in Whitman, Massachusetts, enjoyed immediate and continued popularity in country kitchens.

CHOCOLATE DROPS

1¾ c. flour
¾ t. salt
½ t. baking soda
2 T. cocoa
½ c. butter
¾ c. firmly packed brown sugar
1 egg
1 t. vanilla
½ c. milk
½ c. chopped pecans
  Confectioners' sugar frosting
  Flaked coconut or nuts

Sift together flour, salt, soda and cocoa. Cream butter thoroughly. Add sugar gradually and cream until light and fluffy. Add egg and vanilla; beat well. Blend sifted dry ingredients and milk alternately into creamed mixture. Stir in nuts. Drop by tablespoonfuls onto greased baking sheet. Bake in 350° oven for 10 to 15 minutes. Cool on rack. Frost with confectioners' sugar frosting and sprinkle with coconut or chopped nuts. Makes 4 dozen.

CHOCOLATE CHIP COOKIES

¾ c. butter, soft
1 c. brown sugar, firmly packed
½ c. granulated sugar
1 egg
1 t. vanilla
2 T. milk
1 c. flour
½ t. salt
½ t. baking soda
2 c. rolled oats
  (quick or old-fashioned, uncooked)
1 c. semisweet chocolate pieces
½ c. chopped nutmeats

Heat oven to 375°. Beat butter, sugars, egg, vanilla and milk together until creamy. Sift together flour, salt and soda. Add to creamed mixture, blending well. Stir in oats, chocolate pieces and nutmeats. Drop by teaspoonfuls onto greased cookie sheets. Bake in preheated 375° oven 12 to 15 minutes. Makes 4½ dozen.

UNIQUE DATE COOKIES

1 c. granulated sugar	1 t. vanilla
1 c. brown sugar, packed	1 t. salt
	1 t. baking soda
1 c. butter	4 c. flour
3 eggs	

FILLING

1 lb. dates, finely chopped
½ c. granulated sugar
½ c. water

Combine filling ingredients in saucepan. Bring to boil over medium heat, stirring constantly. Boil 1 minute, remove from heat and set aside to cool.

Cream butter until soft; blend in sugars. Add eggs and beat until light and fluffy. Add vanilla and mix. Stir in flour, salt and soda. Mix well. Chill dough. Roll out on lightly floured board and spread with filling. Roll up like jelly roll. Chill again overnight or in freezer. Slice ⅛-inch thick and place on lightly greased baking sheets. Bake in 375° oven for 10 to 12 minutes or until lightly browned. Makes about 6 dozen cookies.

CHOCOLATE CHIP BARS

3 c. flour
1 t. baking soda
½ t. salt
1 t. cinnamon
½ t. nutmeg
1 c. brown sugar, firmly packed
1 c. granulated sugar
¾ c. soft butter
1 egg
3 t. vanilla
½ c. sour cream
1 c. semisweet chocolate chips
1 to 1½ c. raisins
½ c. finely chopped nuts

Spoon flour into measuring cup and level off. Pour onto waxed paper. Add soda, salt and spices to flour. Stir well to blend. Cream sugars, butter, egg and vanilla thoroughly. Add blended dry ingredients to creamed mixture alternately with sour cream. Stir in chocolate chips, raisins and nuts. Spread in waxed-paper-lined 15 x 10 x 1-inch pan. Refrigerate at least three hours. Invert pan and remove chilled cookie mixture. Peel off waxed paper. Cut into 2 x 1½-inch rectangles. Place two inches apart on ungreased baking sheet. Bake at 400° for 10 to 12 minutes. Remove from baking sheets. Cool on rack. Makes 50 bars.

SALTED PEANUT CRISPS

1 c. butter	3 c. flour
1½ c. brown sugar, packed	½ t. baking soda
	1 t. salt
2 eggs	2 c. salted peanuts
2 t. vanilla	

Heat oven to 375°. Mix butter, sugar, eggs and vanilla thoroughly. Blend together flour, soda and salt; stir in. Mix in peanuts. Drop rounded teaspoonfuls of dough about 2 inches apart on lightly greased baking sheet. Flatten with bottom of greased glass dipped in sugar. Bake 8 to 10 minutes or until golden brown. Makes about 6 dozen 2-inch cookies.

MARBLE SQUARES

1 c. plus 2 T. sifted flour
½ t. baking soda
½ t. salt
½ c. soft butter
6 T. granulated sugar
6 T. firmly packed brown sugar
½ t. vanilla
¼ t. water
1 egg
½ c. coarsely chopped nuts
1 c. semisweet chocolate morsels

Sift together flour, baking soda and salt; set aside. Blend butter, sugars, vanilla and water. Beat in egg; add flour mixture and mix well. Stir in nuts; spread in greased 13 x 9 x 2-inch pan. Sprinkle semisweet chocolate morsels over top of batter. Bake in 375° oven 1 minute. Remove from oven and run knife through batter to marbleize. Return to oven and continue baking for 12 to 14 minutes. Cool. Cut in 2-inch squares. Makes 2 dozen.

CREAMY FUDGE BARS

1 c. butter
2 c. light brown sugar
2 eggs
2 t. vanilla
2½ c. flour
1 t. soda
1 t. salt
3 c. quick rolled oats, uncooked

FILLING

1 12-oz. pkg. semisweet chocolate pieces
1 c. sweetened condensed milk
2 T. butter
½ t. salt
1 c. chopped nuts
2 t. vanilla

Cream together butter and sugar. Mix in eggs and vanilla. Sift together flour, soda and salt; stir in rolled oats. Add dry ingredients to creamed mixture. Set aside. In a saucepan over boiling water, mix together chocolate pieces, sweetened condensed milk, butter and salt. Stir until mixture is smooth. Stir in nuts and vanilla. Spread about ⅔ of oatmeal mixture in bottom of a greased 15½ x 10½ x 1-inch jelly roll pan. Cover with chocolate mixture. Dot with remainder of oatmeal mixture and swirl it over chocolate filling. Bake in 350° oven for 25 to 30 minutes. Makes 60 2 x 1-inch bars.

SPRINGERLE

2 eggs
1 c. sugar
2¼ c. flour
Anise seed

Beat eggs and sugar together thoroughly. Stir in flour until dough is well blended and very stiff. Refrigerate the dough for 3 to 4 hours. Roll out dough about ⅛-inch thick on lightly floured board. Press well-floured "springerle" board or rolling pin down firmly on dough to emboss the designs. Cut out the little squares; let dry on lightly floured board sprinkled with anise for at least 10 hours, at room temperature. Heat oven to 325°. Transfer to lightly greased baking sheet. Bake 12 to 15 minutes. Makes 4 to 5 dozen cookies.

HICKORY NUT COOKIES

1 c. butter
½ c. confectioners' sugar
2 c. flour
2 t. vanilla
1 c. hickory nuts, finely crushed
Confectioners' sugar

Cream together butter and sugar. Blend in flour and vanilla. Mix well. Add crushed nuts, blending well. Roll dough into balls the size of large marbles. Place on ungreased cookie sheet. Bake in 325° oven about 8 minutes or until set. Remove from oven and carefully roll, while still warm, in confectioners' sugar. Cool. Roll again in sugar. Makes about 6 dozen cookies.

MINCEMEAT GEMS

1 c. butter, softened
½ c. sugar
½ c. finely chopped walnuts
1 egg
1 t. vanilla
2¼ c. flour
1 t. salt
2¼ c. prepared mincemeat
21 maraschino cherries, drained and halved

Cream together butter and sugar until light and fluffy. Blend in walnuts, egg and vanilla. Stir together flour and salt, gradually beat into creamed mixture. Drop dough by level tablespoonfuls onto ungreased baking sheets. Flatten each cookie. Place rounded teaspoonful of mincemeat in center of each cookie; top with cherry half. Bake in preheated 400° oven 10 to 12 minutes. Makes 3½ dozen cookies.

CUTOUT SUGAR COOKIES

½ c. butter
1 c. sugar
1 egg
3 c. flour
¾ t. salt
3 t. baking powder
½ c. milk
1 t. vanilla

Thoroughly cream butter and sugar; add egg and beat well. Add sifted dry ingredients alternately with milk and vanilla; mix thoroughly. Roll ⅛-inch thick on lightly floured surface. Cut with floured cookie cutter; sprinkle with sugar, if desired. Bake on greased cookie sheet in 375° oven about 15 minutes. Makes 3 dozen cookies. These may be decorated before or after baking.

BUTTER ICING

4 T. vegetable shortening
2 c. sifted powdered sugar
3 T. milk
½ t. vanilla
Pinch of salt

Cream shortening; add sugar, salt, milk, and vanilla gradually, beating until smooth and stiff enough to spread or use in pastry tube.

OLD-FASHIONED MOLASSES COOKIES

4 c. sifted all-purpose flour
2 t. baking soda
1½ t. ground ginger
½ t. ground cinnamon
¾ t. salt
1½ c. molasses
½ c. lard, melted
¼ c. butter, melted
⅓ c. boiling water

Sift together flour, baking soda, spices and salt. Combine molasses, lard, butter and water in large bowl. Add dry ingredients to liquid and blend well. Cover and chill several hours or overnight. Turn onto well-floured board. Using floured rolling pin, roll to ¼-inch thickness. Cut with 3½-inch floured cookie cutter. Sprinkle with sugar and place on ungreased baking sheets. Bake in 375° oven 12 minutes. Cool on racks. Makes about 3 dozen 3½-inch cookies.

Book I Index

Book II

From Mama's Kitchen
COOKBOOK

CONTENTS

Book I Country Kitchen Cookbook

Book II From Mama's Kitchen Cookbook

Book III Farmhouse Cookbook

Potato Salad

Salads

RHUBARB SALAD

    2 c. fresh rhubarb slices, 1 inch thick
    ⅓ c. sugar
    ½ c. water
    2½ c. pineapple tidbits in syrup
    1 pkg. raspberry gelatin
    1 pkg. lemon gelatin
    ½ c. chopped nuts

Combine rhubarb and sugar; cook in water until tender. Drain, reserving syrup. Drain pineapple and reserve syrup. Combine syrups and add water to make 3½ cups. Heat to boiling. Add both packages of gelatin and stir until dissolved. Chill until syrupy. Fold in rhubarb, pineapple and nuts. Pour into a 6-cup ring mold. Chill until firm. Unmold. Serve with mayonnaise as a salad or with whipped cream as a dessert.

MANDARIN BEAN RELISH

    1 1-lb. can cut green beans
    ½ c. mandarin orange segments
    3 T. sliced celery
    ¼ c. diced onion
    ½ t. sugar (more, if desired)
    ½ t. salt
      Dash of pepper
    2 T. vinegar
    ¼ c. salad oil

Drain beans. Combine in shallow dish with orange segments, celery and onion. Combine all remaining ingredients in a jar; cover and shake to blend. Pour over bean mixture. Cover and chill several hours, stirring occasionally.

TUNA-FRUIT SALAD

    1 7-oz. can tuna, drained
    1 unpeeled apple, chopped
    1 c. seedless grapes, halved
    1 13½-oz. can pineapple tidbits, drained
    1 c. chopped celery
    1 T. lemon juice
    ¼ t. salt
    1 c. sour cream
      Salad greens
      Chopped nuts

In a bowl, combine tuna, apple, grapes, pineapple and celery. In a small bowl, gently blend lemon juice and salt into sour cream. Fold into fruit. Serve on greens and top with chopped nuts.

POTATO SALAD

    8 medium potatoes   ½ t. salt
    ¼ c. chopped onion   ¼ t. seasoned salt
    6 slices bacon   1 c. mayonnaise
    4 eggs, hard-boiled   ¼ c. sweet pickle relish

Boil potatoes until done. Cool and dice. Add onion. Fry bacon until crisp. Crumble into potatoes. Add eggs, seasonings, mayonnaise and relish. Mix well and chill.

4

BEET SALAD

2 c. beets, cooked and diced
1 c. beet juice, chilled
1 pkg. lemon gelatin
1 c. boiling water
½ c. diced celery (optional)
1 small can crushed pineapple, drained

Dissolve gelatin in boiling water. Add chilled beet juice and stir in. Add diced beets, celery and pineapple. Chill until set. Serve with a bit of sour cream on top.

HOLIDAY SALAD

1 c. coarsely chopped cranberries
5 c. shredded cabbage
1 T. grated orange peel
2 T. sugar
½ t. salt
⅓ c. mayonnaise

Mix first 5 ingredients, tossing well. Add mayonnaise and mix. Cover and chill before serving.

BEAN-BEET SALAD

2 1-lb. cans green beans
2 1-lb. cans shoestring beets
2 small onions

Drain green beans and beets. Slice onions into thin rings. Toss lightly.

DRESSING

½ c. salad oil
⅔ c. vinegar
  Salt and pepper to taste
1 t. Worcestershire sauce
½ c. sugar
1 small clove garlic *or* dash of garlic salt

Mix ingredients for dressing. Let vegetables marinate in dressing 4 or 5 hours before serving.

TASTY FRENCH DRESSING

1 can condensed tomato soup
1 c. salad oil
¾ c. vinegar
½ c. sugar
1 t. dry mustard
1 t. paprika
1 t. salt
1 t. celery seed
2 cloves garlic, crushed

Mix all ingredients in a fruit jar and shake.

MACARONI SALAD

1 1-lb. package macaroni
1 tomato, chopped
1 c. celery, finely chopped
3 hard-boiled eggs, chopped
1 c. mayonnaise
1 c. shredded cheese
  Salt and pepper to taste

Cook macaroni according to directions on package. Drain and cool. Add tomato, celery, eggs, mayonnaise, cheese and seasonings. Mix well. Chill and serve.

PICKLED BEET SALAD

2 pkg. lemon gelatin
2 c. hot water
1 T. lemon juice
2 pt. pickled beets
1½ c. diced celery
½ c. chopped nuts
1 t. horseradish
  Pinch of salt

Dissolve gelatin in hot water. Add lemon juice. Drain pickled beets, reserving 2 cups liquid. Add liquid to gelatin. Dice beets. Chill gelatin until partially set and then add remaining ingredients. Chill.

Soups

HAMBURGER SOUP

1½ lbs. hamburger
1 small onion, diced
3 carrots, sliced
2 c. chopped celery stalks and leaves
2 potatoes, peeled and cubed
½ c. barley
½ t. garlic salt
½ t. salt
¼ t. pepper

Crumble hamburger into a saucepan. Add all other ingredients. Cover with water and bring to boil. Cook slowly until vegetables and barley are well done—about 1½ hours.

NAVY BEAN SOUP

1 lb. navy beans
2 qt. cold water
   Ham hocks or meaty ham bones
1 chopped onion
½ c. chopped celery tops (optional)
1 bay leaf

Wash beans, add cold water and soak overnight. Add remaining ingredients the next morning; bring to a boil. Turn heat to simmer, cover and cook about 3 hours. Remove ham hocks, chop the meat, and return to the soup. Season to taste. Note: More water may have to be added during the cooking process.

CHEESE SOUP

2 T. chopped onion
4 T. butter or margarine
4 T. flour
¼ t. salt
¼ t. dry mustard
2 c. milk
2 c. chicken broth or bouillon
2 c. grated cheddar cheese

Brown onion in butter. Blend in flour and seasonings. Gradually stir in milk and broth. Bring to a boil and boil 1 minute, stirring constantly. Add cheese. Cook slowly, stirring constantly, until cheese is melted.

TURKEY SOUP

2 c. cooked, chopped turkey meat
1 T. chopped onion
½ c. chopped celery
2 carrots, washed and diced
2 potatoes, peeled and diced
½ t. seasoning salt
½ t. salt

Combine all ingredients in a saucepan, cover with water, and cook together until vegetables are well done. Some water may have to be added while cooking. Serve hot with your favorite crackers. An excellent way to use leftover Thanksgiving turkey.

Pictured opposite
Cheese Soup

Fruits and Vegetables

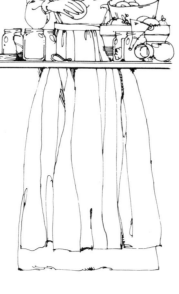

FRIED EGGPLANT

1 eggplant
1 egg
1 T. cold water
¾ c. fine bread crumbs
½ t. salt
    Dash of pepper
½ c. fat or oil

Wash and pare eggplant. Cut in half, then into long slices, ½ inch thick by 1 inch wide. Beat egg. Add water. Dip eggplant into egg, then into combined bread crumbs and seasonings. Cook slices in hot oil, browning on both sides. Drain on paper. Serve at once.

TURNIP CASSEROLE

3 c. sliced turnips
2 t. sugar
½ t. salt
2 to 2½ c. water
    Milk
3 T. butter or margarine
3 T. flour
½ c. crushed dry cereal
2 T. melted butter
2 tablespoons grated cheese

Cook turnips with sugar and salt in just enough water to cover. Drain, reserving liquid. Measure and add enough milk to make 1½ cups. Melt 3 tablespoons butter; blend in flour. Pour in liquids and cook, stirring, until thickened. Combine with turnips in greased baking dish. Cover with cereal, 2 tablespoons butter, and cheese. Bake at 325° about 25 minutes, or until brown.

FRIED GREEN TOMATOES

6 green tomatoes
3 T. flour
1¼ t. salt
1¼ t. sugar
    Pepper to taste
4 T. bacon fat
1 c. evaporated milk

Wash but do not peel tomatoes. Cut in halves crosswise. Mix flour, salt, sugar and pepper. Roll tomatoes, one at a time, in flour. Brown on both sides in hot bacon fat. Remove to hot serving dish and keep warm. Add evaporated milk to the same frying pan. Boil slowly, stirring constantly until thick (about 2 minutes). Pour over tomatoes.

SCALLOPED POTATOES

6 to 8 medium potatoes
1 T. minced onion
  Salt and pepper to taste
2 c. milk
½ c. grated cheese

Wash, pare and thinly slice potatoes. Arrange in layers in greased baking dish. Sprinkle each layer with a bit of onion, salt and pepper. Heat milk and pour over potatoes but do not fill to top of potatoes. Bake uncovered at 350° for about 1 hour and 15 minutes. Crumble grated cheese on top and bake 10 minutes longer.

SCALLOPED CORN

2 c. fresh or canned corn
1 c. milk
1 c. cracker crumbs
2 T. diced onion
2 eggs, well beaten
1 t. salt
  Pepper to taste
2 T. melted butter

Combine all ingredients and pour into a buttered baking dish. Bake at 350° for 1 hour.

CANDIED SWEET POTATOES

6 medium sweet potatoes or yams
¾ c. brown sugar
¼ c. butter
1 t. salt
5 or 6 marshmallows, if desired

Wash and boil sweet potatoes in enough water to cover until just tender. As soon as they are cool enough, peel and cut in ½-inch slices. Place in buttered baking dish. Sprinkle brown sugar and salt over slices and dot with butter. Bake at 375° about 30 minutes. Top with marshmallows the last 5 minutes. Variation: 1 cup drained crushed pineapple may be spread over the slices of sweet potato, then the brown sugar and butter.

QUICK BAKED BEANS

2 large (#2½) cans pork and beans
2 T. chopped onion
½ c. brown sugar
¼ c. dark corn syrup or mild sorghum
½ c. tomato catsup
4 slices bacon

Combine all ingredients except bacon slices. Pour into baking dish. Arrange bacon slices over the top. Bake uncovered for 2 hours at 325°.

CORN PUDDING CASSEROLE

3 eggs
2 c. drained cooked or canned corn
2 c. milk, scalded
1 T. melted butter
1 t. salt
2 T. chopped onion

Beat eggs. Add corn. Gradually stir in scalded milk. Add remaining ingredients and mix well. Pour into 1½-quart buttered casserole. Set in shallow pan and fill pan to 1 inch with hot water. Bake in preheated oven at 350° for 45 minutes, or until knife inserted near center comes out clean. Let stand 5 minutes and serve hot.

NINE DAY PICKLES

7 lbs. cucumbers (small to medium)
1 pt. (2 cups) coarse salt
1 gallon boiled and cooled water
2 c. vinegar
8 green grape leaves
1 t. alum

Wash cucumbers and place in stone jars in brine made of the salt and water. Let stand 4 days, then drain. Cover with clear, fresh water each morning for 3 consecutive days. Wash and split each pickle, regardless of size. Put in kettle with the vinegar and enough water to cover the pickles. Add grape leaves and alum and simmer for 2 hours. Do not boil. Drain and place in stone jars.

SYRUP

3 pt. vinegar (6 cups)
6 c. sugar
1 oz. whole allspice

Boil vinegar, sugar and allspice to make a syrup. Pour over pickles and let stand overnight. Pour off liquid, reheat and pour over again. Let stand overnight and on the third morning put pickles in hot sterilized jars. Heat the same liquid, pour over pickles, and seal immediately.

BREAD-AND-BUTTER PICKLES

3 qt. sliced cucumbers
3 onions, sliced
½ c. coarse salt
3 c. vinegar
1 c. water
3 c. sugar
1 t. cinnamon
½ t. ginger
2 T. mustard seed
2 t. turmeric
½ T. celery seed
1 piece horseradish (optional)

Mix cucumbers, onions, and salt. Let stand at least 5 hours. Drain. Boil vinegar, water, sugar and seasonings for 3 minutes. Add cucumbers and onions and simmer 10 to 20 minutes. Do not boil. Pack into hot sterilized jars and seal immediately.

LIME SWEET PICKLES

7 lbs. cucumbers
2 c. hydrated lime
2 gallons water
2 qt. vinegar
9 c. sugar
1 T. salt
1 t. celery seed
1 t. whole cloves
1 t. mixed pickling spice

Slice cucumbers thin. Cover with the lime and water and soak 24 hours. Drain. Rinse and soak 3 hours in clear water. Drain and rinse again. Bring remaining ingredients to a boil. Pour over cucumbers and soak overnight. Bring to a boil. Boil gently 40 minutes. Pack in hot sterilized jars and seal. Note: Be sure to soak all the lime out.

GRAPE CONSERVE

8 c. Concord grapes
3 c. water
4 c. sugar
1 c. raisins
½ c. orange juice
¼ c. lemon juice
½ c. nuts
¼ t. salt

Wash grapes. Add water and simmer, covered, for 30 minutes. Press skins and pulp through a coarse strainer. Only the seeds should be discarded. Add remaining ingredients and boil 15 minutes or until thick.

CRISPY LUNCH PICKLES

25 medium-sized cucumbers
 8 large onions
 2 large sweet peppers
½ c. salt
 5 c. sugar
 5 c. cider vinegar
 2 T. mustard seed
 1 t. turmeric
¼ t. cloves

Wash fresh cucumbers and slice thin. Chop onions and peppers. Mix with cucumbers and salt; let stand for 3 hours. Drain. Combine sugar, vinegar and spices in large kettle. Bring to a boil. Add drained cucumbers; heat thoroughly but do not boil. Pack while hot into hot sterilized jars and seal at once.

TOMATO CATSUP

1 bushel tomatoes
1 doz. onions
3 green peppers
2 t. mixed pickling spices
2 t. cinnamon
4 sticks cinnamon
2 t. cloves
2 t. dry mustard

2 t. celery seed
2 t. allspice
5 c. sugar
1 qt. vinegar
2 t. red pepper
4 T. salt
⅔ c. cornstarch

Wash and cook tomatoes, onions and green peppers until tender. Run through sieve, discarding seeds and skins. Place sieved pulp in large cooking kettle. Tie all spices in a cloth bag and drop into pulp. Add sugar, vinegar, red pepper and salt. Cook all together and boil ½ hour. Add cornstarch dissolved in small amount of cold water. Stir in, cook until thickened, and seal while hot.

PUMPKIN BUTTER

10 c. raw pumpkin
2 lemons
1 t. ground ginger
1 t. ground cinnamon
½ t. ground allspice
¾ t. salt
2½ lbs. brown sugar
1 c. water

Peel pumpkin and grind in food chopper. Extract juice from lemons; add to pumpkin along with spices, salt and sugar. Let stand overnight. Then add water and boil gently until pumpkin is clear and the mixture is thick. Pour into sterilized jars and seal while hot. This is good on toast.

PICCALILLI

1 gallon green tomatoes, chopped
2 T. coarse salt
1 gallon cabbage, finely chopped
1 qt. onions, finely chopped
2 or 3 green peppers, finely chopped
½ T. cinnamon
1 T. ground mustard
1 t. ginger
1 T. cloves
1½ oz. turmeric
½ oz. celery seed
6 c. sugar
Vinegar

Chop green tomatoes, sprinkle with salt, and let stand 2 hours. Drain. Mix tomatoes with other vegetables. Add spices and sugar and mix well. Cover with vinegar (not too much) and boil slowly until vegetables are done. Seal while hot.

STRAWBERRY LEMON PRESERVES

4 c. fresh strawberries
4 c. sugar
2 T. lemon juice

Heat berries and 2 cups of the sugar to the boiling point, stirring occasionally. Boil 2 minutes. Add remaining sugar and again heat to boiling. Boil 3 minutes. Stir in lemon juice and pour into shallow bowl. Stir occasionally while cooling. Let stand overnight to plump berries.

GREEN PEPPER RELISH

1 large head cabbage
½ doz. medium onions
1 doz. sweet green peppers
1 T. mustard seed, mashed
1 T. celery seed
½ t. black pepper
4 c. water
1 qt. white vinegar

Finely chop the cabbage, onions and peppers. Mix and let stand several hours in a little salt water. Drain. Add remaining ingredients and mix well. Do not cook.

EASY ROLLS

2 c. milk
¼ c. sugar
¼ c. shortening
1 pkg. yeast
  Flour
1 t. baking powder
½ t. baking soda
1 t. salt

Scald milk. While cooling, add sugar and shortening. When cool, add yeast and enough flour to make a batter. Let rise about 1½ hours. Add baking powder, soda, and salt and enough flour to make a soft dough. Roll out on lightly floured board, cut like biscuits, place on greased baking sheet and let rise until doubled. Bake at 375° about 25 minutes.

Yeast Breads

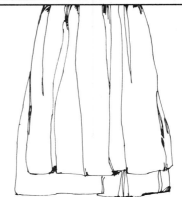

QUICK ROLLS

2 c. milk
4 T. sugar
1 pkg. yeast
4 T. melted fat
1 t. salt
6 c. flour (approximately)

Scald milk and cool to lukewarm. Dissolve yeast and sugar in the lukewarm milk. Add melted fat and salt and 3 cups flour. Beat until very smooth. Cover and let rise in a warm place for one hour. Add enough flour to make a firm dough. Let rise again for 30 to 45 minutes. Make into rolls or shape into balls about the size of walnuts. Cover and let rise to the top. Bake at 350° for 20 minutes. Remove from oven and brush tops with butter.

BASIC ROLLS

1 c. sugar
¼ c. shortening
1 t. salt
2 c. boiling water
2 pkg. yeast
¼ c. warm water
1 T. sugar
2 eggs, beaten
8 c. flour

Mix sugar, shortening, salt and boiling water together. Cool. Dissolve yeast in ¼ cup warm water and stir in 1 tablespoon sugar. Add to cooled first mixture. Beat in eggs and 4 cups flour. Add remaining 4 cups flour and mix to make a smooth dough. Knead slightly. Shape into rolls, allow to double in bulk and bake at 425° for about 20 minutes. This dough may be kept in refrigerator, covered, for a week to 10 days. A good basic dough for rolls, coffee cake or cinnamon rolls.

Pictured opposite
Yeast Breads and Rolls

ONION BREAD

1 c. warm water
1 pkg. yeast
2 t. sugar
½ t. salt
1 onion, grated
2½ c. flour

Dissolve yeast in warm water. Add sugar and salt and blend in. Beat in 2 cups of the flour and mix well. Add remainder of flour and grated onion. Turn dough onto lightly floured board and knead until smooth—5 to 7 minutes. You may have to add up to ½ cup more flour while kneading. Place dough in greased bowl and set in a warm place to rise until doubled in size. Punch down and divide in half. Place in 2 greased 9-inch cake pans and brush tops with melted buter. Let rise 5 minutes. Punch dough down again and let rise until double. Dust with paprika. Bake at 375° for 20-25 minutes.

WHITE BREAD

2 c. warm water or potato water
3 T. butter
½ c. sugar
1 T. salt
2 pkg. yeast
6½ to 7 c. flour

Dissolve yeast in ¼ cup of the water. Heat remainder of water with sugar, butter and salt. Cool to lukewarm. Add dissolved yeast and stir. Add 4 cups flour and beat well. Add the remaining flour 1 cup at a time. Knead on lightly floured board. Let rise in greased bowl until doubled in size. Punch down, shape into loaves, and let rise again. Bake at 375° for 5 minutes, then at 350° for 30 minutes.

ANADAMA BREAD

½ c. yellow cornmeal
2 c. water
1 t. salt
2 T. shortening
⅓ c. molasses
1 pkg. yeast
5 cups flour (approximately)

Stir cornmeal into water and salt. Mix well and bring to a boil, stirring constantly. Lower heat and cook 5 minutes. Add shortening and molasses; cool. When lukewarm, add yeast that has been dissolved in ½ cup warm water. Add enough flour to make a stiff dough. Place in greased bowl and let rise until double. Bake at 400° for 1 hour. Butter when removed from oven and cover with a cloth.

BATTER BREAD

1 c. milk
2 T. shortening
3 T. sugar
1 t. salt
1 c. lukewarm water
2 pkg. yeast
4½ c. flour

Scald milk. Add shortening, sugar and salt; cool to lukewarm. Measure warm water into a large bowl. Dissolve yeast in water. Add lukewarm milk mixture. Stir in enough flour to make a stiff batter. Beat about 2 minutes. Cover and let rise in a warm place about 40 minutes, until more than doubled in bulk. Stir batter down and beat vigorously ½ minute. Pour into 2 greased 9" x 5" x 3" loaf pans. Bake at 375° about 50 minutes.

FRENCH BREAD

1¼ c. warm water
1 pkg. yeast
1 T. shortening
1 T. sugar
1½ t. salt
3½ c. flour

Measure water into a large bowl. Add the yeast and stir until dissolved. Add shortening, sugar and salt. Stir in flour. Turn out onto a lightly floured board. Knead until the dough is springy and elastic. Place in a greased bowl and brush the top lightly with shortening. Cover and let rise in a warm place until doubled in bulk. Punch down. Let rise again until doubled. Punch down and turn out onto a floured board. Cut into 2 equal portions. Roll each half into an oblong, 8" x 10". Beginning with the wide side, roll up tightly and seal the edge by pinching. Lengthen and taper loaves. Place loaves on a greased baking sheet and sprinkle lightly with cornmeal. Brush with a cornstarch glaze made by mixing 1 teaspoon cornstarch with 2 tablespoons water. Let rise 1½ hours. Take a sharp knife and make ¼-inch-deep slashes at 2-inch intervals. Bake at 375° for 45 minutes.

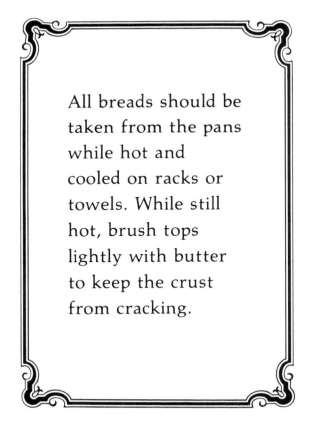

All breads should be taken from the pans while hot and cooled on racks or towels. While still hot, brush tops lightly with butter to keep the crust from cracking.

DANISH PASTRY

1 c. sugar
½ t. salt
3 eggs, beaten
½ c. butter
2 t. vanilla
2 pkg. yeast
8 c. flour
½ lb. butter

Heat the first 5 ingredients together for one minute, and then add yeast which has been dissolved in 2 cups lukewarm water. Add flour. Mix in thoroughly and knead until smooth. Let rise for 1 hour in a warm place. Roll out 1 inch thick. Dot with butter, fold together four times, roll out to same thickness. Continue this procedure until one-half pound of butter has been added to the dough. Form into any shape of rolls desired. Let rise one hour before baking. Bake 25 to 35 minutes in 400° oven.

Quick Breads

BANANA NUT BREAD

1 c. sugar
½ c. shortening
2 eggs
1 c. mashed bananas
1 t. lemon juice
2 c. flour
1 T. baking powder
½ t. salt
1 c. chopped nuts

Cream the sugar and shortening. Add eggs and beat well. Add bananas and lemon juice. Sift dry ingredients together and add to banana mixture. Add nuts. Bake in greased loaf pan at 350° for one hour.

SKILLET CAKE

¼ c. butter
¾ c. brown sugar
8 canned pineapple slices
1 c. nutmeats
2 eggs
1 c. granulated sugar
¼ t. salt
½ c. milk
1 T. melted shortening
1 c. sifted cake flour
1 t. baking powder
1 t. vanilla

Melt butter in iron skillet. Remove from heat. Sprinkle brown sugar over the bottom and arrange pineapple slices. Sprinkle with nuts. Beat eggs until light. Gradually add granulated sugar and salt. Heat milk to the boiling point. Add shortening and beat into the egg mixture. Add flour and baking powder sifted together. Beat in vanilla. Pour batter over fruit. Bake about ½ hour at 350°. Turn out while hot and serve upside down.

APPLE NUT BREAD

1 c. sugar
½ c. shortening
2 eggs
1 c. grated raw apples (unpeeled)
2 c. flour
1 t. baking powder
1 t. baking soda
¼ t. salt
½ c. nuts

Cream sugar and shortening. Add eggs and beat well. Mix in grated apple. Sift dry ingredients together and add to first mixture. Add nuts and mix well. Bake in greased loaf pan at 350° for 50 to 60 minutes.

18

Pictured opposite
Banana Nut Bread

BROWN BREAD

1½ c. buttermilk
1½ t. baking soda
½ t. salt
1½ c. thick molasses or sorghum
4 c. whole wheat flour
1 c. raisins (optional)

Mix buttermilk, soda and salt. Add molasses, then flour, and mix well. Add raisins if desired. Pour into well-greased coffee cans, filling ⅔ full. Set in boiling water. Let water come within 1½ inches of top of can. Boil about 2 hours. Test done with toothpick.

COFFEE CAKE

¾ c. sugar
½ c. shortening
1 t. vanilla
3 eggs
2 c. flour
1 t. baking soda
1 t. baking powder
1 c. sour cream

Combine sugar, shortening and vanilla; mix well. Add eggs, one at a time, beating well after each. Sift dry ingredients together. Add to egg mixture alternately with sour cream. Spread half of batter in greased tube pan. Spread half of topping on batter, cover with remaining batter, and top with remaining topping.

TOPPING

1 c. brown sugar
6 T. butter
2 t. cinnamon
1 c. chopped nuts

Cream together brown sugar and butter. Add cinnamon and chopped nuts and mix well. Bake at 350° for 50 minutes.

RICH COFFEE CAKE

1 c. shortening
1 c. brown sugar
1 c. white sugar
2 c. flour
2 eggs
1 c. sour cream
1 t. baking soda
½ t. salt

Cream shortening and sugars together. Add flour and mix until crumbly. Set aside 1 cup of this mixture. Beat eggs. Add sour cream, soda and salt; mix well. Combine with first mixture and beat well. Pour into a greased 9" x 13" cake pan and sprinkle top with the reserved mixture. Bake at 350° for 40 minutes.

CAKE DOUGHNUTS

2 eggs
1 c. sugar
2 T. soft shortening
¾ c. buttermilk
3½ c. flour
1 t. baking soda
2 t. baking powder
¼ t. cinnamon
¼ t. nutmeg
½ t. salt

Beat eggs. Add sugar and shortening and beat. Stir in buttermilk. Sift dry ingredients and add gradually to egg mixture to make a stiff dough. Chill 2 hours. Roll out on floured board to ⅓-inch thickness. Cut with doughnut cutter. Brown on each side about one minute in 3 inches of 370° shortening in a deep saucepan. Drain on paper or towel and dust with powdered sugar.

RAISED DOUGHNUTS

1 c. mashed potatoes
1½ c. milk, scalded
½ c. sugar
⅓ c. shortening
2 eggs
¼ c. warm water
2 pkg. yeast
1 t. salt
4½ to 5 c. flour

Dissolve yeast in warm water. Boil and mash potatoes and measure 1 cup into a bowl. Add yeast, milk, sugar, shortening and well-beaten eggs. When lukewarm, add flour and salt. Mix and then knead on a lightly floured board. Place in greased bowl and let rise until doubled. Roll out and cut with doughnut cutter and fry in deep hot fat.

GLAZE

1 lb. powdered sugar
1 T. cornstarch
2 T. soft butter
1 T. cream
1 t. vanilla

Combine ingredients. Stir in enough warm water to make a thick liquid. Dip warm doughnuts in glaze and let drip off.

APPLE PLUMPLINGS

2 c. flour
1 t. baking powder
1 c. milk
1 egg, beaten
6 large apples

Mix all ingredients except apples. Peel and core apples; cut into ½" cubes. Add to batter. Drop mixture into deep, hot fat by table-spoonfuls. Be sure you have some apple pieces in each spoonful. When brown, lift out of fat and place on brown paper to drain. Serve while hot.

DROP DOUGHNUTS

2 c. flour
½ c. sugar
2 t. baking powder
¼ t. baking soda
1 t. cinnamon
½ t. salt
1 egg
½ c. applesauce
½ c. milk
1½ T. melted shortening

Sift dry ingredients together. Beat egg. Add applesauce and milk. Add dry ingredients and mix well. Stir in shortening. Drop batter into hot fat (375°) by teaspoonfuls, frying until golden brown on all sides.

DOUGHNUTS

3 eggs
1 c. milk
1 c. sour cream
1 c. sugar
½ t. salt
2 t. baking powder
1 t. baking soda
½ t. nutmeg
1 c. flour

Beat eggs until light. Add milk and sour cream and blend. Sift the dry ingredients together and add to egg mixture. Beat until smooth. Add enough flour to make a soft dough. Pat out dough to ½ inch thick. Cut with doughnut cutter and fry in hot deep fat. May be rolled in sugar while warm.

BISCUITS

2 c. flour
2 t. baking powder
¾ t. salt
⅓ c. fat
¾ c. milk (approximately)

Sift dry ingredients together. Cut in fat until well blended. Stir in milk slowly, using just enough to make dough soft but not sticky. Turn dough onto lightly floured board and knead a few strokes. Roll to ½-inch thickness and cut with biscuit cutter. Place on baking sheet and bake at 450° about 15 minutes.

BAKING POWDER BISCUITS

3 c. flour
4 t. baking powder
1 t. salt
6 T. shortening
1 c. milk

Sift dry ingredients into a bowl. Cut in shortening and add milk. Stir only until moistened. Turn onto lightly floured board. Knead lightly and roll out ½ inch thick. Cut with floured biscuit cutter. Bake at 400° until lightly browned.

QUICK MUFFINS

1½ c. flour
½ t. salt
4 t. baking powder
1 T. sugar
2 eggs, well beaten
¾ c. milk
¼ c. melted butter

Sift dry ingredients together. Add eggs, milk and butter. Mix just until blended. Drop into greased muffin tins, filling ½ to ⅔ full. Bake at 425° for 25 minutes.

APPLE MUFFINS

2 c. flour
4 t. baking powder
½ c. sugar
1 t. salt
½ t. cinnamon
1 egg
1 c. milk
1 c. chopped raw apples (unpeeled)
2 T. melted shortening

Sift dry ingredients together into a bowl. In a separate bowl beat egg; add milk, chopped apples and melted shortening. Add to dry ingredients and mix lightly until blended. Fill greased muffin tins ⅔ full and bake at 425° for 20 to 25 minutes. Serve hot.

BREAKFAST MUFFINS

1½ c. flour
½ t. salt
2¼ t. baking powder
2 T. sugar
1 egg
¾ c. milk
2 T. melted butter

Sift dry ingredients together into a bowl. Beat egg in separate bowl and add the milk and butter. Add this mixture to the dry ingredients. Stir until just mixed; batter should be lumpy. Fill greased muffin tins ⅔ full. Bake at 425° for 25 minutes. Loosen from pan and serve hot with butter and jam, jelly or honey. Makes 8.

Breakfast Muffins

CRISPY CORN BREAD

1 c. flour
4 t. baking powder
1 t. salt
¼ c. brown sugar
1 c. yellow cornmeal
1 egg, well beaten
1 c. milk
¼ c. melted shortening

Sift the first three ingredients into a bowl. Add the brown sugar and cornmeal and mix. Combine egg, milk and shortening, add to dry ingredients and stir just until moist. Pour into a greased 8-inch pan and bake at 450° for 25 minutes.

DELUXE CORN BREAD

2 c. cornmeal
1 t. salt
4 T. sugar
4 T. flour
2 t. baking powder
2 c. boiling water
4 T. melted shortening
4 eggs, separated

Mix dry ingredients together. Gradually add boiling water, stirring well. Stir in shortening. Beat yolks into cornmeal mixture. Beat egg whites and fold in last. Bake in a loaf pan at 350° for 30 to 40 minutes.

Corn Bread

SWEET MILK PANCAKES

1½ c. flour
2 t. baking powder
1 T. sugar
½ t. salt
1 egg
1½ c. milk
2 T. melted buter

Sift dry ingredients together. Separate egg and beat yolk. Combine yolk with milk and melted butter; beat. Add to dry ingredients and mix well. Beat egg white until soft peaks form. Fold into batter. Bake on hot griddle. Serve with your favorite syrup.

CORN PANCAKES

1½ c. flour
1 t. baking soda
2 T. sugar
1 t. salt
½ c. yellow cornmeal
2 eggs, slightly beaten
2 c. buttermilk
2 T. melted butter or bacon fat

Sift first four ingredients into mixing bowl. Stir in the cornmeal. Add eggs, buttermilk and melted fat, stirring until flour is barely moistened. Pour batter from ¼ cup or ⅓ cup measure onto a hot, lightly greased griddle. Turn once. Serve hot.

BUTTERMILK PANCAKES

1 c. buttermilk
1 t. baking soda
¼ t. salt
¼ c. sour cream
1 egg
¼ c. quick oatmeal, uncooked
½ c. plus 1 T. flour
½ t. baking powder
⅓ c. sugar
2 T. cornmeal

Pour buttermilk into a bowl. Add soda and salt. Add sour cream and stir until it foams. Beat in egg with a spoon. Add oatmeal. Sift dry ingredients into the mixture and stir until no flour lumps remain. Fry on hot griddle. Serve with your favorite syrup, honey, jam or jelly.

FRENCH TOAST

2 eggs
1 c. milk
8 slices bread
Margarine

Beat eggs and add milk. Pour into a flat, shallow dish. Dip bread in mixture on both sides and fry in melted margarine in skillet until golden brown. Add margarine as needed. Serve toast hot with your favorite syrup.

JOHNNYCAKE

1 c. cornmeal
½ c. sugar
¼ t. salt
Lukewarm water
6 eggs
4 c. milk

Mix cornmeal, sugar and salt in large bowl. Add just enough lukewarm water to moisten the cornmeal mixture, being careful not to use enough to make mixture wet. Beat the eggs until light and foamy. Add milk. Stir milk mixture into cornmeal mixture and stir together thoroughly. Pour into two ungreased pie pans and bake at 350° until set, 30 to 40 minutes. The cornmeal settles to the bottom of the pan and the eggs and milk form a custard on top. Cut pie in wedges and serve warm with your favorite syrup.

Spinach Special

Main Dishes

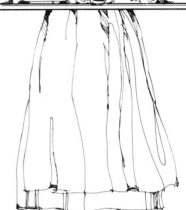

GROUND BEEF CASSEROLE

1½ lbs. ground beef
1 c. raw rice
1 onion, chopped
¼ t. diced dried garlic
1 t. salt
½ t. pepper
2½ c. tomato juice
1 c. boiling water

Brown beef, rice and onion together in frying pan, adding fat if necessary. Add seasonings, tomato juice and water. Pour into a 2-quart covered casserole. Bake for 1 hour in 300° oven.

SPINACH SPECIAL

1½ lbs. ground beef
2 onions, chopped
1 green pepper, chopped
2 c. chopped spinach
3 eggs, beaten
½ c. grated cheese
½ t. salt
Dash of pepper
½ t. oregano
¼ t. nutmeg

Brown ground beef. Sauté onions and green pepper; add to beef. Add chopped spinach. Cook over low heat just until done. Add eggs, grated cheese and seasonings. Cook until eggs are done. Serve immediately with French bread.

HAMBURGER DINNER

1 lb. ground beef
1 small onion, chopped
½ c. washed raw rice
½ t. salt
Dash of pepper
2 T. chopped parsley
Flour
1 c. sliced carrots
½ c. chopped celery
1 c. green beans
2 c. tomato juice or tomatoes

Mix together the first 6 ingredients and shape into balls. Roll meatballs in flour and place in casserole. Arrange the vegetables between the meatballs. Pour tomato juice or tomatoes over all. Cover and bake at 325° for 1 hour. Uncover and bake 30 minutes longer.

MEAT LOAF

2 lbs. ground beef
2 T. finely chopped onion
2 eggs, well beaten
4 slices bread
¾ c. milk
1 t. salt
¼ t. pepper

Mix beef, onion and eggs. Soften bread in the milk and add to meat. Add salt and pepper and mix well. Bake in loaf pan at 325° for 1 hour.

HAM LOAF

1 lb. cured ham, ground
1 lb. fresh pork, ground
2 eggs
⅔ c. cracker crumbs *or* quick-cooking rolled oats
⅓ c. quick-cooking tapioca
1¼ c. milk
1 t. salt

Mix all ingredients together and form into a loaf in a loaf pan.

DRESSING

¼ c. vinegar
½ c. water
½ c. brown sugar
1 T. prepared mustard

Mix all ingredients together and boil for 5 minutes. Pour over the loaf and bake at 350° for 2 hours, basting occasionally. The dressing should become thick and syrupy.

DELUXE MEAT LOAF

2 lbs. ground beef
2 eggs, beaten
2 c. bread crumbs
5 T. chopped onion
1 t. salt
¼ t. pepper
¼ t. dry mustard
¼ t. sage
¼ t. chili powder
½ c. tomato puree
½ finely chopped celery

Mix together all ingredients. Blend thoroughly. Pack into greased loaf pan, shaping into a loaf. Bake at 350° about 1½ hours, or until well done.

SALMON LOAF

1 1-lb. can salmon
2 T. soft butter or margarine
1 T. lemon juice
1 T. finely chopped onion
1 t. parsley flakes
¼ t. oregano
  Dash of pepper
2 T. flour
2 eggs

Mix salmon, butter or margarine, lemon juice and onion. Combine seasonings and flour and add to salmon. Beat eggs until light and fluffy and fold in. Pour into greased baking dish and bake at 350° for 45 minutes.

SKILLET DINNER

½ lb. ground beef
1 c. finely diced onion
2 T. fat
¼ t. garlic salt
½ c. uncooked rice
5 to 6 cups water
1 c. finely diced carrots
1 c. finely diced potatoes
1 t. soy sauce
1 t. salt
Pepper to taste

Brown ground beef and onion in fat. Sprinkle with garlic salt. Add rice and water and simmer uncovered over low heat for 40 minutes. Add carrots and potatoes and continue to simmer until tender, adding more water if necessary. Add seasonings. Serve hot.

MARINATED MEATBALLS

1½ lbs. ground chuck
1 large egg, beaten
¼ c. fine, dry bread crumbs
1 t. salt
Dash of pepper
½ c. salad oil
2 T. chopped parsley
1 T. chopped onion
½ t. celery salt
¼ t. salt
¼ t. garlic powder

Combine meat, egg, bread crumbs, salt and pepper. Shape into 1½-inch balls. Place in bowl. Mix remaining ingredients and pour over meatballs. Refrigerate for 3 to 5 hours. Broil in oven. Turn and baste with marinade as often as meat appears dry.

Variety may be added to fish by sprinkling with tarragon, marjoram or curry powder before cooking.

BARBEQUE HAMBURGER
(FOR FIFTY)

8 lbs. ground beef
2 t. salt
½ c. shortening or oil
1½ c. chopped onion
1½ c. chopped celery
½ c. brown sugar
2 T. prepared mustard
½ c. vinegar
2 qt. tomato sauce

Brown the beef in a heavy skillet, stirring to keep crumbly. Add the salt. In another skillet, melt shortening and sauté onion and celery until tender. Add to hamburger. Add remaining ingredients and simmer for 15 minutes. Serve on hot hamburger buns.

OVEN-COOKED CHICKEN IN SOUR CREAM

1 cut-up frying chicken, 2½ to 3 pounds
1 c. sour cream
1 t. Worcestershire sauce
1 t. lemon juice
1 t. celery salt
1 t. paprika
½ t. salt
¼ t. pepper
1 c. fine bread crumbs
⅓ c. melted butter or margarine

Combine sour cream with seasonings. Dip chicken pieces in sour cream mixture. Coat pieces in bread crumbs. Pour melted butter into baking pan. Place chicken pieces in pan skin side up. Bake in 400° oven for 1 hour or until tender.

BEEF SCRAMBLE

1 T. fat
½ lb. ground beef
¼ c. chopped onion
½ t. salt
Pepper to taste
3 eggs
2 T. cold water

Mix beef, onion, salt and pepper; brown in the fat. Drain. Beat eggs slightly with the water. Pour over the cooked beef and cook over low heat just until eggs are set. Serve on hot buttered toast.

GRANDMA'S GOULASH

½ lb. ground beef
½ c. chopped onion
1 t. salt
¼ t. pepper
4 c. cooked tomatoes
1 c. uncooked macaroni

Brown ground beef and onion. Add seasonings and tomatoes and bring to a boil. Add macaroni. Simmer until macaroni is done, stirring often.

SMOTHERED CHICKEN

1 2½ to 3-pound frying chicken, prepared for frying
1½ c. flour
1 t. salt
¼ t. pepper
1 t. minced onion
2 to 3 c. hot milk
¾ c. hot fat

Mix flour, salt and pepper. Roll chicken pieces in mixture until coated; brown quickly in skillet in hot fat. Place in baking dish, sprinkle with minced onion and cover with hot milk. (There should be enough to cover chicken.) Bake at 350° for 1½ hours. If chicken becomes dry during first hour, dot with butter and add a little more hot milk. By the time it is ready to serve, the chicken should have completely absorbed the milk

STUFFED CABBAGE LEAVES

8 large cabbage leaves
1 lb. ground beef
1 beaten egg
½ t. salt
¼ t. pepper
1½ c. finely chopped celery
1 T. chopped onion
1 c. bread crumbs
1 large tomato, peeled and chopped, *or*
 ¾ c. canned tomatoes
2 T. brown sugar
3 T. lemon juice
1 c. beef broth or bouillon
¼ t. salt

Cook cabbage leaves in a large kettle of slightly salted water just until cabbage is limp (about 3 minutes). Drain. Combine ground beef, egg, salt, pepper, celery, onion and bread crumbs. Place about ⅓ cup of the meat mixture in center of each cabbage leaf. Fold the sides over the filling, then fold over the ends. Place in a large skillet with the seam side down. Mix the remaining ingredients and pour over the rolls. Cover and simmer 45 minutes, occasionally spooning the sauce over the rolls.

SPANISH RICE

1 lb. ground beef
2 T. onion, finely chopped
¼ c. green pepper, finely chopped
2 t. brown sugar
1 t. salt
¼ t. pepper
½ t. chili powder
4 c. canned tomatoes
½ c. catsup
¾ c. uncooked rice

Cook ground beef, onion, green pepper, brown sugar, salt, pepper and chili powder in heavy frying pan until beef is browned. Add tomatoes and catsup, then the uncooked rice. Cover and simmer until rice is tender—about 40 minutes—stirring occasionally.

STUFFED BAKED SQUASH

2 acorn squash
2 c. chopped ham
1 c. crushed pineapple
2 T. brown sugar

Wash squash and split them in half lengthwise. Clean out and wash seed cavity. Place cut side down on a baking sheet and bake at 350° for 30 to 40 minutes. Remove from oven. Turn cut side up. Mix ham, pineapple and brown sugar. Place equal portions of the mixture in the squash halves. Return to oven and bake 25 to 30 minutes longer, or until squash is tender.

TUNA CASSEROLE

2 7-oz. cans tuna, flaked
2 eggs, beaten
2 T. chopped onion
2 T. chopped celery
1 c. cooked peas
1 t. salt
¼ t. pepper
1 T. Worcestershire sauce
1 c. quick-cooking rolled oats
1 c. milk

Combine all ingredients. Pour into a well-greased casserole dish. Bake at 350° for 50 minutes or until set.

BAKED HOMINY

1½ lbs. ground beef
1 T. diced onion
1 T. flour
1 t. salt
¼ t. pepper
2 c. canned tomatoes
2 T. fat
1 large can hominy (2½ c.), drained
¼ lb. American cheese, grated

Brown beef and onion. Add flour, seasonings, and tomatoes. In a separate skillet, brown the hominy in the fat. Add to meat mixture. Place in a greased casserole and sprinkle with grated cheese. Bake at 350° for 30 minutes.

CHILI CON CARNE

2½ c. uncooked pinto beans
    or 2 1-lb. cans red kidney beans
1½ lbs. ground beef
  1 c. chopped onion
  ½ c. chopped green pepper
  4 c. canned tomatoes
  1 6-oz. can tomato paste
2½ t. chili powder
  1 bay leaf
  ¼ t. cumin
  1 t. salt

Soak the pinto beans overnight in 6 cups water. Or bring beans and water to a boil, cover, and let stand 1 hour. In either case, simmer for 2 hours or until tender. Drain, reserving 1 cup of the liquid. Cook and stir ground beef, onion and green pepper in a large skillet until meat is brown and onion and peppers are tender. Add all the rest of ingredients and the 1 cup of bean liquid; cover and simmer for 1 hour. Serve with hot cornbread made from your favorite recipe.

BAKED LIVER WITH VEGETABLES

1½ lbs. sliced beef liver
  ¾ c. flour
  ½ t. salt
    Dash of pepper
  2 T. fat
  2 small onions, thinly sliced
  4 small carrots, pared and chunked
  2 c. tomatoes
  2 c. mashed potatoes

Dredge liver with seasoned flour. Brown in hot fat, adding a little more fat if necessary. Place browned slices in a greased casserole. Add onions and carrots; pour tomatoes over all. Cover and bake at 350° for one hour. While the liver is baking, boil 3 or 4 medium-sized pared potatoes. Drain and mash, adding ¼ cup milk and 1 teaspoon butter; beat until fluffy. Cover the baked liver with the hot mashed potatoes. Bake at 400° until the potatoes are brown.

BROWNED HASH

2 c. cooked meat, chopped (beef, turkey, ham, chicken or lamb)
2 c. boiled potatoes, chopped
1 T. chopped onion
  Salt and pepper to taste
1 T. minced parsley (optional)
1 c. milk
2 T. fat

Mix all ingredients except milk and fat. Melt fat in a heavy skillet over medium heat. When the fat is very hot, spread hash mixture evenly in the skillet. The bottom of the hash should brown quickly. Add the milk and mix. Cover and cook slowly until crisp, about 10 minutes.

CHICKEN PIE

1 frying chicken, cut up *or* chicken parts
½ t. salt
¼ t. pepper
1 t. chopped parsley

Wash chicken thoroughly and cut up, trimming off any excess fat. Place in pan with a tight cover. Add just enough water to cover the chicken pieces. Add seasonings. Bring to a boil, then reduce heat to keep bubbling; cover and cook until tender, about 40 minutes. Cool. Pick all meat from the bones and chop into small chunks.

GRAVY

Measure the remaining broth in which the chicken was cooked. For each cup of broth, mix smooth ¼ cup cold water and 1 tablespoon flour. Stir the flour and water into the broth; heat to a boil, stirring constantly. Add chopped chicken. Pour the chicken mixture into a Dutch oven or a large baking pan, such as a cake pan. Top with your favorite baking powder biscuit dough, cutting small rounds of dough and placing on top of the chicken. Bake in preheated 400° oven until the biscuit topping is browned, about 12 to 15 minutes. Serve piping hot.

Desserts

ICE CREAM

4 eggs
1 c. sugar
Dash salt
1 qt. light cream or half-and-half
1 c. whipping cream
1 c. milk
2 T. vanilla

Beat eggs. Add sugar and salt and mix well. Add all liquids and vanilla. Freeze in hand-turned or electric ice-cream freezer according to manufacturer's directions.

ICE CREAM TOPPING

2 c. applesauce
1/3 c. red cinnamon candies
2 T. sugar
1 T. lemon juice

Combine all ingredients. Heat to melt candies. Cool and chill. Stir before spooning over vanilla ice cream.

PEANUT BUTTER FUDGE

2 c. brown sugar
1/8 t. salt
2 T. light corn syrup
3/4 c. milk
4 T. peanut butter
1 t. vanilla

Combine brown sugar, salt, corn syrup and milk. Cook to soft ball stage (test in cold water). Cool to lukewarm. Add peanut butter and vanilla. Beat until the gloss is gone. Pour into 8" square pan. When set, cut into squares.

MARSHMALLOW SNOW

1/2 c. milk
30 large marshmallows
1 c. whipping cream
1 c. crushed pineapple, drained

Melt marshmallows in milk. Cool. Whip cream until stiff. Add marshmallow mixture and whip together until stiff. Fold in pineapple. Chill overnight. Cut in squares to serve.

APPLE PANDOWDY

1 c. brown sugar
¼ c. flour
¼ t. salt
1 t. vinegar
1 c. water
1 c. flour
2 t. baking powder
¾ t. salt
¼ c. butter or margarine
¾ c. milk
5 c. pared, sliced apples
¼ t. cinnamon
  Dash of nutmeg
1 t. lemon juice
1 t. vanilla
2 T. butter, melted

Mix sugar, flour and salt in a saucepan. Stir in vinegar and water. Cook over low heat, stirring constantly, until thickened. Set aside. Heat oven to 375°. Sift flour, baking powder and salt together. Cut in butter. Add milk and stir until moistened. Arrange apple slices in well-greased 8" x 12" x 2" baking dish. Add cinnamon, nutmeg, lemon juice, vanilla and butter to sauce. Pour over apples. Drop dough on top of apples. Bake 40 minutes or until topping is brown. Serve warm. Serves 6.

STRAWBERRY-RHUBARB COBBLER

2 c. sugar
¼ c. quick-cooking tapioca
¼ t. salt
3 c. fresh rhubarb, cut into 1-inch pieces
3 c. halved strawberries
2 T. butter
1½ c. flour
1 T. sugar
¼ t. salt
3 t. baking powder
¼ t. cream of tartar
⅓ c. shortening
½ c. milk

Combine sugar, tapioca, salt, rhubarb and strawberries in an 8-inch square baking dish. Let stand about 15 minutes. Then dot with butter and bake at 400° for 15 minutes. While fruit mixture bakes, sift together dry ingredients. Cut in shortening until mixture resembles coarse crumbs. Add milk and stir until all is moistened and clings together when pressed into a ball. Pat or roll on floured board into an 8-inch square. Cut into 9 squares and place squares on top of hot fruit. Bake at 400° for 30 minutes or until brown.

MARSHMALLOW-POPCORN BALLS

6 qts. popped corn
½ c. butter
1 lb. marshmallows

Melt butter in double boiler. Add the marshmallows and stir until melted. Pour over the popped corn and stir until well mixed. Form into balls.

KOOL-AID SHERBET

1 c. sugar
1 pkg. Kool-Aid
3 c. milk

Dissolve sugar and Kool-Aid in the milk. Pour into refrigerator freezing tray. Freeze until partially firm. Spoon into cold bowl and beat with an eggbeater until smooth but not melted. Return to tray. Freeze until firm, about 2 hours. Makes ¾ quart.

APPLE BROWN BETTY

 2 c. finely chopped apples
½ c. brown sugar
½ c. bread crumbs
½ c. chopped nuts
½ t. cinnamon
 2 T. butter

Place a layer of apples in a greased baking dish. Mix dry ingredients together. Sprinkle apples with the mixture. Alternate layers until all is used, ending with the crumbs on top. Dot with butter. Cover and bake at 350° for 45 minutes. Uncover to brown. Serve warm or cold with cream.

APPLE-NUT COBBLER

½ c. sugar
½ t. cinnamon
 1 c. nutmeats
 4 c. pared, thinly sliced, tart apples
 1 c. flour
 1 c. sugar
 1 t. baking powder
¼ t. salt
 1 egg, well beaten
½ c. evaporated milk
⅓ c. butter or margarine, melted

Mix sugar, cinnamon and ½ cup of the nuts. Place apple slices in bottom of 8-inch round baking dish. Sprinkle with the cinnamon mixture. Sift dry ingredients together. Combine egg, milk and melted butter. Add dry ingredients and mix until smooth. Pour over apples. Sprinkle with the remaining nuts. Bake at 325° for about 55 minutes.

QUICK COBBLER

 3 to 4 c. canned fruit (any kind)
⅓ c. sugar
½ c. butter or margarine
 1 c. flour
 1 c. sugar
 2 t. baking powder
 1 t. salt
 1 c. milk

Heat fruit in its syrup with ⅓ cup sugar. Stir until sugar is dissolved. Melt butter in 9" x 13" pan. Mix flour, sugar, baking powder, salt and milk. Pour into pan. Then pour fruit over the batter. Bake at 350° for 1 hour.

APPLE DUMPLINGS

1½ c. sugar
1½ c. water
¼ t. cinnamon
¼ t. nutmeg
½ t. red food coloring
2 T. butter
2 c. flour
2 t. baking powder
1 t. salt
⅔ c. shortening
½ c. milk
6 medium apples, pared and cored

Combine sugar, water, spices and food coloring; bring to a boil and add butter. Cool. Sift dry ingredients together. Cut in shortening until mixture resembles coarse meal. Add milk and stir just until flour is moistened. Roll on lightly floured board into rectangle about 18" x 12" x ¼". Cut into 6-inch squares. Place a whole apple in each square. Sprinkle generously with sugar. Dot with butter. Moisten edges of squares. Fold in corners to center and pinch edges together. Place 1 inch apart in baking dish. Pour the syrup over the dumplings. Bake at 375° for 35 minutes or until apples are tender. Serve with cream.

DUTCH CRACKER PUDDING

2 c. salted crackers
4 c. milk
3 eggs, separated
½ c. sugar
1 c. flaked coconut
1½ t. vanilla
6 T. sugar

Break crackers into coarse crumbs; set aside. Scald milk in 3-quart saucepan. Beat egg yolks until light. Add hot milk to yolks, stirring well. Return to saucepan. Stir in ½ cup sugar and cook about 2 minutes, stirring constantly. Add cracker crumbs and coconut. Cook and stir until crumbs are soft and pudding has thickened. Stir in vanilla and pour into lightly buttered baking dish, about 8 inches square. Beat egg whites until frothy. Gradually add the 6 tablespoons sugar, beating until the mixture holds stiff peaks. Spread over pudding and swirl. Bake at 350° until meringue is brown, about 15 minutes. Cool to serve.

STRAWBERRY SHORTCAKE

2 c. flour
3 t. baking powder
½ t. salt
5 T. sugar
½ c. shortening
1 egg, beaten
⅓ c. milk
4 c. sweetened, crushed strawberries
1 c. cream

Mix flour, baking powder, salt and sugar. Cut in the shortening until mixture has the texture of cornmeal. Add egg and then enough milk to make the dough easy to handle. Roll or pat dough into rounds for individual shortcakes (about ½ inch thick). Place on cookie sheet and bake at 450° for 12 to 15 minutes. Split shortcakes, cover with strawberries, and serve with cream.

Pictured opposite
Apple Dumplings

DATE PUDDING

½ c. chopped, pitted dates
⅓ c. sugar
3 T. cornstarch
¼ t. salt
2¼ c. milk
1½ t. vanilla
¼ c. chopped nuts
1 c. whipped cream (optional)

Combine dates, sugar, cornstarch and salt in a saucepan. Add milk. Stir and cook until the mixture is smooth and thick. Boil vigorously for about 1 minute. Remove from heat and add vanilla and nuts. Chill and serve topped with whipped cream.

CARROT PUDDING

½ c. sugar
½ c. butter
2 eggs
1 c. grated raw carrots
1 c. grated raw potatoes
1 t. baking soda
2 T. hot water
1½ c. flour
½ t. nutmeg
½ t. cinnamon
½ t. cloves
½ t. salt
½ c. raisins, washed and drained

Cream sugar and butter. Beat in eggs. Add grated vegetables and soda dissolved in hot water. Sift dry ingredients together, combine with raisins, and add to first mixture. Mix thoroughly. Pour into buttered double boiler. Steam for 2 to 3 hours.

RICE PUDDING

¼ c. uncooked rice
2 c. milk
½ t. salt
2 eggs, separated
2 T. butter
½ c. sugar
1 T. lemon juice
1 c. raisins
½ t. mace
½ c. whipping cream

Wash rice. Soak in milk for 30 minutes in top of double boiler. Add salt. Cook over hot water until rice is tender and milk is almost all absorbed, stirring often. Beat egg yolks. Add a little hot rice to egg yolks and stir in. Add to mixture in double boiler. Cook 2 minutes, stirring. Cream butter and sugar. Blend in lemon juice and mace. Stir in washed and drained raisins. Add to rice mixture and blend well. Whip cream and fold in. Beat egg whites until they form soft peaks. Fold into rice mixture. Turn into buttered 1-quart casserole. Bake at 325° for 30 minutes or until set. Serve warm or cold with cream, if desired.

CREAMY BAKED CUSTARD

2 eggs (or 4 egg yolks)
⅓ c. sugar
¼ t. salt
2 c. milk, scalded
1 t. vanilla

Beat eggs slightly. Add sugar and salt and beat well. Add scalded milk gradually, stirring constantly. Stir in vanilla. Pour into lightly buttered 5-6-ounce custard cups. Place in warm water in a shallow pan. Bake at 350° for 25 or 30 minutes, or until a silver knife inserted 1 inch from edge of dish comes out clean.

CANNED CHERRY PIE

Pastry for 2-crust 9-inch pie
1 c. sugar
3 T. cornstarch
Dash of salt
4 c. pitted cherries
6 to 8 drops red food coloring
½ t. almond extract
1 T. butter

Roll pastry and line pie pan. Mix sugar, cornstarch, and salt together. Pour cherries into heavy saucepan. Add sugar mixture and food coloring and stir in. Cook over medium heat, stirring constantly, until thick. Add extract and butter. Pour into pastry-lined pan. Top with slitted crust, seal edges, and bake at 400° until nicely browned.

Pies

BUTTERMILK PIE

1 c. sugar
1½ T. flour
1½ c. buttermilk
1½ t. lemon extract
¼ t. salt
1½ t. lemon juice
3 eggs, beaten
1 t. grated lemon rind
1 unbaked 8-inch pie shell

Combine sugar and flour. Add buttermilk, lemon extract, salt, lemon juice and beaten eggs. Mix well. Pour into pastry-lined pan. Sprinkle top with grated lemon rind. Bake at 425° until inserted knife comes out clean.

PLAIN PIE CRUST

2 c. flour
¾ t. salt
¾ c. shortening
5 T. cold water

Sift flour and salt together into a bowl. Cut in shortening with a pastry blender. Add water and mix just until mixture will hold together. Divide dough into two parts. Roll out on floured board to desired size, being careful to use no more flour than absolutely necessary. Fit into pans, press edges and cut off excess dough. Prick dough in pan with a fork. Bake at 400° until lightly browned. Makes 2 single crusts or one double-crust pie.

MINCEMEAT

1 lb. beef
½ lb. suet
4 lbs. apples
½ lb. currants
1 lb. raisins
1½ lbs. brown sugar
1 qt. cider
1 c. meat stock
2 t. salt
1 t. cloves
1 t. nutmeg
2 t. cinnamon
5 T. lemon juice

Grind beef and suet (or use 1½ pounds fatty ground beef). Pare, core and chop apples. Chop together currants and raisins. Mix apples, currants, raisins, sugar, cider and meat stock. Cook about 5 minutes. Add beef, suet and seasonings to apple mixture. Simmer 1 hour, stirring frequently to keep from burning. Add lemon juice.

GREEN TOMATO MINCEMEAT

5½ c. chopped green tomatoes
5½ c. chopped apples
8 c. brown sugar
½ t. cloves
1 t. nutmeg
1 t. cinnamon
2 lbs. chopped raisins
2 t. salt
1 c. chopped suet or ground beef
1 c. vinegar
1 orange rind, grated

Chop tomatoes and drain thoroughly. Measure juice and add an equal amount of water to the pulp. Heat until scalding hot. Drain off liquid. Repeat two times: adding fresh water, scalding and draining. Add the chopped apples to the tomatoes. Add sugar mixed with spices, raisins, salt, and suet. Cook until clear. Add remaining ingredients and cook until mixture thickens and flavors are blended. Pack into hot, sterilized jars and seal.

MINCE PIE WITH OATMEAL CRUST

CRUST
¾ c. flour
½ t. salt
½ c. quick-cooking rolled oats
⅓ c. shortening
4 T. cold water

Sift together flour and salt. Stir in rolled oats. Cut in shortening and sprinkle on cold water. Stir until just dampened. Roll out on floured board and fit into 9-inch pie pan.

FILLING
2½ c. prepared mincemeat
⅓ c. brown sugar
2 T. flour
¾ c. whipping cream
½ c. chopped pecans

Pour mincemeat into unbaked pie shell. Combine brown sugar and flour. Add whipping cream and blend well. Pour cream mixture over mincemeat. Sprinkle with pecans. Bake at 425° for 15 minutes. Reduce heat to 325° and bake 15 to 20 minutes longer or until done.

PUMPKIN-MINCEMEAT PIE

1 unbaked 9-inch pie shell
2 c. cooked pumpkin
¾ c. brown sugar
¾ t. cinnamon
¼ t. nutmeg
⅛ t. ginger
⅛ t. cloves
½ t. salt
2 eggs, beaten
1 c. evaporated milk
1 c. mincemeat

Combine pumpkin, sugar, spices and salt. Add beaten eggs and mix well. Gradually add evaporated milk, stirring until well blended. Set aside. Spread mincemeat over bottom of pie shell. Pour pumpkin mixture over mincemeat. Bake at 375° for 45 minutes or until a metal knife inserted into center of pie comes out clean. Cool. Garnish with whipped cream if desired.

JELLY PUDDING PIE

For each serving desired, use 2 slices homemade bread which has been buttered, sprinkled with sugar and toasted in a slow oven until crisp. Place the toasted bread in a bowl.

When a jelly jar is nearly empty, use a bit of hot water to rinse out the jelly that clings to the jar. Save and pour hot over the toasted bread. Or use a fresh new jar of jelly or preserves—or any leftover fruits. This makes a delicious fruit pudding when doused with rich milk.

CUSTARD PIE

1 unbaked pie shell
3 eggs
½ c. sugar
2 c. milk
1 t. vanilla
⅛ t. salt
Dash of nutmeg

Beat eggs until light and frothy. Add sugar, milk, vanilla and salt. Mix well. Brush pie shell with melted butter. Add custard and sprinkle with ground nutmeg. Bake at 450° for 10 minutes, then reduce heat to 350° and bake for about 40 minutes, or until custard is set.

CHOCOLATE PIE

3 eggs, separated
1 c. sugar
2 T. butter
4 T. cocoa
4 T. flour
2 c. milk
¼ t. salt
2 t. vanilla
3 T. sugar
1 baked 9-inch pie shell

Beat egg yolks until light. Beat in sugar, butter, cocoa and flour. Add milk and salt and cook in double boiler until thick. Add 1 teaspoon vanilla. Pour into baked pie shell. Beat egg whites until stiff. Add 3 tablespoons sugar and 1 teaspoon vanilla. Beat into peaks. Spread on top of pie and bake until brown at 375°.

GRAPE PIE

Pastry for 2-crust 9-inch pie
6 c. Concord grapes
1 c. sugar
¼ c. flour
¼ t. salt
1 t. lemon juice
1 T. butter

Wash and peel grapes, saving skins. Cook pulp in a saucepan with no water; bring to a hard boil. Rub through a strainer to remove seeds. Mix strained pulp with the reserved skins. Mix flour, sugar and salt; stir into grapes. Add lemon juice and butter. Pour into pastry-lined 9-inch pie pan. Top with second crust. Slit top crust and seal edges. Bake at 400° for about 40 minutes or until crust is browned and pie is bubbly.

APPLE-BUTTERSCOTCH PIE

Pastry for 2-crust pie
⅔ c. brown sugar
⅓ c. cream
2 T. flour
¼ t. salt
¼ c. sugar
6 to 8 cooking apples
Juice of ½ lemon

Combine brown sugar and cream and cook in double boiler for 20 minutes. Roll out pie crust and fit into 9-inch pie pan. Mix flour, salt and sugar and sprinkle over the bottom crust. Peel and core apples, slice thin, and fill pie. Squeeze lemon juice into brown sugar-cream mixture. Pour ⅔ of mixture over apples. Cut 2-inch hole in top crust and place over apples; seal edges. Bake 20 minutes at 425°, then reduce heat to 350° and bake 25 minutes more. When baked, pour remaining brown sugar mixture into hole in top crust. Serve warm.

PINEAPPLE CREAM PIE

1 baked 9-inch pie shell
½ c. sugar
3 T. cornstarch
½ t. salt
2½ c. milk
3 eggs, separated
1 T. butter
1 t. vanilla
1 c. crushed pineapple (1 small can)
3 T. sugar
½ t. vanilla

Mix ½ cup sugar, cornstarch and salt. Combine with milk in a heavy saucepan. Beat in egg yolks. Cook over medium heat, stirring constantly, until mixture thickens. Add butter and vanilla; stir in pineapple. Pour mixture into baked pie shell. Beat egg whites until frothy. Add 3 tablespoons sugar and beat until mixture forms soft peaks. Add vanilla. Spread on top of pie filling, being sure to seal edges. Bake at 375° until delicately browned.

BLACKBERRY DEEP DISH PIE

Pastry for single-crust pie
1 qt. fresh blackberries
¾ c. sugar
2½ T. quick-cooking tapioca
¼ t. salt
1 T. butter

Combine blackberries, sugar, tapioca and salt. Pour into an 8-inch square baking dish. Dot with butter. Let stand 15 minutes. Roll pastry ⅛ inch thick (to fit top of baking dish). Cut several slits in center. Place on top of filling. Bake at 425° for 25 minutes. Serve warm.

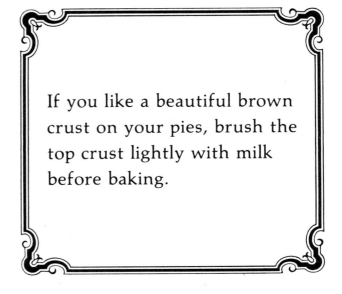

If you like a beautiful brown crust on your pies, brush the top crust lightly with milk before baking.

Cookies

GOOD COOKIES

1 c. shortening
1 c. brown sugar
1 c. white sugar
2 eggs, beaten
1½ c. flour
1 t. baking powder
1 t. baking soda
½ t. salt
1 T. vanilla
2 c. crisp rice cereal
2 c. quick-cooking rolled oats

Cream shortening and sugars. Add eggs, beating well. Sift flour, baking powder, soda and salt together. Add to egg mixture. Mix in vanilla, rice cereal and rolled oats. Bake at 375° for about 12 minutes.

Cookies

FRUIT PATS

1½ c. sugar
¾ c. shortening
3 eggs, beaten
2 T. sour milk or buttermilk
3 c. flour
1 t. baking soda
½ t. salt
1 t. cinnamon
1 t. vanilla
1 c. whole wheat flour *or* rolled oats
2 c. raisins, washed and drained
1 c. nutmeats

Cream sugar and shortening. Add eggs and beat well. Add sour milk. Sift flour, soda, salt and cinnamon together and stir into first mixture. Add vanilla. Stir in whole wheat flour or rolled oats. Add raisins and nuts. Drop by teaspoonfuls on greased cookie sheet and bake at 375° until brown.

PINEAPPLE CRUNCHIES

1 c. sugar
½ c. shortening
2 eggs, beaten
1½ c. flour
¼ t. baking soda
¼ t. salt
1 t. baking powder
⅜ c. sour cream
1 c. quick-cooking rolled oats
1 c. nuts
1 c. raisins
⅔ c. drained crushed pineapple

Cream sugar and shortening. Add eggs. Sift flour, soda, salt and baking powder together. Add to egg mixture alternately with sour cream. Add remaining ingredients and mix well. Drop by small spoonfuls on greased cookie sheet. Bake at 375° for 10 to 12 minutes.

APPLESAUCE SQUARES

½ c. shortening
1 c. sugar
1 egg, beaten
1 c. raisins, moistened in hot water
   and drained
1 c. applesauce
1 t. baking soda
1½ c. flour
1 t. baking powder
1 t. cinnamon
½ t. salt
½ c. nuts

Cream shortening and sugar. Add beaten egg and mix well. Heat applesauce and add soda while hot. Cool to warm and add to sugar mixture. Sift dry ingredients over nuts and raisins; add to above mixture. Bake in greased cookie sheet at 375° for 20 to 30 minutes or until done. While hot, sprinkle with powdered sugar and cut into squares.

BROWN SUGAR REFRIGERATOR COOKIES

1 c. butter
1½ c. brown sugar
2 eggs
1 t. vanilla
2 c. flour
2 t. baking soda
2 t. cream of tartar

Cream butter and sugar. Add eggs and vanilla and beat well. Sift together dry ingredients; stir into sugar-butter mixture. Chill. Make into walnut-sized balls and bake at 400° until lightly browned.

RAISIN HONEY DROPS

¾ c. sugar
¾ c. butter or margarine
¾ c. honey
1 egg
2 c. flour
1 t. cinnamon
1 t. salt
½ t. baking soda
2 c. quick-cooking rolled oats
1 c. raisins

Cream sugar and butter. Add honey and egg. Sift flour, cinnamon, salt, and soda into creamed mixture. Add rolled oats and raisins. Drop by teaspoonfuls onto baking sheet and bake at 375° for 12 to 14 minutes.

OATMEAL CRISPIES

1 c. shortening
1 c. brown sugar
1 c. white sugar
2 eggs, well beaten
1 t. vanilla
1½ c. flour
1 t. salt
1 t. baking soda
3 c. quick-cooking rolled oats
½ c. chopped nuts

Cream shortening and sugars. Beat in eggs and vanilla. Add sifted dry ingredients. Mix in oatmeal and nuts. Shape into rolls. Chill overnight. Slice and bake at 375° for 8 to 10 minutes or until lightly browned.

COCONUT COOKIES

½ c. white sugar
½ c. brown sugar
½ c. shortening
1 egg, beaten
1 c. flour
½ t. salt
½ t. baking powder
½ t. baking soda
1 c. quick-cooking rolled oats
½ c. shredded coconut
½ c. chopped nuts
1 t. vanilla

Cream sugars and shortening. Beat in egg. Sift flour, salt, baking powder and soda together; add to sugar mixture. Blend in rolled oats, coconut, nuts and vanilla. Place on greased cookie sheets, flatten a little and bake at 325° for 15 minutes.

OATMEAL COOKIES

2 c. brown sugar
1 c. shortening
2 eggs
2 c. flour
2 t. baking soda
1 t. baking powder
½ t. salt
3 c. quick-cooking rolled oats
1 t. vanilla
1 c. nuts

Cream the sugar and shortening. Add eggs and beat until creamy. Sift together flour, salt, baking powder and soda. Add to first mixture and blend well. Blend in rolled oats. Add vanilla and nuts. Drop by teaspoonfuls on baking sheet and bake at 375° for about 12 minutes.

NO-BAKE CHOCOLATE OATMEAL COOKIES

½ c. butter or margarine
2 c. sugar
6 T. cocoa
½ c. milk
3 c. quick-cooking rolled oats
1 t. vanilla
½ c. nuts

Place butter in saucepan. Mix sugar and cocoa together and add to butter. Add milk. Heat until butter melts, then boil 4 or 5 minutes. Stir in rolled oats, vanilla and nuts. Drop by teaspoonfuls on waxed paper.

MOLASSES SUGAR COOKIES

¾ c. shortening
1 c. sugar
¼ c. molasses
1 egg, beaten
2 c. flour
2 t. baking soda
1 t. cinnamon
½ t. cloves
¼ t. ginger
½ t. salt

Melt shortening over low heat. Cool. Add sugar, molasses and egg. Beat well. Sift dry ingredients together and add to first mixture. Mix well and chill thoroughly. Form into 1-inch balls, roll in sugar, and place on cookie sheet 2 inches apart. Bake at 375° for 8 to 10 minutes. Makes about 4 dozen cookies.

HARVEST BARS

¼ c. butter
1 c. brown sugar
1 t. vanilla
2 eggs
⅔ c. pumpkin
½ c. chopped dates
½ c. nuts
2 T. flour
½ c. flour
½ t. baking powder
¼ t. baking soda
½ t. salt
½ t. each cinnamon, nutmeg, and ginger

Cream butter, brown sugar, and vanilla together. Add eggs. Beat well and add pumpkin. Dredge dates and nuts in the 2 tablespoons flour. Sift together remaining dry ingredients and add to pumpkin mixture. Add dates and nuts. Bake in greased pan for 30 minutes at 350°. Frost with lemon icing and cut into bars.

LEMON ICING

1½ c. powdered sugar
1 t. lemon flavoring
Cream

Combine sugar and lemon flavoring. Stir in enough cream to spread easily.

CARROT COOKIES

1 c. soft shortening
¾ c. sugar
1 egg
1 c. cooked carrots, mashed
¼ c. milk
1 t. vanilla
½ t. lemon flavoring
2 c. flour
2 t. baking powder
½ t. salt
1 c. bran flakes

Cream shortening and sugar. Add egg and beat well. Stir in carrots, milk and flavorings. Sift flour, baking powder, and salt together and combine with the bran flakes. Add to first mixture and mix well. Drop by teaspoonfuls onto baking sheets and bake at 375° about 18 minutes. Grated raw carrots may be used instead of cooked carrots. Decrease baking time to about 12 minutes. Cookies may be frosted if desired.

FROSTING

1 c. sifted powdered sugar
2 T. orange juice

Beat until smooth and spread on cooled cookies.

For most cookie recipes, it is not necessary to grease the baking sheet. The shortening in the cookies is sufficient.

*Pictured opposite
Harvest Bars*

COCONUT BARS

½ c. flour
¾ c. brown sugar
½ c. white sugar
½ t. salt
½ t. baking soda
2 eggs, beaten
½ c. grated coconut
½ c. nuts
½ c. powdered sugar, sifted

Sift flour; add sugars, salt and soda. Beat in eggs, nuts and grated coconut. Place in shallow greased pan and bake in 350° oven for 30 minutes. Cut into strips. When cool, roll in powdered sugar.

POPCORN-PEANUT SQUARES

4 qts. popped corn
1 c. peanuts
1½ c. sugar
½ c. corn syrup
½ c. water
1 T. vinegar
1 t. butter
¼ t. baking soda

Force enough freshly popped popcorn through a food chopper, using the medium blade, to make 2 quarts. Grind the peanuts also. Combine sugar, corn syrup, water and vinegar; boil until a little of the mixture cracks when tested in cold water. Remove from heat, add butter and soda, and stir. Pour over the corn and peanuts, mixing thoroughly. Press firmly into a buttered pan so that the mixture is about 1 inch thick. Cut into squares or break into pieces as desired.

SHORTCUT SUGAR COOKIES

¾ c. sugar
⅔ c. shortening
1 egg
2 c. flour
1½ t. baking powder
¼ t. salt
4 t. milk
½ t. vanilla

Cream sugar and shortening together. Beat in egg. Sift together flour, baking powder and salt; add to first mixture. Stir in milk and vanilla. Chill 3 hours. Roll out ¼ inch thick on lightly floured board. Cut into squares or diamonds. Bake on cookie sheets at 375° for 5 to 6 minutes. Cool slightly on cookie sheet before removing to cooling rack.

SOUR CREAM DROP COOKIES

1 c. brown sugar
1 c. white sugar
1 c. shortening
1 c. sour cream
2 eggs, beaten
4½ c. flour
½ t. salt
½ t. nutmeg
½ t. baking soda
3 t. baking powder

Cream sugars and shortening. Add sour cream and beat well. Add eggs and beat in. Sift dry ingredients together and stir into first mixture. Coconut, nuts, or chocolate chips may be added if desired. Drop by teaspoonfuls on greased cookie sheet and bake at 375° for about 12 minutes.

POUND CAKE

1 c. butter or margarine
2 c. sugar
6 eggs
2 c. flour
1 t. vanilla
1 t. almond flavoring
1 t. lemon flavoring

Cream butter and sugar. Add eggs one at a time, beating after each addition. Add sifted flour and flavorings. Bake in angel food pan at 350° nearly an hour.

CHOPPED APPLE CAKE

2 c. sugar
½ c. shortening
2 eggs
4 c. chopped apples
1 c. chopped nuts
2 c. flour
2 t. baking soda
2 t. cinnamon
1 t. nutmeg
1 t. salt

Cream sugar and shortening together. Add beaten eggs and mix well. Add apples and nuts to first mixture but do not stir in. Sift combined dry ingredients over the apples and nuts. Stir all in until thoroughly mixed. This is a very stiff batter. Bake in greased 9" x 13" pan at 350° for 15 minutes. Reduce heat to 325° and bake 25 minutes longer. To serve, cut in squares and top with sauce. Cake may also be served without sauce.

SAUCE

1 c. sugar
½ c. butter or margarine
½ c. light cream or half-and-half

Cook together until thick. Add 1 teaspoon vanilla. Spoon over cake pieces and top with whipped cream.

Cakes

GOLD CAKE

½ c. shortening
1 c. sugar
½ c. milk
8 egg yolks
2 t. lemon extract
⅛ t. salt
2 c. flour
3 t. baking powder

Cream shortening and sugar. Add remaining ingredients and beat vigorously for 3 minutes. Pour into two 8-inch cake pans. Bake at 350° until cake tests done. Note: This is a good way to use up egg yolks left from making angel food cakes, meringues or white cakes.

SPICE CAKE

2 c. flour
½ t. cinnamon
½ t. cloves
¼ t. ginger
2 t. baking powder
¼ t. salt
½ c. shortening
1 c. sugar
2 eggs
¾ c. milk

Sift dry ingredients together. Cream sugar and shortening and beat in eggs until light and fluffy. Add the milk alternately with the flour mixture. Bake in 2 greased 9" layer pans at 375° for 25 to 30 minutes. May be baked in loaf pan.

GINGERBREAD

½ c. sugar
½ c. shortening
1 c. molasses
1 t. baking soda
1 c. boiling water
2½ c. flour
½ t. cinnamon
½ t. ginger
½ t. cloves
2 eggs, well beaten

Cream sugar and shortening. Add molasses. Dissolve soda in hot water and add to the sugar mixture. Sift flour and spices together and beat in well. Add beaten eggs and mix well. Bake in a 9-inch square pan at 350° for about 40 minutes. Cut in squares and serve hot topped with whipped cream.

APPLE CREAM TOPPING
(for Spice Cake or Gingerbread)

1 c. canned applesauce
½ c. sugar
½ t. cinnamon
1 c. whipping cream

Beat cream until thickened. Add sugar and cinnamon blended together and beat cream until it peaks. Fold in drained applesauce. Chill. Top cut pieces of spice cake or gingerbread.

CREAM CAKE

2 eggs
1 c. sugar
1¼ c. cream
2 c. flour
2 t. baking powder
¼ t. salt
1 t. vanilla

Beat eggs. Add sugar and beat in. Sift flour, baking powder, and salt together and add to egg mixture alternately with the cream. Beat well. Add vanilla. Pour into 2 greased and floured 9" pans and bake at 350° until cakes test done.

Pictured opposite
Gingerbread

DATE CAKE

1 c. boiling water
1 c. chopped dates
1 t. baking soda
1 c. sugar
⅓ c. softened butter
1 egg
1 t. vanilla
1½ c. flour
1 t. baking powder
½ t. salt
½ c. chopped nuts

Pour boiling water over dates. Stir in soda and allow to cool. Cream sugar and butter. Add egg and vanilla and beat well. Sift flour with baking powder and salt; mix with creamed mixture until well blended. Stir in date mixture. Add nuts. Bake in greased and floured 9″ x 13″ pan at 350° for 35 minutes.

WHITE CAKE

1½ c. sugar
½ c. butter
2½ c. flour
2 t. baking powder
¼ t. salt
1 c. milk
1 t. vanilla
4 egg whites

Cream sugar and butter. Sift flour, baking powder, and salt together and add alternately with the milk. Add vanilla. Beat egg whites until stiff but not dry and fold in last. Pour into greased 9″ x 13″ x 2″ cake pan. Bake at 375° for about 40 minutes.

TWO EGG CAKE

1 c. sugar
½ c. shortening
1 t. vanilla
2 eggs
2 c. flour
2½ t. baking powder
⅔ c. milk

Cream sugar and shortening. Beat in eggs and add vanilla. Sift flour and baking powder together and add to egg mixture alternately with milk. Beat until smooth. Bake in 2 greased 8″ layer pans or make cupcakes. Bake at 350°.

MASHED POTATO CAKE

1 c. shortening
2 c. sugar
4 eggs
1 c. hot mashed potatoes
2 c. flour
3 t. baking powder
½ t. salt
½ c. cocoa
½ t. cinnamon
½ t. cloves
½ c. milk
½ c. nuts

Cream shortening and sugar together. Add eggs one at a time, beating after each addition. Add potatoes and beat until just blended. Sift all dry ingredients together and add alternately with the milk. Fold in nuts. Bake in greased and floured 10″ x 13″ pan at 350° for 45 minutes.

APPLE CAKE

1⅔ c. sugar
¾ c. butter or margarine
2 eggs
2 large apples, diced
1⅔ c. flour
1 t. baking soda
½ t. salt
1 t. cinnamon
1 t. cloves
½ c. nuts

Cream sugar and butter. Beat in eggs. Add apples. Sift dry ingredients together and add to apple mixture. Beat well. Stir in nuts. Bake in greased 9" x 13" pan at 350° for about 30 minutes.

CARAMEL ANGEL CAKE

1½ c. brown sugar
½ c. water
1¼ c. egg whites
¼ t. salt
1 t. cream of tartar
1 t. vanilla
1 c. sifted cake flour

Cook sugar and water until it becomes thick and will spin a thread when dropped from the tip of a spoon (220° F.). Beat egg whites with salt until frothy. Add cream of tartar and beat until whites are stiff but not dry. Pour sugar syrup slowly over egg whites, beating continuously until all the syrup is used. Fold flour in gradually. Add vanilla and pour into ungreased angel food pan. Bake at 300° for an hour, or until cake tests done.

RED DEVIL'S FOOD CAKE

1 c. sugar
1¾ c. cake flour
⅓ c. cocoa
1¼ t. baking soda
1 t. salt
½ c. soft shortening
1 c. milk
2 eggs
1 t. vanilla

Blend together sugar, flour, cocoa, soda and salt. Add shortening and ⅔ cup of milk and beat 2 minutes. Beat in remaining ingredients. Bake in greased and floured 9" x 13" x 2" pan at 350° for 30 to 45 minutes.

OATMEAL COCOA CAKE

1½ c. boiling water
1 c. quick-cooking rolled oats
½ c. shortening
1½ c. sugar
2 eggs
1 t. vanilla
1 c. flour
½ t. salt
1 t. baking soda
½ c. cocoa

Pour boiling water over rolled oats. Set aside. Cream sugar and shortening. Add eggs and vanilla and beat well. Add rolled oats mixture. Sift dry ingredients together and beat in. Bake in greased 9" x 13" pan at 350° for 35 minutes.

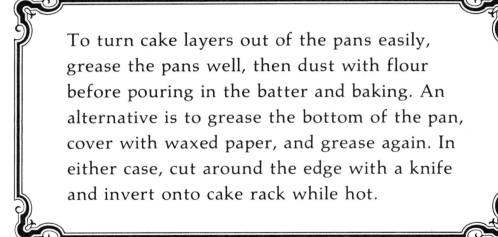

To turn cake layers out of the pans easily, grease the pans well, then dust with flour before pouring in the batter and baking. An alternative is to grease the bottom of the pan, cover with waxed paper, and grease again. In either case, cut around the edge with a knife and invert onto cake rack while hot.

BUTTERMILK CAKE

2 c. sugar
½ c. shortening
½ c. butter or margarine
5 eggs, separated
1 c. buttermilk
1 t. vanilla
2 c. flour
1 t. baking soda
1 t. salt
2 c. coconut
1 c. chopped nuts

Cream sugar, shortening and butter or margarine. Add the egg yolks and beat well. Add buttermilk and vanilla. Sift flour, soda, and salt together and add to first mixture. Beat well. Add coconut and nuts. Beat the egg whites stiff and fold into the batter. Pour into 3 greased and floured layer cake pans. Bake at 350° for 35 to 40 minutes.

FROSTING

2 c. sifted powdered sugar
¼ c. butter or margarine (softened)
1 t. vanilla
Buttermilk

Mix all ingredients together, using just enough buttermilk to make spreading consistency. Beat smooth. Spread between layers and top and sides of cake.

QUICK CHOCOLATE CAKE

1½ c. sugar
4 T. cocoa
½ c. butter
1 c. milk
2 eggs, beaten
1½ c. flour
1 t. baking soda
½ c. cold coffee

Mix sugar and cocoa in a saucepan. Cream butter into this mixture. Add milk and cook until smooth. Let cool. When cool add eggs, flour, soda and coffee. Beat well. Bake in greased shallow 9" x 13" pan at 350° until done when tested with a toothpick. Remove from oven and cover with icing while warm.

CHOCOLATE ICING

2 c. sifted powdered sugar
6 t. cocoa
4 T. soft butter
Dash of salt
3 T. cold coffee
½ t. vanilla

Mix together powdered sugar and cocoa. Add remaining ingredients and beat smooth. Spread on cake.

Pictured opposite
Buttermilk Cake and Frosting

59

CARROT CAKE

1 c. margarine
2 c. sugar
1½ c. grated raw carrots
1 c. nuts
1 T. grated orange rind
3 c. flour
3 t. baking powder
1 t. cinnamon
1 t. nutmeg
½ t. salt
⅔ c. orange juice
4 egg whites, stiffly beaten

Cream margarine and sugar. Add carrots, nuts and orange rind. Sift dry ingredients together and blend into carrot mixture alternately with the orange juice. Fold in egg whites last. Bake in greased and floured 10-inch tube pan at 350° for 60 to 70 minutes. Cool in pan 20 minutes, then turn out of pan onto rack to completely cool.

PUMPKIN CAKE

4 eggs
2 c. sugar
1 c. salad oil
2 c. flour
½ t. salt
2 t. cinnamon
2 t. baking soda
2 c. cooked or canned pumpkin

Beat eggs. Add sugar and oil. Sift dry ingredients and add to egg mixture. Blend in pumpkin. Pour into greased and floured tube pan. Bake at 350° for 1 hour. Remove from oven. Let stand 10 minutes before removing from pan to cool.

COLD WATER CHOCOLATE CAKE

½ c. butter or margarine
1 c. sugar
1 t. vanilla
⅛ t. salt
½ c. cocoa
⅓ c. cold water
2½ c. flour
1¼ t. baking soda
1 c. cold water
3 egg whites
¾ c. sugar

Cream together the butter and sugar. Add vanilla and salt. Combine the cocoa with the ⅓ cup of cold water. Mix well and add to the creamed mixture. Sift flour and soda together and add to the creamed mixture alternately with the 1 cup cold water. Beat until just blended after each addition. If using an electric mixer, set at medium speed. Beat the egg whites until stiff but not dry. Add the ¾ cup sugar gradually, beating after each addition. Fold egg whites into batter. Bake in 10" x 14" greased pan at 350° until cake tests done.

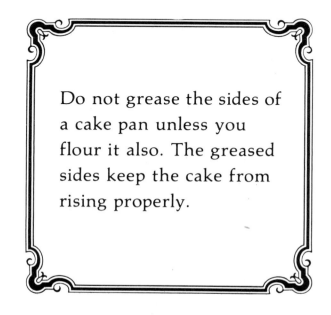

Do not grease the sides of a cake pan unless you flour it also. The greased sides keep the cake from rising properly.

Book II Index

Continued on page 63

MAMA'S KITCHEN

The smell of cookies baking
Brings back thoughts of Mama's kitchen;
Her suppers were so tasty
We could hardly keep from snitchin'.
Fresh-baked bread and apple pie,
Beef or chicken dishes;
Noodle soup to chocolate cake—
Her meals were just delicious.
But, oh, what fun it was to watch
As Mama stirred and measured.
Helping her to cook and bake
Were moments that I treasured.
Meals that were prepared with love—
These memories I'm rich in.
It's certain that no feasts compare
To those from Mama's kitchen!

Book III

Farmhouse
COOKBOOK

by Clarice L. Moon

CONTENTS

Book I Country Kitchen Cookbook

Book II From Mama's Kitchen Cookbook

Book III Farmhouse Cookbook

Appetizers and Beverages

ANCHOVY PECANS

Toast pecan halves in a 350° oven for 5 minutes. Spread bottoms with thin layer of anchovy paste. Press each 2 halves together. Serve immediately.

CAVIAR ROUNDS

Rye bread, toasted rounds
Caviar
Finely minced onion
Hard-boiled egg

Butter rounds of rye toast. Press on these rounds, slices of the egg white. Fill the inside of the egg white with caviar. Sprinkle finely minced onion over caviar. Surround egg white with grated yolk.

ASPARAGUS CANAPÉ

2 T. mayonnaise
2 hard-boiled eggs
  Pimiento strips
5 asparagus tips
  Toast triangles

Spread toast with mayonnaise. Chop egg yolks and whites separately. Arrange the chopped egg white and the chopped egg yolk in alternate rows across toast. Lay asparagus tips on top. Garnish with pimiento strips.

HOT TUNA CANAPÉS

Mix flaked tuna with mayonnaise or salad dressing. Add chopped stuffed olives. Add a few drops of Worcestershire sauce. Spread on toast strips and sprinkle with American cheese. Place under broiler until cheese melts. Serve hot.

CORNUCOPIAS

2 3-oz. pkgs. cream cheese
1 T. pickle relish
1 T. minced onion
12 thin slices boiled ham

Mash cheese with onion and drained pickle relish. Spread on a slice of boiled ham. Roll cornucopia fashion. Chill.

CHEESE SAVORY CANAPÉS

4 T. Roquefort cheese
2 T. butter
½ t. salt
⅛ t. pepper
  Mayonnaise
  Gherkins, thinly sliced
  Celery, minced
  Pimiento strips

Cream cheese and butter together. Add salt and pepper. Spread on toasted bread. Cover with celery mixed with a little mayonnaise. Garnish with sliced gherkins and a cross made of pimiento strips.

CHEESE BEEF STICKS

Cut American cheese in strips 2 inches long and ⅜ inch wide. Wrap each stick in a dried beef square. Place rolls on a cookie sheet, 3 inches below broiler. Broil until cheese is slightly melted.

EGGNOG

12 eggs, separated
1½ pt. cream or half and half
4 c. sugar
1½ c. whisky
1 t. nutmeg
1 t. salt
6 qts. milk

Beat egg yolks until lemon colored. Beat in sugar and salt. Slowly add whisky, cream, nutmeg and milk. Fold in well-beaten egg whites. Makes 2 gallons.

DIET SHAKE

1 12-oz. can diet soda, any flavor
⅓ c. instant nonfat dry milk
½ c. fresh fruit
⅛ t. artificial sweetener
½ t. vanilla
½ t. extract, strawberry, almond, rum or brandy
1 c. coarsely crushed ice

Combine all ingredients in blender. Whirl at high speed until frothy and blended.

SKINNY FRUIT WHIRL

1 12-oz. can diet creme soda
½ c. nonfat milk
1 t. lemon juice
⅛ t. artificial sweetener
⅛ t. salt
2 c. sliced nectarines, peaches or other fruit

Whirl all ingredients together in blender until smooth. Makes about 1 quart. Mixture may be frozen to make sherbet.

HOT TODDY

Juice of 1 lemon
2 T. honey or sugar
3 oz. bourbon or rye whisky
Boiling water

Put juice of 1 lemon in tall glass or mug. Sweeten with honey or sugar. Add whisky or rye. Fill glass with boiling water. Stir and drink.

RUSSIAN TEA

1 c. Tang
1 t. cinnamon
¼ c. instant tea
½ t. cloves
½ pkg. lemonade mix with sugar

Mix all ingredients together and keep in a tightly sealed jar. Use 1½ teaspoonsful in a teacup of hot water or 2 heaping teaspoonsful in a mug.

SKINNY MARY

¾ c. tomato juice
1 T. Worcestershire sauce
¼ c. sauerkraut juice
Ice cubes

Pour tomato and sauerkraut juice over ice cubes in glass. Add Worcestershire sauce and stir. Serve at once. Makes 1 serving.

LEMONADE

½ c. lemon juice (2 lemons)
3 c. cold water
½ c. sugar
Ice cubes

Add sugar to juice. Stir in cold water. Pour over ice in glasses. For hot lemonade, use hot water instead of cold.

Note: Roll lemons on table to make more juice.

Salads and Dressings

STUFFED PRUNE SALAD

12 large cooked prunes
2 3-oz. pkgs. cream cheese
2 c. grapefruit sections
¼ c. mayonnaise
¼ c. chopped nuts
   Lettuce

Drain prunes and remove the pits. Blend cream cheese and mayonnaise; fill centers of prunes. Sprinkle with nuts. Arrange on lettuce leaves with grapefruit sections and serve with a salad dressing of your choice. Serves 4.

GERMAN POTATO SALAD

¼ c. sugar
1 T. flour
2 t. salt
¼ t. pepper
¼ c. vinegar
⅔ c. water
4 slices bacon, diced and browned
¼ c. bacon drippings
4 c. cold, cooked, cubed potatoes
1 hard-boiled egg
2 T. chopped onion
   Sprig parsley

Combine sugar, flour, salt and pepper in the top of a double boiler. Stir in vinegar, water, bacon and bacon drippings. Cook, stirring constantly, about 5 minutes, or until thick. Place potatoes, onions, egg and parsley in a greased casserole or baking pan. Pour dressing over and mix to coat all. Heat in a 350° oven for 30 minutes. Serves 6 to 8.

PERFECTION SALAD

2 T. unflavored gelatin
2½ c. cold water
1 c. boiling water
⅓ c. sugar
1 t. salt
¼ c. tarragon vinegar
2½ T. lemon juice
½ t. prepared horseradish
3 carrots, grated
1 c. thinly sliced celery
1 2-oz. jar diced pimiento
2 c. finely shredded cabbage
½ green pepper, chopped
2 green onions and tops, thinly sliced

Soften gelatin in ½ cup cold water. Stir in boiling water, sugar and salt. Stir until dissolved. If necessary, place over low heat to dissolve. Add remaining 2 cups cold water, vinegar, lemon juice, and horseradish. Chill to a soft set. Fold in remaining ingredients. Turn into a 6-cup mold. Chill overnight. Unmold to serve. Serves 6.

CELEBRATION SALAD

2 c. diced cooked chicken
2 c. diced cooked ham
2 c. diced celery
1 c. salted almonds
½ c. mayonnaise
1 hard-boiled egg
2 T. pimiento slices
   Lettuce

Combine chicken, ham, celery, almonds and mayonnaise. Serve on lettuce leaves. Cut egg lengthwise into eighths. Garnish salad with egg wedges and pimiento. Serve with hot biscuits. Serves 6.

Pictured opposite
Celebration Salad
(page 6)

FROSTED FRUIT SALAD

1 3-oz. pkg. lemon gelatin
1 3-oz. pkg. orange gelatin
Juice of 1 lemon
2 c. boiling water
2 c. cold water
2 bananas, diced
1 No. 2 can crushed pineapple, drained
1 c. minature marshmallows

Dissolve gelatin in boiling water. Add cold water and lemon juice. Chill until partly set. Fold in pineapple, marshmallows and bananas. Pour into a 9 x 12 x 3-inch loaf pan. Chill until set. When gelatin is firm frost with Frosting. Serves 8.

FROSTING

2 T. flour
½ c. sugar
1 egg, beaten
½ c. milk
1 c. pineapple juice
1 c. heavy cream, whipped

Combine flour and sugar. Slowly stir in egg and milk. Stir in pineapple juice. Cook, stirring constantly, until thickened. Cool. Fold in whipped cream.

HAM SALAD

1 3-oz. pkg. lemon gelatin
1⅔ c. boiling water
1 T. lemon juice
¼ t. salt
1 c. chopped, cooked ham
¼ c. chopped celery
2 T. chopped green pepper
½ t. chopped onion
2 T. chopped pimiento

Dissolve gelatin in boiling water; add lemon juice and salt. Cool until slightly thickened. Pour half the gelatin into individual molds or one large mold, filling molds only half full. Chill just until set. Stir ham and vegetables into remaining gelatin and gently pour on top of set gelatin. Refrigerate until completely set. Unmold on rings of pineapple or garnish with pineapple. Serves 8.

JELLIED BEET SALAD

1 3-oz. pkg. lemon or lime gelatin
1 c. boiling water
1 c. cold beet juice
3 T. vinegar
2 T. minced onion
1 T. horseradish
¾ c. celery
1 16-oz. can diced beets, drained

Dissolve gelatin in boiling water. Stir in beet juice and vinegar. Add onion, horseradish, celery and diced beets. Refrigerate overnight. Serve on a bed of lettuce. Serves 4.

POTATO SALAD

4 c. potatoes, cooked and diced
6 hard-boiled eggs, chopped
½ c. chopped green pepper
2 T. chopped ripe olives
1½ to 2 c. mayonnaise
1 t. salt
1 c. diced celery
½ c. diced pimiento
1 large onion, chopped
Paprika

Mix together all ingredients, stirring thoroughly to coat all with mayonnaise. Place in serving dish. Sprinkle with paprika. Refrigerate until serving time. Serves 6.

THREE BEAN SALAD

1 16-oz. can green beans
1 16-oz. can wax beans
1 16-oz. can kidney beans
½ c. sugar
½ c. vinegar
½ t. celery seed
1 T. vegetable oil
1 medium onion, chopped

Combine beans. Slowly stir vinegar into sugar, blending until smooth. Add celery seed, oil and onion. Refrigerate.

SEA SALAD SURPRISE

2 c. tuna fish
1 c. lobster meat
2 c. shrimp, cooked and deveined
1 lemon, cut in wedges
2 c. diced celery
¾ c. mayonnaise
1 bunch watercress

Clean and slice fish. Reserve 12 whole shrimp for garnish. Combine all with mayonnaise and serve on watercress. Garnish with whole shrimp and lemon wedges. Serve with hot hard rolls. Serves 6.

MOLDED CRANBERRY SALAD

1 16-oz. can whole cranberry sauce
1 c. boiling water
1 3-oz. pkg. strawberry gelatin
1 T. lemon juice
¼ t. salt
½ c. mayonnaise
1 apple, diced
½ c. finely chopped celery
¼ c. chopped nuts

Heat cranberry sauce. Strain. Mix cranberry liquid, boiling water and gelatin, stirring until gelatin is dissolved. Add lemon juice and salt. Chill mixture until slightly thickened. Stir in mayonnaise; beat until fluffy. Fold in reserved cranberries, apple, celery and nuts. Pour into a mold or a flat pan; cut in squares to serve. Refrigerate until firm. Makes 6 servings.

FRENCH DRESSING

¼ c. vegetable oil
1 T. sugar
½ t. pepper
2 T. cider vinegar
1 t. salt
½ t. paprika

Place all ingredients in a pint jar; shake vigorously until thick. Serves 4.

LO-CAL TOMATO JUICE DRESSING

½ c. canned tomato juice
2 T. lemon juice or vinegar
1 t. salt
1½ T. Worcestershire sauce
2 to 4 T. vegetable oil
½ t. dry mustard
1 t. minced onion
3 T. sugar substitute

Combine all ingredients and beat until well blended. Makes 1 cup. Contains 25 calories per tablespoon.

BOILED SALAD DRESSING

2 T. flour
1 t. salt
¾ t. dry mustard
1 T. sugar
⅛ t. pepper
½ t. paprika
1 egg, slightly beaten
1 c. milk
¼ c. cider vinegar
2 T. butter or margarine

In the top of a double boiler, mix together flour, salt, mustard, sugar, pepper and paprika. Gradually stir in egg and milk. Cook over boiling water, stirring constantly, until thick. Add vinegar and butter. Cool. Makes 1⅔ cups.

NEW ORLEANS DRESSING

½ t. salt
½ t. dry mustard
¼ c. vinegar
¼ t. sugar
¾ c. vegetable oil
¼ t. pepper

Combine all ingredients in a screw-top jar. Shake vigorously. Rub bowl with clove of garlic before tossing green salad with dressing.

CELERY SEED DRESSING

2½ c. sugar
4 t. dry mustard
4 t. salt
1¼ c. vinegar
1 small onion, grated
4 c. vegetable oil
¼ c. celery seed

Combine sugar, mustard and salt. Add half the vinegar and onion to dry mixture. Beat on medium speed of mixer for 15 minutes. Stir in oil, then remainder of vinegar. Mix until well blended. Fold in celery seed. Refrigerate. Makes 3 pints.

MAYONNAISE

2 egg yolks
1 t. salt
1 t. dry mustard
2 c. vegetable oil
2 T. lemon juice or vinegar

Beat egg yolks, salt and mustard until light and lemon colored. Add oil, a small amount at a time. Beat until mixture is emulsified. Stir in lemon juice or vinegar. Refrigerate until needed. Makes 1 pint.

FRENCH DRESSING

1 10¾-oz. can tomato soup
1 c. sugar
1 c. cider vinegar
1 c. vegetable oil
2 T. Worcestershire sauce
1 t. salt
1 t. dry mustard
1 t. paprika
1 t. dry onion flakes *or* 1 T. minced onion

Place all ingredients in a screw-top jar. Shake well. Store in refrigerator. Makes 1 quart.

*Pictured opposite
from left
Mrs. Smith's Salad Dressing
Russian Dressing
Roquefort Cheese Dressing (on salad)
(page 11)*

ROQUEFORT CHEESE DRESSING

1 t. salt
1 t. celery seed
1 t. paprika
1 t. dry mustard
1 t. minced onion
4 T. sugar
¼ c. grated Roquefort cheese
⅔ c. vegetable oil
4 T. lemon juice

Mix dry ingredients together. Blend with a little of the oil. Stir in remaining oil, alternating with lemon juice. When ready to serve, add cheese.

MRS. SMITH'S SALAD DRESSING

3 whole eggs, slightly beaten
1 T. flour, rounded
¾ t. salt
2 T. butter
⅓ c. sugar
½ t. dry mustard
½ c. cider vinegar

Mix all ingredients in top of a double boiler. Cook over boiling water, stirring constantly, until thick and smooth. Cool.

RUSSIAN DRESSING

¼ c. white corn syrup
½ t. salt
½ t. celery seed
1 T. vinegar
1 T. Worcestershire sauce
1 medium onion, finely chopped
⅓ c. sugar
½ t. paprika
2 T. lemon juice
½ c. catsup
1 c. salad oil

Combine all ingredients in a screw-top jar. Shake well. Refrigerate.

Vegetable Dishes

FRIED GREEN TOMATOES

4 medium-size green tomatoes
1 t. salt
½ c. flour
2 T. vegetable oil

Wash and slice green tomatoes in ½-inch thick slices. Sprinkle with salt. Roll each slice in flour until coated on each side. Place oil in a skillet and heat. Place floured tomato slices in skillet. Fry over low heat until browned on both sides. Serve hot. Serves 4.

STUFFED CUCUMBER

1 large cucumber
2 3-oz. pkgs. cream cheese
1 T. chopped pimiento
3 T. mayonnaise
1 T. chopped stuffed olives
1 T. chopped ripe olives
Lettuce leaves

Cut cucumber in half lengthwise. With a spoon scoop out seeds and membrane. Soften cream cheese with mayonnaise. Mix in olives and pimiento. Fill the cucumber cavity with the cream cheese mixture until level. Press cucumber halves together. Refrigerate for at least 2 hours. To serve, slice thin and place on lettuce leaf. Serve with Roquefort cheese dressing.

GLAZED PARSNIPS

3 c. parsnips, sliced diagonally in ½-inch slices
¾ c. boiling water
½ t. salt
2 T. butter
¼ c. orange juice
1 t. grated orange rind

Place parsnips in water with salt. Bring to a boil. Simmer, covered, about 20 minutes. Drain. Heat remaining ingredients together in a saucepan. Pour over parsnips in serving dish. Serves 6.

SPINACH BALLS

2 c. chopped spinach, cooked and drained
2 T. grated cheese
2 T. melted butter
1½ c. bread crumbs
2 eggs
¼ c. water
⅓ t. pepper
½ t. salt
¼ c. margarine
Bread crumbs

Combine spinach, cheese, butter, bread crumbs and 1 beaten egg. Roll into balls. To other egg, add water and seasoning and beat. Dip spinach balls into additional bread crumbs, then into egg mixture, and again in bread crumbs. Brown balls on both sides in margarine. Serves 4.

POTATO CROQUETTES

2 c. mashed potatoes
1 egg
1 t. salt
¼ t. black pepper
2 T. chopped parsley
1 T. Parmesan cheese
1 clove garlic, minced (optional)
¾ c. bread crumbs
1 egg, beaten
1 T. water

Thoroughly mix potatoes, 1 egg, salt, pepper, parsley, cheese and garlic, if desired. Shape into small balls. Dip balls in bread crumbs, then into egg mixed with water, and again in the bread crumbs. Let stand on waxed paper 20 minutes. Fry in deep fat until browned on all sides. Serves 4.

SAUERKRAUT STUFFING FOR GOOSE

2½ lbs. sauerkraut
1 grated carrot
1 c. salami or other sausage
1 T. goose or bacon fat
1 potato, grated
1 onion, minced
½ c. dried bread crumbs

Mix all ingredients together. Stuff into goose that has been prepared for roasting. Sew up. Place in roasting pan. Roast, uncovered, in a 350° oven for 2 hours or until goose is done. Pour off fat occasionally.

POLENTA

3 c. water
1½ t. salt
1 c. yellow cornmeal
1 c. cold water
2 T. vegetable oil
1 lb. Italian sausage, casings removed
1 lb. mushrooms, cleaned and
   sliced lengthwise
2½ c. tomatoes
1 t. salt
¼ t. pepper
½ c. grated Parmesan or Romano cheese

Bring water and salt to a boil. Mix cornmeal with cold water; gradually stir into boiling water. Continue boiling, stirring constantly, until mixture thickens. Cover; lower heat. Simmer 10 minutes. Meanwhile, to make sauce, place oil in heavy skillet. Crumble sausages in skillet; add mushrooms. Cook until mushrooms and sausages are lightly browned. Stir in tomatoes, salt and pepper; simmer 20 to 30 minutes. To serve, transfer cooked cornmeal to a warm platter. Top with tomato sauce and sprinkle with grated Parmesan or Romano cheese. Serves 6 to 8.

MAPLE-GLAZED SQUASH AND PARSNIPS

8 parsnips (1½ lbs.)
2 small acorn squash
1¼ c. maple syrup
   Water
1 t. salt
3 T. butter or margarine
1 T. chopped parsley
¼ t. nutmeg

Pare parsnips; cut in quarters, lengthwise then crosswise into thirds. Halve squash crosswise; scoop out seeds and stringy membrane. Cut squash into ½-inch slices. Do not peel. Cook parsnips and squash in a large skillet in boiling salted water for 10 minutes or until almost tender. Drain. Heat maple syrup in same skillet. Add butter or margarine. Stir until melted. Return parsnips and squash to skillet. Simmer over medium heat, basting frequently, until vegetables are tender and glazed. Remove squash with slotted spoon. Arrange slices around edges of heated platter. Spoon parsnips into the center. Drizzle remaining syrup over vegetables. Sprinkle with parsley and nutmeg. Serves 8.

STUFFED CABBAGE LEAVES

12 large cabbage leaves
 1 lb. ground beef
 1 c. cooked rice
⅔ c. milk
 1 egg
¼ c. onion, finely chopped
 1 t. chopped parsley
 1 t. salt
½ t. sage
 2 T. brown sugar
⅔ c. water
 4 whole cloves
 1 10½-oz. can condensed tomato soup

Drop cabbage leaves into boiling water. Boil for 5 minutes; drain. Cut thick vein from each leaf. Brown ground beef. Mix beef, rice, milk, egg, 2 tablespoons of the onion, parsley, salt and sage. Place a spoonful on each leaf. Roll up the leaf and secure with a toothpick. Place rolls in a buttered 13 x 9 x 2-inch pan. Sprinkle with brown sugar. Mix the remaining onion with soup, water and cloves. Pour over cabbage rolls. Bake uncovered in a 325° oven for 1½ hours. Serves 6.

RED CABBAGE

 3 strips bacon
1½ lbs. red cabbage
 1 medium onion, finely chopped
 7 bay leaves
 2 T. mixed pickling spice
 3 T. honey or sugar
   Juice of 2 lemons or ¼ c. vinegar
½ t. salt
⅛ t. pepper

Fry bacon until crisp. Remove from pan and break into small pieces. Shred cabbage leaves in ¼-inch wide strips. Add to bacon grease along with crumbled bacon. Cover tightly and simmer for 20 minutes. Add onion, bay leaves and pickling spice, tied in cheesecloth. Stir in honey, lemon juice or vinegar. Cover and simmer slowly for about 1½ hours. Add salt and pepper and steam ½ hour. Serves 4.

Pictured opposite
Red Cabbage (page 15)
with a pork roast and potatoes

CORN AND TOMATOES

 6 large, fresh tomatoes
 2 c. fresh corn
½ t. salt
 1 t. chopped chives
½ t. pepper
¼ t. sweet basil

Pour boiling water over tomatoes. Cool slightly; slip off tomato skins. Chop tomatoes. Combine corn and tomatoes in a saucepan. Add salt, pepper, chives and basil. Simmer over low heat for 20 minutes or until vegetables are tender. Serves 6.

STUFFED GREEN PEPPERS

 4 large green peppers
 1 lb. ground beef
¼ c. vegetable oil
½ t. salt
¼ t. pepper
 1 T. minced parsley
⅔ c. cooked rice
1½ c. tomatoes, sieved
¼ c. minced onion
½ t. salt
¼ c. water
¼ t. pepper
 2 slices mozzarella cheese

Grease a 2-quart baking dish. Rinse peppers. Cut a thin slice from the stem end of each green pepper and remove inner white fiber and seeds. Rinse cavity. Drop peppers in boiling salted water to cover. Simmer for 5 minutes. Remove and set aside to drain. Brown ground beef in oil. Stir in parsley, salt, pepper and cooked rice. Lightly fill pepper shells with the mixture, heaping slightly. Place in a baking dish. Combine tomatoes, onion, salt, water and pepper, mixing well. Pour over peppers. Place a strip of cheese on top of each pepper. Bake in a 350° oven for 30 minutes. Serves 4.

EGGPLANT WITH SHRIMP OR HAM FILLING

1 1½ to 2-lb. eggplant
2 T. butter or margarine
¼ c. chopped onion
2 T. chopped green pepper
1 clove garlic, minced
2 c. shrimp or ham
1 c. soft bread crumbs
2 T. pimiento, chopped
½ t. salt
¼ t. pepper
1 c. Buttered Bread Crumbs

Split eggplant in half lengthwise. Cook, covered, in a small amount of boiling water for 10 minutes or until slightly tender. Remove from water and drain. Scoop out pulp from center of eggplant, leaving ¼-inch shell. Set shells aside. Finely chop the pulp. Melt butter; add pulp, onion, green pepper and garlic. Sauté until onion is transparent. Chop shrimp or ham. Add shrimp, bread crumbs, pimiento, salt and pepper to onion mixture. Blend thoroughly. Spoon mixture into eggplant shells, heaping slightly. Cover tops with buttered bread crumbs. Bake in a 375° oven for 20 to 30 minutes or until crumbs are browned. Serves 6 to 8.

BUTTERED BREAD CRUMBS

2 T. melted butter
1 c. soft bread crumbs

Melt butter. Add bread crumbs and sauté until slightly browned.

PAPRIKA BROWNED POTATOES

2 c. boiled potatoes, thinly sliced
3 T. margarine
¼ t. pepper
½ t. salt
1 t. paprika

Melt margarine in a heavy skillet. Add potatoes, salt, pepper and paprika. Mix well and brown lightly over low heat until potatoes are warmed through and reddish brown in color. Serves 4.

BAKED STUFFED TOMATOES

2 T. vegetable oil
1 t. chopped onion
¼ c. ground beef
½ c. grated cheese
1 t. salt
1 c. cooked rice
6 large ripe tomatoes

Grease an 8 x 8 x 2-inch baking dish. Heat oil in skillet; brown onion and ground beef. Stir in cheese, seasonings and rice. Set aside. With a sharp knife, cut a ¼-inch slice from top of each tomato. Cut around inside of tomatoes, being careful not to cut through the bottom. Scoop out center pulp. Sieve the tomato pulp and set aside the liquid. Sprinkle each tomato with salt. Lightly fill the tomatoes with filling. Place tomatoes in baking dish. Pour the tomato juice over tomatoes. Bake in a 375° oven for 20 to 25 minutes. Garnish with parsley. Serves 6.

STUFFED GRAPE LEAVES

12 large grape leaves
½ lb. ground beef
1 medium onion, minced
2 T. vegetable oil
1 T. grated lemon rind
1 t. salt
⅛ t. pepper
½ c. white raisins
2 c. cooked rice

Grease a 1½-quart casserole. Wash grape leaves. Blanch the grape leaves in boiling water for 30 seconds. Drain. Plunge in cold water; drain and set aside. Brown ground beef and onion in oil. Stir in lemon rind, salt, pepper, raisins and rice. Place one-third cup filling on each grape leaf. Fold leaves around the filling. Place in the casserole with folded side down. Continue until all grape leaves and filling are gone. Add 1 cup water. Cover and bake in a 350° oven 20 to 30 minutes until liquid is almost gone. Serves 4.

GREEN BEAN CASSEROLE

    3 6-oz. pkgs. frozen green
       beans, French cut
    1 8-oz. can water chestnuts
    ½ c. butter
    4 green onions *or* 1 medium onion,
       chopped
    2 4-oz. cans mushrooms
    ½ c. flour
    2 c. milk
    ¾ c. shredded Cheddar cheese
    2 t. soy sauce
    ½ t. Tabasco sauce
    1 t. salt
    ¾ c. slivered almonds

Cook frozen beans according to package directions. Drain. Chop water chestnuts and add to beans. Sauté onion and mushrooms in butter. Stir in flour, milk and cheese. Cook over low heat until thickened, stirring occasionally. Stir in soy sauce, Tabasco sauce and salt. Pour sauce over beans and mix gently. Turn into a 2-quart buttered casserole. Sprinkle almonds over top. Bake for 20 minutes in a 375° oven. Serves 8 to 10.

SCALLOPED POTATOES

    3 or 4 large white potatoes, thinly sliced
    1 small onion, sliced
    ½ t. pepper
    1 t. salt
    ⅓ c. flour
    ½ c. bread crumbs
    2 c. milk or more
    4 to 5 T. butter or margarine

Grease a 2-quart casserole. Alternate layers of sliced potatoes and onion. Sprinkle each layer with salt, pepper and flour. Dot with butter. Repeat until casserole is full. Pour milk over, barely covering potatoes. Sprinkle top with bread crumbs and dot with additional butter. Bake in a 375° oven 45 to 60 minutes or until potatoes are tender. Serves 4.

LEFSE

    1 T. melted butter
    1 T. sugar
    ¼ t. salt
    1 c. cream
   10 c. mashed potatoes
       Flour

Add butter, sugar, salt and cream to mashed potatoes. Blend well. Add enough flour to handle without being sticky. Dough will be similar to pie dough. Cool completely and roll very thin in 8 to 9-inch circles. (To prevent sticking, dough must be rolled with a covered rolling pin.) Bake dough on *lefse* grill or pancake grill. Turn only once when underside is brown spotted. Makes about 35 circles. To serve, cut circles into wedges. Butter and roll up. The *lefse* pieces were traditionally used to wrap around a piece of fish or meat before eating. Serves 8 to 10.

BAKED FILLED SWEET POTATOES

    6 medium-size yams
    1 T. shortening
   12 pork sausage links
    ½ c. hot orange juice
    3 T. butter or margarine
    2 T. brown sugar
    1 t. grated orange peel
    1 t. salt
    ½ t. nutmeg

Rub potato skins with shortening. Bake in a 450° oven for 45 to 60 minutes. While potatoes are baking, pan broil pork sausage links. Drain on paper towels and keep warm. When sweet potatoes are tender, cut each potato in half lengthwise. Scoop out inside of the potato without breaking skin. Mash or rice potato; whip in hot orange juice, butter, brown sugar, orange peel, salt and nutmeg. Pile mixture lightly into potato shells. Top each with 2 sausage links. Bake in a 350° oven 8 to 10 minutes longer, or until potatoes are reheated and browned lightly. Serves 6.

BLUSHING CAULIFLOWER

1 head cauliflower
½ t. salt
2 T. butter
1 clove garlic, crushed
1 10-oz. can condensed tomato soup
½ c. grated American cheese
1 T. chopped parsley

Place cauliflower in a large kettle. Add salted water to cover bottom of the pan. Simmer over low heat for about 20 to 30 minutes, or until tender. Melt butter in a saucepan. Sauté garlic until lightly browned. Add soup and cheese; heat, stirring occasionally, over low heat until cheese is melted. Pour sauce over cauliflower; sprinkle with parsley. Serves 6.

POTATO CAKES

6 large potatoes
¼ c. milk
3 eggs, beaten
½ t. salt
3 T. butter
1 t. baking powder
2 c. flour
Cream Sauce

Peel and boil potatoes in salted water until tender. Drain and mash. Beat in milk, eggs, salt, flour and baking powder. Form into patties. Brown potato patties lightly in hot butter. Serve with Cream Sauce. Serves 6.

CREAM SAUCE

4 c. milk, heated
3 T. flour
⅓ c. sugar
¼ c. cold milk
2 T. butter
1 t. caraway seed

Heat milk in saucepan. Mix flour and sugar with the cold milk. Stir into hot milk, stirring until mixture boils and thickens. Add butter and caraway seed, stirring to melt butter.

BAKED STUFFED MUSHROOMS

1 lb. mushrooms with 1 to 2-inch caps
2 T. vegetable oil
¼ c. chopped onion
⅓ c. bread crumbs
3 T. grated Parmesan cheese
1 T. chopped parsley
½ t. salt
⅛ t. oregano
2 T. vegetable oil

Clean mushrooms; remove stems. Place caps, open side up, in a greased 1½-quart casserole. Set aside. Finely chop mushroom stems. In a skillet heat oil; add mushroom stems and onion. Sauté over low heat until onion is lightly browned. Combine bread crumbs, cheese, parsley, salt and oregano. Add to mushroom stems and onions. Pile mixture lightly into mushroom caps. Drizzle remaining oil over caps. Bake in a 400° oven for 15 to 20 minutes or until mushrooms are tender and tops are browned. Serves 6 to 8.

EGGPLANT PARMIGIANA

2 medium-size eggplants
1 c. vegetable oil
2 6-oz. cans tomato paste
2 c. water
½ c. grated Parmesan cheese
1 3-oz. can mushrooms
1 lb. mozzarella cheese

Peel eggplant and slice into ½-inch slices. Fry in oil until lightly browned. Drain on paper towels. Cover bottom of a 13 x 9 x 2-inch buttered pan with a layer of eggplant slices. Combine tomato paste and water, mixing well. Pour over eggplant. Sprinkle with Parmesan cheese, mushrooms and mozzarella cheese. Repeat layers, ending with mozzarella cheese. Bake in a 400° oven for 20 minutes or until cheese is bubbly. Makes 10 servings.

*Pictured opposite
Baked Stuffed Onions
(page 19)*

BAKED STUFFED ONIONS

- 6 large onions
- ½ t. salt
- 2 T. vegetable oil
- ¼ lb. ground beef
- 1 c. cooked rice
- 1 egg yolk
- ½ c. soft bread crumbs
- ½ t. salt
- ½ t. pepper
- 2 T. melted butter
- 2 T. grated Parmesan cheese
- ½ c. soft bread crumbs
- 1 T. chopped parsley

Cut off root; peel and rinse onions. Cut a ½-inch slice from the top of each onion. Cook onion, uncovered, in salted water to cover for 10 to 15 minutes or until slightly tender. Drain well; cool. Heat oil in skillet; add ground beef and sauté until browned. Scoop centers out of onions; chop and add to ground beef. Sauté until golden. Combine rice, egg yolk, salt, pepper and bread crumbs with meat mixture. Fill onions. Mix together melted butter, cheese, parsley and bread crumbs. Spread over top of onions. Bake in a greased casserole in a 350° oven for 1 hour. Serves 6.

FRIED ZUCCHINI WITH ONIONS

2 T. margarine
2 medium-size onions, sliced
1 fresh zucchini squash
1 t. salt
¼ t. pepper
¼ c. water

In a heavy skillet, melt margarine; lightly sauté onion slices. Wash zucchini; slice in thin rounds, leaving skin on. Add to onion with salt and pepper. Fry over low heat, turning as slices brown. Add water and lower heat. Cover tightly and steam for 20 to 25 minutes, stirring occasionally, until tender. Serves 4.

FRIED PARSNIPS

6 to 8 parsnips (1½ lbs.)
½ t. salt
3 T. butter

Pare parsnips. Cut in half lengthwise and then in half crosswise. Put in kettle with water to cover; add salt. Cook until tender; drain. Melt butter in skillet. Arrange parsnips in one layer in skillet. Brown on all sides, turning to keep from burning. Serves 8. Can use carrots this way, too.

CARROTS AND CELERY

2 c. diced celery
4 to 6 carrots, diced
½ t. salt
Water
2 T. melted butter
1 t. chopped parsley

Place celery and carrots in a saucepan with enough salted water to cover. Simmer over low heat 30 minutes or until carrots and celery are tender. Drain. Pour into a serving dish. Pour melted butter over carrots and sprinkle with parsley. Serves 4.

POTATO DUMPLINGS

6 large potatoes, boiled and mashed
1 c. flour
1 t. salt
½ t. nutmeg
3 eggs, beaten slightly
½ lb. ground beef

To cooled potatoes, add flour, salt, nutmeg and eggs. Roll ground beef into balls, ½ inch in diameter. Mold potato mixture around meatballs. Drop in boiling water. Cover tightly and continue boiling for 15 minutes. Do not lift lid. Serve with vegetable soup. Serves 6.

HONEYED SWEET POTATOES

1½ lbs. sweet potatoes
⅓ c. butter
⅔ c. honey
Salted water

Scrub sweet potatoes and cut into quarters. Place in a stewing kettle. Cover with salted water and boil until almost done, about 30 minutes. Drain; cool slightly. Remove skins and slice crosswise in ½-inch slices. Place in a 1½-quart buttered casserole. Mix honey and butter together. Bake in a 350° oven for 20 to 25 minutes or until lightly browned. Serve at once. Serves 4 to 6.

SOUTHERN CORN PUDDING

2 eggs
2 c. fresh corn
2 c. milk
½ t. salt
½ t. pepper
1 T. vegetable oil

Beat eggs until light. Add milk, corn, seasonings and oil in a large mixing bowl. Mix well. Turn into a 1-quart buttered casserole. Bake in a 350° oven for 30 minutes. Serves 6.

CUCUMBERS IN SOUR CREAM

3 medium-size cucumbers
½ c. sour cream
2 T. cider vinegar
1 t. sugar
½ t. salt
½ t. black pepper

Peel cucumbers and slice thin. Layer cucumbers in a medium-size bowl. Cover with 3 cups water, or enough to cover, and 1½ teaspoon salt. Chill. Pour off salted water and rinse in clear water. Drain. Blend sour cream, vinegar, and sugar. Fold into cucumbers. Serve with a sprinkling of salt and pepper.

STEWED SAUERKRAUT

1 30-oz. can sauerkraut
3 T. caraway seed
1 c. water
1 medium onion, sliced
¼ c. sugar
1 medium potato, grated

Mix all ingredients except potato in a saucepan. Let simmer, stirring occasionally, until onion is soft and transparent. Stir in potato. Just bring mixture to a boil; cover. Let stand for 10 minutes before serving. Serves 4 to 6.

SKILLET SALAD

4 slices bacon
¼ c. vinegar
1 T. brown sugar
1 t. salt
1 T. finely chopped onion
4 c. shredded cabbage
¼ c. chopped parsley

Cook bacon until crisp; drain and crumble. To fat in skillet, add vinegar, sugar, salt and onion. Bring to a boil. Remove from heat; toss cabbage and parsley in hot mixture. Makes 6 servings.

BROCCOLI PARMESAN

1 bunch fresh broccoli
2 T. butter
2 T. minced onion
¼ t. pepper
½ t. dry mustard
½ c. grated Parmesan cheese
½ t. salt
¼ t. marjoram
3 T. flour
1 chicken bouillon cube
2½ c. milk
2 T. grated Parmesan cheese
1 t. paprika

Cook broccoli in boiling salted water until tender. Drain. Arrange broccoli in a shallow greased baking dish. Melt butter in a saucepan. Add onion and sauté over low heat until tender. Blend in seasonings and flour. Add bouillon cube and milk. Cook over medium heat, stirring constantly, until mixture thickens and comes to a boil. Add cheese and stir well, until melted. Pour sauce over broccoli. Sprinkle with paprika and additional Parmesan cheese. Bake in a 375° oven for 20 to 25 minutes or until browned. Serves 4 to 6.

RAW FRIED POTATOES

6 to 8 medium-size potatoes, peeled and thinly sliced
3 T. shortening
1 t. salt
½ t. pepper
1 c. chopped onion, optional
¼ c. water

Heat shortening in large skillet. Add sliced potatoes, salt and pepper and onion, if desired. Fry on medium-low heat, stirring potatoes up from the bottom as they brown. Fry about 15 minutes. Add water and cover tightly. Cook over low heat until potatoes are tender, stirring occasionally. Serves 4 to 6.

HOT COLE SLAW

½ c. cider vinegar
¼ c. water
½ t. salt
¼ c. sugar
¼ t. paprika
¼ t. dry mustard
¼ c. vegetable oil
¼ c. heavy cream
2 eggs, slightly beaten
1 head cabbage, shredded fine
½ c. pickle relish
1 2-oz. jar pimiento, diced

Place vinegar, water, salt, sugar, paprika, mustard and oil in a pan and bring to a boil. Remove from heat. Combine eggs and cream. Stir a little of the hot mixture into egg-cream mixture. Continue stirring and slowly pour remaining hot mixture into the egg mixture. Return to pan and cook on low heat for 5 minutes, stirring constantly. Mix together cabbage, pimiento and pickle relish. Pour hot dressing over and toss lightly. Serve immediately. Serves 8.

BROCCOLI CUSTARD

1 bunch broccoli
½ lb. fresh mushrooms
3 T. butter
1 c. grated Cheddar cheese
3 eggs, well beaten
1 10¾-oz. can condensed cream of
    celery soup
⅓ c. milk
1 t. grated onion
½ t. salt
1 t. Worcestershire sauce
¼ t. pepper
⅓ c. French bread crumbs

Trim and wash broccoli. Cook until barely tender. Drain and set aside. Sauté whole mushrooms in butter. Arrange broccoli and mushrooms in a shallow, greased 1½-quart baking dish. Combine ½ cup of the cheese, eggs, soup, milk and seasonings. Pour over the vegetables. Sprinkle with remaining cheese and bread crumbs. Set dish in shallow pan of water. Bake in a 350° oven for 45 minutes, or until custard is set. Serves 6.

CORN PUDDING

3 eggs, beaten
1 c. milk
2 c. corn
3 T. chopped green pepper
1 t. grated onion
1 T. minced parsley
½ t. salt
¼ t. pepper

In a large mixing bowl, combine eggs and milk; mix well. Add corn, green pepper, onion, parsley and seasonings. Turn into a buttered 1½-quart casserole. Bake in a 350° oven for 1 hour or until firm. Serves 6.

STUFFED ZUCCHINI

4 zucchini squash
1 green pepper, diced
1 small onion, chopped
1 T. butter
½ lb. ground beef
2 c. fresh corn
1 tomato, chopped
1 pimiento, diced
1 egg, slightly beaten
1 c. bread crumbs
1 T. Worcestershire sauce
¼ t. pepper
1 t. salt

Split zucchini in halves lengthwise and scoop out seeds and membrane. Set aside. Sauté green pepper and onion in butter until onion is transparent. Remove and set aside. Brown ground beef, separating with a fork. Add green pepper, onion and remaining ingredients. Place zucchini halves in a well-greased baking pan. Fill each half with corn stuffing. Pour one-half cup water in the bottom of the pan; cover with foil. Bake in a 350° oven until zucchini is tender. Remove foil and bake an additional ½ hour. Serves 6 to 8.

Pictured opposite
Stuffed Zucchini
(page 22)

SQUAW CORN

2 c. whole kernel corn
2 T. margarine
1 green pepper, diced
2 medium onions, chopped
1 small jar pimiento, diced
¼ t. pepper

Melt margarine in skillet. Add green pepper and onion. Sauté slowly over low heat until tender and onion is transparent. Add drained corn, pimiento and seasonings. Cook over low heat for 20 minutes. Serve in a warm bowl. Serves 4.

CARROTS SUPREME

4 c. carrots, chopped
½ t. salt
   Water
½ lb. bacon, diced
1 medium onion, diced
¼ t. pepper

Cook carrots in boiling, salted water until tender. Drain and set aside. Brown bacon in skillet. Drain and set aside. Sauté onion in bacon fat. Remove to dish. Mash carrots with potato masher; stir in bacon, onions, drippings and seasoning. Mix well. Serve hot. Serves 4.

BUTTERED PARSNIPS

8 parsnips (1½ lbs.)
½ t. salt
2 T. melted butter
2 T. parsley, chopped

Pare the parsnips and quarter. Split in half lengthwise. Place in a kettle with salted water to cover. Simmer until tender; drain. Pour melted butter over parsnips in serving dish. Mix to coat all sides. Sprinkle with parsley and serve. Serves 6.

VEGETABLE DISH

2 16-oz. cans green beans
2 16-oz. cans small, whole onions
2 16-oz. cans potatoes
1 16-oz. can small carrot pieces
2 2½-oz. jars mushrooms
1 head cauliflower, broken into flowerets
½ t. salt
½ t. pepper
   Paprika
   Cheese Sauce

Drain all vegetables and combine in a buttered 9 x 13 x 2-inch baking dish. Stir in Cheese Sauce and sprinkle top with paprika. Bake in a 350° oven for 1 hour. Serves 6.

CHEESE SAUCE

4 T. butter
4 T. flour
2 c. milk
1 t. salt
¼ t. pepper
½ lb. Cheddar cheese

Melt butter in saucepan. Add flour, salt and pepper. Gradually stir in milk. Simmer 2 to 3 minutes, or until thickened. Add cheese, stirring to melt. Blend thoroughly.

PEAS AND CARROTS

1 10-oz. pkg. frozen peas *or* 2 c. fresh peas
4 carrots, diced
2 c. water
½ t. salt
2 T. melted butter *or* 2 c. White Sauce

Cook peas and carrots in salted water until carrots are tender, about 15 minutes. Drain. Add melted butter or White Sauce. Serve hot. Serves 8.

WHITE SAUCE

2 T. butter
2 T. flour
2 c. milk

Melt butter in saucepan; add flour. Stir in milk and cook, stirring, until thick.

SNOW PEAS

4 c. fresh snow peas *or* 2 6-oz. pkgs.
  frozen snow peas
2 c. water
½ t. salt
2 T. melted butter

Prepare fresh snow peas by breaking off tips and tails. Wash and place in saucepan in salted water. Drain. Drop frozen snow peas in boiling salted water and cook until tender. Drain. Add melted butter and serve. Serves 4.

SNOW PEAS AND MUSHROOMS

1 6-oz. pkg. frozen snow peas *or* 2 c. fresh
  snow peas
  Water to cover
1 t. salt
1 4-oz. can mushroom bits and pieces
2 T. melted butter

Cook frozen snow peas or fresh snow peas in salted water to cover for 20 minutes or until tender. Add drained mushrooms. Mix well. Heat through. Drain. Pour into warm serving dish. Pour melted butter over peas. Serve hot. Serves 4.

CAULIFLOWER WITH
BUTTERED CRUMBS

1 head cauliflower
1 t. salt
  Water to cover
3 T. margarine
¾ c. bread crumbs

Soak cauliflower in salted cold water, head down for 30 minutes. Rinse in clear water. Place in kettle. Add salt and enough water to cover. Simmer slowly for 20 to 30 minutes, until tender but still firm. Drain. Carefully remove cauliflower to a warm serving dish. Melt margarine in saucepan or small skillet and mix with bread crumbs. Heat through, but do not burn. Pour over cauliflower and serve hot. Serves 6.

STEWED TOMATOES WITH
BREAD CUBES

1 30-oz. can tomatoes *or* 2 c.
  fresh tomatoes
1 c. stale bread, cut in cubes
1 t. salt
1 T. butter
½ t. pepper

Heat tomatoes in a saucepan or cook fresh tomatoes 20 minutes. Add bread cubes, butter, and seasonings. Bring to a boil. Serve hot. Serves 4.

STEWED TOMATOES

1 30-oz. can tomatoes *or* 2 c. fresh
  tomatoes
1 t. salt
1 T. butter
½ t. pepper

Combine tomatoes, seasonings and butter in a saucepan. Bring to a boil. Serve hot. Serves 4.

PARSNIP PATTIES

8 to 10 parsnips
½ t. salt
  Boiling water
½ t. onion salt
⅛ t. pepper
½ t. salt
1 egg, beaten
⅓ c. fine bread crumbs
2 T. butter or margarine
¼ c. bread crumbs

Peel parsnips and cook in boiling salted water until tender. Drain and mash. Beat in seasonings and egg. Add bread crumbs. Chill well. Make into 6 patties. Coat with additional bread crumbs and fry in melted butter until golden brown on both sides. Serves 6.

Meats and Main Dishes

CHICKEN-BROCCOLI CASSEROLE

JG

- 3 lb. frying chicken
- 2 10-oz. pkgs. frozen broccoli *or*
  2 bunches fresh broccoli
- 1 c. mayonnaise
- 2 10¾-oz. cans condensed cream of
  chicken soup
- ¼ t. curry powder
- 1 T. lemon juice
- ½ c. grated Cheddar cheese
- ½ c. bread crumbs
- 1 T. melted butter

Stew chicken; cool and bone. Steam broccoli until tender; drain. Grease an 11 x 7-inch casserole. Place chicken on the bottom, broccoli on top. Combine mayonnaise, soup, curry powder and lemon juice. Pour over broccoli. Sprinkle with a mixture of cheese and bread crumbs combined with butter. Bake in a 350° oven for 30 minutes. Serves 6.

BIG BOY PIE

- ½ c. chopped onion
- ¼ c. shortening
- 1 lb. ground beef
- 2 T. catsup or chili sauce
- 1 t. salt
- 2 c. biscuit mix
- ⅔ c. milk
- 1 c. cooked tomatoes, drained
- 1 c. grated cheese

Sauté onion in shortening until golden. Add meat and brown. Stir in catsup and salt. Set aside. Stir milk into the biscuit mix, stirring until well blended. Turn onto a lightly floured board. Knead six times. Roll into a circular shape and place in a 9-inch pie pan. Fill with meat and onion. Cover with tomatoes and top with grated cheese. Bake in a 450° oven for 30 minutes. Serves 6.

SAUERBRATEN

- 5 lbs. boneless round, chuck or
  rump roast
- 2 onions, sliced
- 2 carrots, pared and sliced
- 1 stalk celery, chopped
- 1 T. meat tenderizer
- 1 T. salt
- 2 T. sugar
- 6 peppercorns
- 3 bay leaves
- 6 whole cloves
- 1½ c. red wine vinegar
- 1½ c. water
- 2 T. flour
- 4 T. butter
- ½ c. gingersnap crumbs

Place meat in earthenware, glass or enamel bowl. Add vegetables, meat tenderizer, seasonings, vinegar and water. Cover and refrigerate for 2 to 4 days, turning meat each day. When ready to cook, remove meat from marinade and pat dry. Strain marinade and save both marinade and vegetables. Flour meat. In a deep pot, melt butter and brown meat on all sides. Add 2 cups marinade and the vegetables. Cover tightly and simmer over low heat for 3½ to 4 hours, or until meat is tender. Add a bit more marinade if needed to replenish liquid. Remove meat to a heated platter and keep warm. To make gravy, strain vegetables from marinade. Add enough of the marinade to make 2 cups. Bring to a boil; add gingersnap crumbs. Cook, stirring constantly until thickened. Serve with vegetables, gravy and potato dumplings. Serves 12.

Pictured opposite
Chicken-Broccoli Casserole
(page 27)

LASAGNA

1 lb. ground beef
¼ c. butter
1 c. chopped onion
1 garlic bud, minced
3 6-oz. cans tomato paste
2 c. water
2½ T. salt
1 No. 2 can tomatoes
1 lb. broad noodles, boiled
1 lb. mozzarella cheese, shredded
2 lbs. dry cottage cheese
1 c. Parmesan cheese

Brown meat in butter. Add onion and garlic. Stir in tomato paste, water, salt, and tomatoes. Cook over low heat for 45 minutes. Cook noodles, rinse and drain. Butter a 13 x 9 x 2-inch baking dish. Line dish with layer of noodles, sauce and cheese, ending with sauce and cheese. Bake in a 375° oven for 30 minutes. Let stand for 10 minutes before cutting. Serves 8 to 10.

VEAL PARMIGIANA

1½ lbs. veal, thinly sliced
3 T. vegetable oil
½ c. chopped onion
2 8-oz. cans tomato sauce
¼ t. crushed basil leaves
½ t. oregano
¼ t. thyme
½ lb. sliced mozzarella cheese
¼ c. grated Parmesan cheese

Over medium heat, brown veal lightly on both sides in the hot oil. Remove meat to a shallow 2-quart buttered dish. Add more oil as needed. Add onion and sauté until tender. Stir in tomato sauce, basil, oregano and thyme. Remove from heat. Pour sauce over veal and top with mozzarella and Parmesan cheese. Bake in a 350° oven for 40 minutes or until browned and tender. Serves 6.

CHOW MEIN CASSEROLE

1 lb. ground beef
1 onion, chopped
1 large can chow mein noodles
2 c. diced celery
2 T. vegetable oil
1 10¾-oz. can condensed cream of mushroom soup
1 10¾-oz. can condensed tomato soup
1 10¾-oz. can condensed cream of chicken soup

Brown beef and onion in oil. Pour into a greased 2-quart casserole. Add celery, noodles and soup. Bake in a 350° oven for 1 hour. Serves 6.

HAM LOAF

2½ c. soft bread crumbs
1 c. milk
1 lb. ground ham
1 lb. ground beef
2 eggs
½ green pepper, chopped
2 T. chopped onion
1 t. salt
½ t. pepper

Soak bread crumbs in milk. Add to meat and mix well. Add remaining ingredients and mix thoroughly. Pack in a greased loaf pan. Bake in a 350° oven for 1½ hours. Serves 6.

BAKED SPARERIBS AND DRESSING

1 c. chopped apple
1 c. hot water
4 c. dry bread crumbs
1 t. sage
½ c. chopped onion
1 t. salt
4 lbs. meaty pork spareribs

In a large bowl, combine all ingredients except spareribs. Add more water if a moist stuffing is desired. Place dressing in the bottom of a greased baking dish. Place ribs on top. Cover tightly with foil. Bake in a 350° oven for 2 hours or until meat is tender. Serves 4 to 6.

CORNED BEEF HASH

4 c. cooked corned beef, diced
2 T. butter
4 c. cooked potatoes, diced
1 medium onion, diced
1 t. salt
½ t. pepper
½ to 1 c. milk
6 poached eggs

Melt butter in a heavy frying pan; add chopped meat, potatoes, onion, seasonings and enough milk to moisten. Stir until well blended. Cook slowly for 1 hour. When brown on bottom, fold over like an omelet and serve on a warm platter. Garnish with poached eggs. Serves 6.

TAMALE PIE

1 onion, chopped
1 green pepper, diced
1 T. shortening
2 8-oz. cans tomato sauce
1 12-oz. can whole kernel corn
½ c. ripe olives, chopped
1 clove garlic, minced
1 T. sugar
1 t. salt
½ t. pepper
1 t. chili powder
1½ c. shredded American cheese
¾ lb. ground beef
¾ c. cornmeal
½ t. salt
2 c. cold water
1 T. butter

Cook onion and green pepper in shortening until tender. Add meat and brown. Add tomato sauce, corn, olives, garlic, sugar, salt, pepper and chili powder. Simmer for 20 to 25 minutes. Add cheese, stirring until melted. Pour into a 10 x 6-inch greased baking dish and set aside. Stir cornmeal and salt into water. Cook and stir until thick. Add butter. Spoon over meat mixture in strips. Bake in a 375° oven for about 40 minutes. Serves 6 to 8.

JAMBALAYA

½ lb. bacon
½ c. finely chopped onion
2 large green peppers, chopped
1 c. uncooked rice
1 clove garlic, minced
1 large can tomatoes
1 t. salt
1 bay leaf
¼ t. thyme
½ lb. baked or cooked ham, cubed
2 T. chopped parsley
½ t. pepper
½ t. Tabasco sauce
2 c. chicken broth, strained
1 lb. shrimp, cooked, shelled, and deveined

Preheat oven to 350°. Cut bacon into ½-inch pieces and cook in a heavy, oven-proof pan or Dutch oven with cover. When browned, remove with slotted spoon to paper towel to drain. Sauté onion until transparent, stirring as needed. Add green pepper; cook for 1 minute. Add rice; stir and cook rice for 3 minutes. Add remaining ingredients and bring to a boil. Cover pot and place in oven. Bake, covered, for 15 to 20 minutes or until liquid is absorbed and rice is tender. Sprinkle with parsley. Serves 4 to 6.

BEEF AND SAUERKRAUT

1 qt. sauerkraut
2 T. flour
3 lbs. beef brisket
1 small onion, minced
1 tart apple, grated
1 T. brown sugar
½ t. salt
¼ t. pepper

In a large Dutch oven, layer half of the sauerkraut; sprinkle with flour. Add meat, onion, apple and sugar. Sprinkle with salt and pepper. Lay remaining sauerkraut on top of meat. Add boiling water to just cover. Cover tightly and simmer for 1½ to 2 hours over low heat. Serves 6.

LAMB STEW WITH MUSHROOM DUMPLINGS

3 lbs. lamb stew meat, cubed
3 T. shortening
½ c. sliced onion
3 carrots, sliced diagonally
5 c. boiling water
1 c. flour
2 t. baking powder
½ c. condensed mushroom soup
3 T. water
3 T. parsley, chopped

Roll lamb in flour. Melt shortening and brown lamb cubes and onion. Add carrots and boiling water. Simmer slowly for 2 hours. To make dumplings, sift together flour and baking powder. Add mushroom soup and water. Mix well. After stew has simmered for 2 hours, drop dumplings by spoonfuls into boiling stew. Cover tightly and cook for 20 minutes. Remove stew to hot platter and surround with dumplings. Garnish with parsley. Serves 6.

BEEF STROGANOFF

3 beef bouillon cubes
1 c. boiling water
2 lbs. round or sirloin steak, cubed
3 T. flour
½ t. salt
⅛ t. pepper
½ c. shortening
1 c. chopped onion
1 14-oz. can mushrooms
1 c. sour cream
1 T. Worcestershire sauce

Dissolve bouillon cubes in water. Set aside. Dredge meat in flour and seasonings. In a large skillet, brown in ¼ cup of the shortening. Sauté onion in remaining shortening; add onion and bouillon to meat. Mix thoroughly. Cover pan and cook slowly for 1½ hours or until meat is tender. Add mushrooms and Worcestershire sauce; fold in sour cream. Heat thoroughly but do not boil. Serve hot on buttered noodles. Serves 6.

LAMB STEW

2 lbs. lamb shoulder, cubed
1 t. salt
4 carrots, cut up
3 potatoes, quartered
1 t. sugar
2 T. flour
1 T. shortening
1 6-oz. can peas

Salt meat thoroughly and place in a stewing pan; add water to cover. Bring to a boil. Reduce heat and simmer until meat is almost tender. Add carrots, potatoes and sugar. Simmer until vegetables and meat are tender. Melt shortening; stir in flour. Add about a cup of hot stew liquid to flour mixture, stirring well. Add to stew, stirring until thickened. Add drained peas. Heat through. Serves 4 to 6.

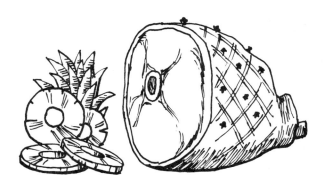

BAKED HAM

5 to 6-lb. ham
½ c. whole cloves
⅓ c. prepared mustard
½ c. brown sugar
6 to 8 pineapple slices
½ c. pineapple juice

Bake ham in roasting pan, uncovered, in a 350° oven for 1½ hours. Remove from oven and cut off skin. With a sharp knife, score fat into diamond shapes. Place a whole clove in the center of each diamond. Spread mustard over ham. Then press on brown sugar. Secure pineapple slices on ham with toothpicks. Bake an additional 30 minutes, basting frequently with pineapple juice. Serves 10 to 12.

Pictured opposite
Beef Stroganoff
(page 31)

NOODLE, KRAUT AND WIENER CASSEROLE

6 wieners
1 c. sauerkraut, rinsed and drained
½ t. caraway seed
⅛ t. celery salt
1 c. cooked noodles
½ t. pepper
½ t. salt
½ t. nutmeg
4 oz. Cheddar cheese, shredded
1 T. margarine

Place wieners in a buttered 1½-quart casserole. Combine sauerkraut, caraway seed and celery salt. Combine noodles, pepper, salt, and nutmeg. Mix well. Place half of the sauerkraut on top of wieners. Cover with noodles. Arrange cheese and margarine over noodles. Top with rest of the sauerkraut. Bake in a 375° oven for 25 minutes. Makes 2 servings.

CHOP SUEY

1 c. pork or veal, cubed
½ c. chopped onion
3 T. shortening
1½ c. water
½ t. salt
1½ c. celery, cut diagonally
1 1-lb. can bean sprouts
1 1-lb. can chop suey vegetables, drained
1 4-oz. can mushrooms
3 T. cornstarch
⅓ c. cold water
1 T. brown sugar
2 T. soy sauce
2 c. cooked rice

Brown cubed meat and onion in shortening. Place in stewing kettle. Add water, salt and celery; simmer until meat is tender. Add bean sprouts, chop suey vegetables, and mushrooms. Heat to boiling. Mix cornstarch and cold water until smooth. Add to boiling mixture, stirring constantly, until thickened and transparent. Add brown sugar and soy sauce. Serve over cooked rice or Chinese noodles. Serves 4.

SAN FRANCISCO STEW

1½ lbs. hamburger
2 T. shortening
1 1-lb. can tomatoes
4 c. Great Northern beans, cooked
1 large onion, sliced
1 c. brown sugar, firmly packed
4 bacon slices

Brown meat in shortening. Drain beans; add to meat with tomatoes. Mash. Pour half the mixture in a 4-quart greased baking dish. Slice a layer of onion to cover; sprinkle brown sugar over onions. Add remaining bean mixture. Bake in a 350° oven for 1 hour. Place bacon slices over top. Bake until bacon is done and juice is absorbed. Serves 6.

PARSNIP CASSEROLE

3 c. mashed, cooked parsnips
½ t. pepper
½ t. salt
1 c. cubed ham
1 c. sliced mushrooms
1 c. shredded cheese
½ c. crushed cornflakes

Season hot parsnips. Mix ham, mushrooms and cheese. Alternate layers of parsnips and ham mixture in a greased 2-quart casserole. Sprinkle top with cornflakes. Bake in a 350° oven for 25 minutes. Serves 6.

MACARONI CASSEROLE

1 lb. ground beef
2 t. dry onion flakes
2 c. elbow macaroni
1 T. diced pimiento
1 3-oz. can tomato sauce
⅔ c. water
2 T. vegetable oil

Brown ground beef in oil. Add onion flakes. Cook macaroni in salted water until done. Drain and rinse with hot water. Combine macaroni and meat. Add tomato sauce, water and pimiento. Pour into a greased baking dish. Cover with foil. Bake for 1 hour in a 350° oven. Serves 6.

ORIENTAL HAMBURGER

1½ lbs. ground beef
2 T. shortening
1 medium onion, chopped
2 t. garlic salt
2 c. water
4 T. soy sauce
1½ T. molasses
1 8-oz. pkg. frozen green beans
4 T. cornstarch
½ c. water
6 to 7 c. cooked rice

Brown ground beef and onion in shortening. Stir in garlic salt, 2 cups water, soy sauce and molasses. Heat to boiling; add green beans. Simmer 20 to 30 minutes until beans are tender. Blend cornstarch with ½ cup water. Stir into meat mixture; cook until thickens. Serve over rice. Serves 4 to 6.

HUNTER'S STEW

2 lbs. lean meat, beef or venison, cubed
Shank bone of beef
½ lb. suet
1½ gal. cold water or 24 c.
1 bunch celery
3 onions, chopped
1½ c. peas
1½ c. corn
1½ c. tomatoes
1½ c. lima beans
5 potatoes, diced
1½ c. diced carrot
¼ c. rice
½ c. chili sauce

Combine meat, bone, suet, celery, onion and water. Simmer 2½ hours. Remove celery and bone. Add vegetables with rice and simmer over low heat until vegetables are done. Before serving, season with ½ cup chili sauce and more salt and pepper if needed. Should be a thick soup. Serves 8 to 10.

SAVORY STEW

2 lbs. beef chuck, cut in 1-inch cubes
1 t. lemon juice
1 clove garlic, minced
1 small bay leaf
¼ t. allspice
8 small whole onions
3 c. water
1 t. Worcestershire sauce
1 medium onion, sliced
2 t. salt
¼ t. pepper
6 carrots, quartered
3 medium potatoes, cut up
½ c. flour
1 c. water

In Dutch oven, combine all ingredients except 1 cup of the water and the flour. Cover and bake in a 325° oven for 4 hours or until meat is tender. Remove stew from oven. In a covered jar, shake 1 cup water and flour until blended. Stir into stew. Heat to boiling, stirring constantly for 1 minute. Serve hot. Serves 4 to 6.

PRIME RIBS AU JUS

5 lbs. prime ribs
1 c. water
¼ c. vinegar
2 stalks celery, diced
1 c. water
⅛ c. vegetable oil
2 carrots, diced
1 onion, chopped
2 bay leaves
½ t. sage
½ t. salt
4 raw potatoes, cut up
1 green pepper, diced
1 clove garlic
½ t. thyme
2 c. tomatoes
¼ t. pepper
1 t. paprika

Place beef in roasting pan with water. Add ingredients in order as above. Bake in a 300° oven for 2½ hours. Baste meat every 30 minutes. Serves 6.

SOY-MARINATED CHUCK STEAK

3½ to 4 lbs. beef blade chuck roast,
    2 inches thick
    Unseasoned meat tenderizer
3 T. brown sugar
4 t. white vinegar
¾ c. soy sauce
3 T. Worcestershire sauce

Early in the day, trim excess fat from steak.
Prepare steak with meat tenderizer as label
directs. Combine brown sugar, vinegar, soy
sauce and Worcestershire sauce in a deep
bowl or pan. Add meat, turning to coat.
Cover and refrigerate at least 4 hours, turning occasionally. Barbecue, basting with
marinade, until tender and browned. Serves
4 to 6.

SWEET-SOUR RIBS

3 lbs. beef short ribs
1 c. sliced onion
1 clove garlic
1 small bay leaf
3 T. brown sugar
¼ c. raisins
⅛ t. pepper
1½ c. hot water
¼ c. vinegar
⅓ c. catsup
1 t. salt

Wipe short ribs with damp cloth. Cut into
individual serving pieces. Remove excess
fat. Dredge in seasoned flour and brown
well on all sides in hot fat in skillet. Remove
ribs. Sauté onion and garlic. Combine remaining ingredients; pour over ribs. Cover
and simmer 2 to 2½ hours or over low heat
until tender. Serves 6.

BAKED HAM HASH

½ lb. boiled ham, ground
1 6-oz. can peas
5 hard-boiled eggs, chopped
1½ c. soft bread crumbs
1 T. melted butter
1 c. milk
2 T. flour
⅛ t. pepper
½ t. salt

In a buttered casserole, layer ham, peas,
eggs and bread crumbs. Melt butter in a
saucepan. Stir in flour. Gradually add milk,
stirring constantly. Cook over medium heat,
stirring constantly, until thickened. Add
salt and pepper. Pour over casserole. Serves
4 to 6.

PIGSPAGOOT

2 T. shortening
2 lbs. pork, cubed
1 stalk celery, chopped
1 27-oz. can tomatoes
1 9-oz. pkg. spaghetti, cooked
1 6-oz. can mushrooms, drained
1 8-oz. can lima beans
1 3-oz. jar stuffed olives and liquid

Slightly brown pork in shortening. Salt very
lightly. Sauté celery in 1 tablespoon shortening. Add to browned pork. Mix in tomatoes. Simmer until meat is tender. Add
cooked spaghetti, mushrooms, lima beans,
olives and liquid. Heat through; serve hot.
Serves 4 to 6.

HORSERADISH MOLD
FOR COLD MEAT

1 3-oz. pkg. lime gelatin
1 c. boiling water
1 c. cold water
¾ c. grated horseradish
1 c. shredded cabbage

Dissolve gelatin in boiling water; add cold
water. Stir in horseradish and cabbage. Pour
into tiny individual molds and chill until
firm. Serve in lettuce nests as a garnish for a
platter of cold meat.

34

Pictured opposite
Sweet-Sour Ribs
(page 34)

NEW ENGLAND BOILED DINNER

2 lbs. ham hocks
6 small beets
3 small turnips
3 carrots
1 t. salt
6 small onions
2 c. shredded cabbage
3 small parsnips
3 small potatoes
½ t. pepper

Wash ham hocks and put in a stewing kettle with enough water to cover. Simmer for 1 hour. Add vegetables in serving sized portions and seasonings. Cover and cook 30 minutes more or until vegetables and meat are tender. Place ham hocks in middle of platter and arrange vegetables around edge. Serves 4 to 6.

STUFFED FLANK STEAK

2 lbs. flank steak
1½ t. salt
1 onion, chopped
2 apples, sliced
6 or 8 prunes
Strips of fat salt pork
2 T. shortening
3 T. flour
½ t. pepper
1 c. cream
Toothpicks

Pound meat; salt. Sprinkle evenly with onions, apples, and prunes and roll tightly. Tie or fasten with toothpicks. Insert strips of pork. Sear on all sides in hot shortening. Cover and simmer, basting with the stock. Cook for 2 hours. Remove meat; add flour to liquid in pan. Add cream and pepper. Simmer until thick. Pour over meat. Serves 4 to 6.

LIVER LOAF

1 lb. ground liver
¼ lb. ground pork
¼ lb. ground beef
2 t. salt
¼ t. nutmeg
4 T. chopped onion
2 T. shortening
2 eggs
2 c. thin cream
¼ t. cinnamon
1 t. pepper
2 c. flour, sifted

Combine all meats, salt and nutmeg; mix well. Sauté onion in shortening until tender. Add to ground meat with eggs. Blend in remaining ingredients. Put mixture in a well-greased loaf pan. Set in a pan with hot water 1-inch deep. Cover loaf pan with foil. Bake in a 350° oven for 1 hour. Uncover and bake 1 additional hour. Serve hot or cold. Serves 8 to 10.

CREAMED CHIPPED BEEF

¼ lb. dried beef
2 T. minced onion
1 4-oz. can mushrooms
¼ c. butter
3 T. flour
1 c. milk
1 c. shredded Cheddar cheese
1 t. salt
⅛ t. pepper
1 c. sour cream

Cut dried beef in strips. Sauté beef, onion and drained mushrooms in butter. Cook over low heat until onions are transparent. Blend in flour. Add milk, stirring constantly. Cook until sauce is thick and smooth. Add cheese, sour cream, salt and pepper. Heat to serving temperature. Serve in popovers, on buttered toast triangles, toasted English muffins, rice or buttered noodles. Garnish with additional cheese, if desired. Serves 5 to 6.

SPANISH RICE

1 lb. ground beef
2 T. vegetable oil
1 green pepper, chopped
1 onion, chopped
1 1-lb. can tomatoes
3 T. parsley
1 c. diced celery
1 c. raw rice
1 c. water
½ t. salt
¼ t. pepper
½ t. chili pepper

Brown ground beef in oil. Add pepper and onion and cook until onion is transparent. Add remaining ingredients, mixing well. Pour mixture into a greased 1½-quart casserole. Bake in a 350° oven for 45 minutes. Serves 4.

SATURDAY NOODLE BAKE

1 lb. ground beef
½ lb. ground pork
2 T. butter or margarine
⅔ c. chopped onion
2 10¾-oz. cans condensed tomato soup
1 3-oz. pkg. cream cheese
2 T. sugar
¼ t. pepper
1 t. salt
1½ T. Worcestershire sauce
2 c. wide noodles
1 c. crushed cornflakes
½ c. melted butter or margarine

Combine meats and brown lightly in butter. Add onion and cook until tender, but not brown. Add soup, cheese, sugar, Worcestershire sauce and seasonings. Simmer for 15 minutes. Cook noodles in boiling water until tender; drain. Place noodles in a 11 x 7 x 1-inch buttered baking dish; pour sauce over noodles. Mix cornflakes with melted butter; sprinkle over the top. Bake in a 350° oven for 20 minutes or until heated through. Serves 8.

PORK ROAST

4 to 5-lb. fresh pork shoulder
½ t. pepper
1 t. salt
¼ c. flour
6 potatoes, quartered
6 medium onions, quartered
6 carrots, halved

Place pork shoulder, fat side up, in a roasting pan. Sprinkle with salt and pepper. Sprinkle flour on fat part of roast. Roast in a 350° oven for 1½ hours. Prepare vegetables and place around meat. Bake an additional 45 minutes or until vegetables are tender and pork is well done. Serves 6 to 8.

PORK, SAUERKRAUT AND DUMPLINGS

3 or 4 pork shanks *or* 3 lbs. meaty spareribs
1 large onion, chopped
1 T. caraway seed
1 t. salt
½ t. pepper
1½ lbs. sauerkraut

Wash pork. Place in a large pot; cover with water. Bring to a boil and simmer for about 15 minutes. Add onion, caraway seed, salt and pepper. Simmer for 60 minutes. Rinse sauerkraut; add to the meat. Bring to a boil and add dumplings. Cover tightly and boil an additional 30 minutes.

Potato Dumplings

1 egg, slightly beaten
½ c. flour
4 large potatoes, peeled and grated
½ t. salt

Drain excess water from grated potatoes by placing on cloth and squeezing out excess water. Place potatoes in a bowl and add egg, salt and flour; mix thoroughly. Drop by spoonfuls on top of pork and sauerkraut mixture. Simmer about 30 minutes. Serves 4 to 6.

STEAK AND KIDNEY PIE

1 lb. round steak
1 beef kidney
¼ c. flour
⅛ t. pepper
1 t. salt
3 T. shortening
1 onion, chopped
¼ c. pimiento, chopped
2 T. Worcestershire sauce
¼ t. thyme
1½ c. water
   Pastry for 1 pie

Cut round steak in ¾ to 1-inch cubes. Remove tubes and fat from kidney. Cut in ¾ to 1-inch cubes. Combine flour, salt and pepper. Dredge steak and kidney cubes in flour, reserving any extra flour. Brown meat in shortening. Remove meat from skillet. Add onion to drippings in skillet and sauté over low heat until transparent. Drain grease. Add pimiento, Worcestershire sauce, thyme and water. Bring to a boil. Stir in browned meat cubes and any remaining seasoned flour. Make crust for pie. Roll out and line pie pan. Roll out top crust, cutting design for steam to escape. Turn meat mixture into crust in pie pan. Moisten edges. Cover with top crust. Seal top crust to edge and flute edges. Paint top with milk. Bake in a 325° oven for 1½ hrs. Makes 6 servings.

SAUERKRAUT CASSEROLE

2 lbs. sauerkraut
½ c. diced smoked sausage
1 large carrot, diced
1 onion, chopped
12 peppercorns
1 c. dry white wine
2 c. diced smoked ham
½ c. diced bacon
1 large apple, diced
1 large potato, pared and grated
1 c. stock or water

Drain sauerkraut. Combine all ingredients and pour in a buttered 2-quart casserole. Cover tightly and bake in a 350° oven for 1½ to 2 hours. It should be fairly dry. Serves 6.

TUNA-POTATO CHIP CASSEROLE

2 c. tuna, flaked
2 T. butter
1 c. sliced fresh mushrooms
½ green pepper, diced
1 t. minced onion
½ c. sliced stuffed olives
1 3-oz. bag potato chips
2 c. White Sauce

Melt butter in skillet. Sauté mushrooms, pepper and onion over low heat for 5 minutes. In a greased casserole, lightly combine all ingredients. Top with crushed potato chips. Bake in a 375° oven for 30 minutes. Serves 4.

WHITE SAUCE

2 T. butter
2 T. flour
2 c. milk

Melt butter; stir in flour. Slowly add milk, blending until smooth. Cook slowly until thickened, stirring constantly.

HUNGARIAN VEAL CUTLET

1 veal steak, 1½-inch thick
1 c. soft bread crumbs
1 egg, slightly beaten
1 T. water
1 clove garlic
¼ c. shortening
1 t. paprika
2 c. sour cream

Cut veal into six serving-size pieces. Dip into crumbs, in egg that has been beaten with water, and again into crumbs. Rub frying pan with garlic; melt shortening. Brown breaded veal quickly on both sides. Add paprika to sour cream. Pour over veal. Cover; and bake in a 325° oven for 1½ hours or until tender. Uncover for the last 15 minutes to brown. Serves 6.

Pictured opposite
Ingredients for
Sauerkraut Casserole
(page 38)

PORK CHOPS
SPANISH STYLE

6 pork chops *or* pork steaks
Pepper
Salt
2 T. shortening
2 16-oz. cans stewed tomatoes
1 c. uncooked rice
2 T. butter
1 t. salt

Sprinkle meat with salt and pepper. Brown meat in hot shortening. Drain. Preheat oven to 350°. In a 1½-quart greased baking dish, combine tomatoes with liquid, rice, butter and 1 teaspoon salt. Arrange meat over rice. Bake for 1 hour or until meat is tender. Serves 4.

MEATBALLS WITH SAUERKRAUT

1 lb. ground beef
1 egg
¼ c. coarse bread crumbs
½ t. salt
¼ t. pepper
1 c. catsup
1 c. water
½ c. gingersnap crumbs
¼ c. brown sugar, firmly packed
½ t. salt
1 8-oz. can sauerkraut

Mix together meat, egg, bread crumbs, salt and pepper. Shape into 1-inch balls. Simmer catsup, water and cookie crumbs for 5 minutes. Add brown sugar, salt and sauerkraut. Heat to boiling; add meatballs. Lower heat and simmer for 45 minutes. Serves 4 to 6.

ENGLISH BEEF STEW

1½ lbs. round steak, cubed
⅛ t. pepper
½ t. salt
3 T. shortening
2 medium onions, sliced
2 c. boiling water
2 c. tomatoes
3 c. sliced potatoes
1 T. Worcestershire sauce
1 c. sliced carrots
3 T. flour
¼ c. water
Pastry or biscuits for topping

Season meat with salt and pepper and roll in flour. Brown in shortening. Add onions and boiling water. Simmer for ½ hour. Add tomatoes, potatoes, Worcestershire sauce and carrots. Simmer over low heat until meat and vegetables are tender. Remove meat and vegetables to a casserole and thicken stock with flour mixed with water. Pour thickened stock over meat and vegetables. Cover with biscuits. Bake in a 425° oven for 20 to 25 minutes. Serve hot. Serves 6.

FRANKY NOODLE

1 lb. frankfurters
1 onion, chopped
½ green pepper, chopped
3 T. margarine
1½ c. tomato juice
¾ c. water
1 T. sugar
2 T. flour
3 c. cooked noodles

Cut frankfurters into 1-inch pieces. Sauté franks, onion and green pepper in margarine. Add tomato juice, water, flour and sugar. Stir until thickened. Simmer slowly for 20 minutes; serve hot over noodles. Serve with salad and rolls. Serves 4.

PORK BIRDS

1 onion, chopped
½ c. chopped celery
1 T. shortening
1 t. sage
2 c. dry bread cubes
2 bouillon cubes
½ to ¾ c. hot water or enough to moisten
   bread
6 boneless pork steaks
2 T. shortening

Brown onion and celery in shortening. Add sage, onion and celery to bread cubes. Dissolve bouillon cubes in hot water and pour over bread mixture. Stir with a fork until moistened. Place a heaping tablespoon of stuffing in middle of pork steak. Roll up and fasten with toothpicks. Brown each steak in additional shortening until all sides are browned. Place in a casserole or baking dish; add ¾ cup water to bottom of pan. Cover and bake in a 350° oven 1½ hours. Serves 6.

FRANKFURTER SPAGHETTI

⅓ c. chopped onion
¼ c. shortening
3 T. flour
¼ t. oregano
½ t. salt
¼ t. pepper
¾ c. water
1 c. evaporated milk
1 t. Worcestershire sauce
1 c. grated American cheese
1 lb. wieners, cut up
1½ c. cooked spaghetti

Sauté onion in shortening until tender. Remove from heat and stir in flour, oregano, salt and pepper. Heat until thick; gradually add water, milk, Worcestershire sauce and cheese. Stir over low heat until cheese melts. Add wieners and spaghetti. Place in 1½-quart greased baking dish. Bake in a 350° oven for 30 minutes. Serves 4 to 6.

QUICK CHILI MAC

1 c. macaroni
1 green pepper, chopped
1 large onion, chopped
2 T. margarine
1 lb. ground beef
1 10¾-oz. can condensed tomato soup
1 1-lb. can kidney beans
½ t. salt
½ t. chili powder

Boil macaroni as directed on package. Drain and set aside. Sauté green pepper and onion in margarine until transparent. Add ground beef and brown. Add tomato soup, kidney beans, salt and chili powder. Simmer over low heat for 20 minutes. Add macaroni and heat through. Serves 4.

THRIFTY TUNA CASSEROLE

1 10¾-oz. can condensed cream of
   mushroom soup
½ c. milk
1 7-oz. can tuna, drained and flaked
1¾ c. potato chips, crushed
1 c. canned peas, drained

Empty soup into small bowl. Add milk and mix. Add tuna, crushed potato chips and peas. Stir well. Turn into a greased 1½-quart casserole. Sprinkle top with crushed potato chips. Bake in a 375° oven for 25 minutes. Serves 4.

VEAL SCALLOPINI

1 c. mushrooms
¼ c. olive oil or vegetable oil
¾ c. flour
2 lbs. veal steak, cut thin
½ t. pepper
1 t. salt
1½ c. white wine

Sauté mushrooms in hot oil. Remove and set aside. Flour meat lightly; brown in hot oil. Add mushrooms, salt, pepper and wine. Cover and simmer 20 minutes. Serves 6.

Quick Breads and Yeast Breads

CRANBERRY NUT LOAF

2 c. flour
1½ t. baking powder
1 t. salt
½ t. baking soda
1 egg
1 c. sugar
¾ c. orange juice
3 T. vegetable oil
1½ c. cranberries, chopped
1 c. chopped nuts

Sift together flour, baking powder, salt and soda. Put egg, sugar, orange juice and oil in blender. Blend only until mixed. Add cranberries and nuts; blend. Add dry ingredients and stir until barely moistened. Turn into a greased 9 x 5 x 3-inch loaf pan. Bake in a 350° oven for 45 minutes or until a tester inserted into the middle comes out clean. Turn out of pan onto a wire rack and cool before slicing.

BANANA BREAD

1 c. sugar
½ c. butter or margarine
1 t. baking soda
1 T. sour milk or orange juice
2 eggs, well beaten
3 mashed, ripe bananas
2 c. flour
¼ c. chopped nuts

Cream together butter and sugar. Stir soda into sour milk or orange juice. Add eggs, bananas, soda mixture and flour, beating thoroughly. Stir in nuts. Pour into a buttered loaf pan. Bake in a 350° oven for 1 hour. Cool before slicing. Freezes well. Makes 1 loaf.

CLUSTER COFFEE CAKE

2 pkgs. dry yeast
¼ c. warm water
1¼ c. milk, scalded and cooled to lukewarm
3½ to 4 c. flour
2 eggs, well beaten
½ c. sugar
½ c. melted butter and margarine
1 t. salt
2 T. grated orange rind
¾ c. sugar
¾ c. pecans, finely chopped

Soften yeast in water for 5 minutes. Add milk and 1 cup of the flour, beating well. Let mixture stand for 20 minutes or until light and bubbly. Blend beaten eggs, ½ cup sugar, melted butter and salt. Add to yeast mixture; mix well. Work in remaining flour and 1 tablespoon orange rind. Knead on floured board until dough is smooth and elastic. Place in a greased bowl and let rise in a warm place, until doubled in bulk. Divide dough in half; form each half into a long roll. Cut each roll into 24 pieces. Roll each piece into a ball. Mix remaining sugar and orange rind. Dip balls into melted butter, then into sugar mixed with rind, then into chopped nuts. Place in a greased tube pan, close together and in layers. Let stand in a warm place for 40 minutes. Bake in a 350° oven for 45 minutes. Turn out of pan onto a cake rack to cool. Break off pieces and butter. The coffee cake may be made in layer cake pans, if desired.

Pictured opposite
Cranberry Nut Loaf (upper shelf)
Banana Bread (lower shelf)
(page 43)

REFRIGERATOR ROLLS

1 c. milk, scalded
¼ c. sugar
1 t. salt
⅓ c. shortening *or* vegetable oil
2 pkgs. dry yeast
½ c. lukewarm water
2 eggs, beaten
5 c. sifted flour (about)

Scald milk. Add sugar, salt, shortening or oil. Stir until dissolved. Cool to lukewarm. Dissolve yeast in lukewarm water; add to milk mixture. Add eggs. Gradually add flour; mix to a smooth, soft dough. Knead on a lightly floured board until smooth and satiny. Shape into a ball and place in a greased bowl; cover with a cloth. Let rise in a warm place until doubled in bulk. (If it is not to be used immediately, dough can be set in refrigerator until needed; then let it rise until doubled in bulk.) Shape into rounds or crescents. Cover. Let rise until doubled in bulk. Bake in a 425° oven for 15 to 20 minutes. Makes 2½ dozen.

POPOVERS

1 c. flour
¼ t. salt
⅞ c. milk
1 t. melted butter or margarine
2 eggs

Sift together flour and salt. Gradually add milk to flour in a bowl. Add butter. Beat eggs well and add to batter. Beat batter for 2 minutes with mixer. Fill hot muffin pans two thirds full. Bake in a 450° oven for 14 minutes. Reduce heat to 350° and bake 20 more minutes. Serve hot. Can be filled with creamed vegetables or creamed meat.

PUMPKIN BREAD

1 c. brown sugar
½ c. sugar
1 c. cooked or canned pumpkin
½ c. vegetable oil
2 eggs, beaten
2 c. sifted flour
1 t. baking soda
½ t. salt
½ t. nutmeg
½ t. cinnamon
¼ t. ginger
1 c. raisins
½ c. chopped nuts
¼ c. water

Combine sugars, pumpkin, oil and eggs. Beat until blended. Sift together flour, soda, salt and spices. Add to pumpkin mixture and mix well. Stir in raisins, nuts and water. Spoon into a well-oiled 9 x 5 x 3-inch loaf pan. Bake in a 350° oven for 65 to 75 minutes or until a toothpick inserted into the bread comes out clean. Turn out on a wire rack to cool thoroughly before slicing.

BAKING POWDER BISCUITS

2 c. flour
1 t. salt
2 T. sugar
4 t. baking powder
2 T. shortening
½ c. milk, or enough to make a stiff dough

Sift flour, salt, sugar and baking powder into a bowl. Cut in shortening. Add milk, a little at a time, to make a stiff dough. Turn out on a floured board. Sprinkle flour over the top if sticky and pat into a circle about 1 inch thick. Cut into rounds with a biscuit cutter dipped in flour. Place in a greased pan; bake in a 400° oven for 15 to 20 minutes. Serve hot with butter and honey. *Note:* For shortcake, bake recipe in a 9-inch pie tin and split into wedges. Top with crushed berries and whipped cream.

BOSTON BROWN BREAD

1 egg
1 t. salt
2 T. sugar
1 T. shortening
1 c. sour milk
1 t. baking soda
2 T. dark molasses
2 T. white flour
1 c. raisins
1½ to 2 c. graham flour

Mix ingredients in order given. Care must be given that not too much graham flour is used as it makes the bread crumble when sliced. The dough should be a little thicker than cake batter. Bake in a greased loaf pan in a 350° oven for 50 to 60 minutes. Turn on wire rack to cool before slicing. Makes 1 loaf.

BRAN MUFFINS

1 c. whole bran
1 c. sour milk
1 c. flour
1 t. baking powder
½ t. salt
½ t. baking soda
½ t. cinnamon
¼ c. sugar
2 T. shortening
1 egg, well beaten

Pour milk over bran and set aside. Sift together flour, baking powder, salt, soda, cinnamon and sugar. Set aside. In a large bowl, beat shortening and egg; add bran mixture, mixing thoroughly. Add dry ingredients, stirring only until moistened. Fill muffin cups two-thirds full. Bake in a 400° oven for 20 to 25 minutes.

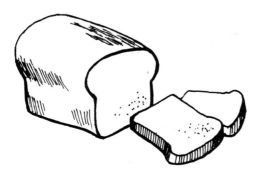

CHEESE BLINTZES

2 eggs
½ t. salt
1 c. water
1 c. sifted flour
¾ lb. cottage cheese
2 T. melted butter
2 T. light cream
⅛ t. salt
Butter for frying

Put 1 egg, salt, water and flour in blender container. Cover and process at mix until smooth. Pour 2 tablespoons of the batter onto a hot griddle. Fry on one side only until lightly browned, using low heat. Remove each pancake onto a clean cloth, cooked side up. Cool. Stir ¾ of the cottage cheese and remaining egg and butter together. Spread a little on each pancake. Fold over from both sides, then roll loosely. Sauté in hot butter. Put the cream, remaining cottage cheese and salt into blender container. Process at blend until smooth. Spoon onto hot blintzes and serve at once. Makes 4 servings.

CREAM PUFFS

¾ c. water
⅓ c. butter or margarine
¾ c. flour
⅛ t. salt
3 eggs

In a small saucepan combine water and butter and bring to a boil over medium heat. Remove from heat and beat in flour and salt, all at once. Over low heat, stir until mixture forms a ball and leaves the sides of the pan. Remove from heat. Add eggs all at once. Beat until smooth and satiny looking. Place dough by large spoonfuls on an ungreased cookie sheet. Bake in a 400° oven for 40 minutes without opening door. Remove from oven and cool in a draft-free place. To serve, cut tops from puffs and take out doughy substance in the middle of each puff and discard. Fill puff with cold vanilla pudding or ice cream. Place tops back on. Can be frosted with chocolate frosting.

DOUGHNUT DROPS

2 c. sifted flour
⅓ c. sugar
3 t. baking powder
½ t. salt
1 t. nutmeg
1 egg, slightly beaten
¾ c. milk
3 T. vegetable oil
Oil for frying
Confectioners' sugar or cinnamon and
sugar mixture

Sift together dry ingredients. Add egg, milk and oil; stir until smooth. Heat 1 inch oil to 365°. Drop dough by teaspoons into hot oil. Turn after a few seconds and fry until browned on both sides, turning once more. Remove with slotted spoon. Drain on paper towels over a pan. Roll in sugar and serve warm. Makes about 3 dozen.

RAISED DOUGHNUTS

½ c. warm water
2 pkgs. dry yeast
½ c. shortening
1½ c. warm milk
½ c. sugar
2 eggs
6 to 6½ c. flour

Dissolve yeast in warm water. Heat shortening, milk and sugar until shortening melts. Remove from heat. Cool slightly; then stir in eggs. Stir in yeast mixture. Add 4 cups flour, mixing well. Add more flour as needed to make a soft dough. Knead until smooth and satiny. Place in a greased bowl and let rise in a warm place for 1 hour and 15 minutes. Punch down. Let rise 55 more minutes. Roll out on floured board to about a ¼-inch thickness. Cut with a doughnut cutter. Let rise for 30 minutes. Deep fry in hot grease at 400° until light brown. Turn to brown other side. Drain on paper towels. Sprinkle with confectioners' sugar, granulated sugar or frost.

POTATO BREAD

3 or 4 large potatoes
2 pkgs. dry yeast
¼ c. warm water
½ c. sugar
2 T. salt
½ c. melted shortening
4 c. scalded milk, cooled
4 to 6 c. flour or more

Dissolve yeast in warm water. Peel and cook potatoes. Drain and save potato water. Mash potatoes until fluffy. Add potato water, sugar, salt, yeast, shortening and milk. Add enough flour to make a thick sponge. Let set overnight in a warm place. In the morning, add enough flour to make a dough that isn't sticky. Make into loaves, biscuits or rolls. Let rise about 1 hour. Bake in a 350° oven 30 minutes for rolls and biscuits, about 1 hour for loaves. Remove from pans and wipe tops with butter, then cover with cloth to soften crust.

POTATO PANCAKES

2 eggs
½ small onion
½ t. salt
⅛ t. pepper
2 T. flour
¼ t. baking powder
3 c. cubed raw potatoes

Put eggs, onion, salt, pepper, flour, baking powder and ½ cup of the potato cubes into blender container. Process at grate until potatoes have gone through the blades. Stop blender and add remaining potatoes. Cover and process at chop just until all potato cubes have passed through the blades. Use a rubber spatula to help guide potatoes into the blades. Do not overblend. Pour onto a hot, well-greased griddle. Cook until golden brown. Drain on absorbent paper. Yield 12 pancakes. Serve hot with applesauce.

Note: Potatoes can be raw grated to make 1 cup. Drain well and use in above recipe.

Cakes and Frostings

BRANDIED FRUIT CAKE

3 c. sifted flour
1 t. salt
1 t. baking soda
1 t. nutmeg
1 t. cinnamon
¾ c. shortening
½ c. honey
½ c. brown sugar, firmly packed
2 eggs
½ c. brandy
1 lb. mixed candied fruit, diced
1 c. whole glacé cherries
1 c. light raisins
1 c. broken walnuts

Sift flour with salt, soda, nutmeg and cinnamon. Cream shortening, honey and sugar until fluffy. Add eggs, one at a time, beating well after each. Stir in brandy, fruits and nuts. Gradually add dry ingredients. Beat well with a spoon until well blended. Spoon into a greased and floured 9-inch tube pan. Bake in a 300° oven for 2½ hours or until a toothpick inserted in center comes out clean. Cool in pan for 15 minutes. Remove to rack to finish cooling. Wrap in foil and store to ripen. Once a week, open foil and sprinkle thoroughly with more brandy. Just before serving, brush with glaze and decorate with candied fruits.

COFFEE CLOUD SPONGE CAKE

1 T. instant coffee
1 c. boiling water
2 c. flour
3 t. baking powder
½ t. salt
6 eggs, separated
½ t. cream of tartar
2 c. sugar
1 t. vanilla
1 c. pecans, chopped

Dissolve instant coffee in boiling water. Set aside to cool. Sift together flour, baking powder and salt. Beat egg whites with cream of tartar. Add ½ cup of the sugar. Set aside. Beat egg yolks until blended. Add sugar and vanilla. Beat 4 to 5 minutes. Add dry ingredients, cooled coffee and egg whites. Fold in pecans. Bake in a greased and floured 10-inch tube pan or a 13 x 9 x 2-inch pan. Bake in a 350° oven for 60 to 70 minutes.

COFFEE ICING

2 T. butter, softened
2 c. confectioners' sugar
1½ t. instant coffee
2 T. milk

Mix the ingredients to a spreading consistency and spread on cake.

FRUIT CAKE GLAZE

2 T. brown sugar
1 T. light corn syrup
2 T. water

Combine ingredients in a saucepan. Bring to a boil and boil for 2 minutes. Cool before using.

48

SALAD DRESSING CAKE

2½ c. flour
1¼ c. sugar
⅓ c. cocoa
1½ t. baking soda
½ t. salt
¾ c. salad dressing
1 c. cold water
1 t. vanilla

Sift together flour, sugar, cocoa, soda and salt. Stir in salad dressing, cold water and vanilla, mixing well. Pour into two greased and floured 9-inch cake pans. Bake in a 400° oven for 35 to 40 minutes.

CARROT CAKE

2 c. sugar
2 c. flour
2 t. baking soda
1 t. salt
3 t. cinnamon
1½ c. vegetable oil
4 eggs
3 c. grated carrot
1 c. chopped nuts (optional)
1 t. vanilla

Sift together sugar, flour, soda, salt and cinnamon. Stir in oil. Add eggs, one at a time, mixing well after each addition. Add carrots, nuts and vanilla, mixing thoroughly. Pour into a floured and greased 13 x 9 x 2-inch cake pan. Bake in a 350° oven for 30 minutes. Cool in pan. Spread with Cream Cheese Icing.

CREAM CHEESE ICING

½ c. melted butter
1 8-oz. pkg. cream cheese, softened
1 t. vanilla
1 1-lb. box confectioners' sugar

Combine butter, cream cheese and vanilla, mixing well. Gradually add confectioners' sugar, beating until smooth. Spread on cooled cake.

LIGHTNING CAKE

2 eggs
  Sweet milk
½ c. shortening
1 c. sugar
2 c. flour
2 t. baking powder
¼ t. salt
1 t. vanilla

Drop eggs in measuring cup and add enough milk to make one cup. Add to sugar and shortening in a mixing bowl. Mix well. Sift together flour, baking powder and salt. Add to batter with vanilla. Mix well. Pour into 2 greased and floured 8-inch cake pans. Bake in a 350° oven for 35 minutes or until done. Frost with favorite icing.

TAKE-ALONG CAKE

1 No. 303 can fruit cocktail
2 eggs
1½ c. sugar
2 c. flour
2 t. baking soda
2 t. baking powder
1 t. salt

Mix all ingredients together, including juice from fruit cocktail. Pour into a greased and floured 13 x 9 x 2-inch cake pan. Bake in a 350° oven for 1 hour. Frost warm cake with Coconut Icing.

COCONUT ICING

1 c. sugar
1 c. coconut
½ c. margarine
1 14½-oz. can evaporated milk
1 t. vanilla

Combine all ingredients and bring to a boil. Take fork and stab holes all over cake. Pour hot frosting over cake as soon as the cake is taken from the oven. When cool, cut and serve.

FLORENCE'S DEVIL'S FOOD

3 T. cocoa
½ c. boiling water
1 t. baking soda
1 c. sugar
½ c. shortening
2 eggs
2 c. flour
½ t. salt
½ c. sour milk
1 t. vanilla

Place cocoa in medium-size bowl; add boiling water. Stir in soda and set aside to cool. Cream sugar and shortening. Beat in eggs and mix well. Mix flour and salt and add to sugar and shortening with sour milk. Add vanilla and cocoa mixture. Spoon into a greased and floured 12 x 9-inch cake pan. Bake in a 350° oven for 35 to 40 minutes. Frost with white, caramel or chocolate icing.

PUZZLE CAKE

1½ c. flour
½ c. brown sugar, firmly packed
¾ c. softened butter

Mix together the flour, sugar and butter until crumbly. Set aside ½ cup. Spread half of the remaining mixture in an 8 x 12-inch pan and pat down. Bake in a 350° oven for 10 minutes. Remove from oven and spread on Filling. Sprinkle reserved crumbs on top. Bake for an additional 25 minutes.

FILLING

½ c. cut-up dates
1 c. shredded coconut
½ c. chopped nuts
2 egg whites
¾ c. sugar
1 t. vanilla

Combine dates, coconut and nuts. Whip egg whites until stiff and add sugar and vanilla. Fold in the date mixture.

RHUBARB CAKE

2 c. flour
2 t. baking powder
½ t. salt
½ c. sugar
1 T. butter
1 egg
½ c. milk
3 c. rhubarb, finely sliced
2 c. sugar
1 T. butter
3 T. flour
1 egg
½ t. nutmeg

Sift flour with baking powder, salt and ½ cup sugar. Stir in butter, egg and milk until dry ingredients are moistened. Spread in a buttered and floured 13 x 9 x 2-inch cake pan. Mix rhubarb, sugar, butter, flour, egg and nutmeg. Spread on top of the batter. Bake in a 350° oven for 45 minutes. Cool and serve.

EGGLESS, MILKLESS, BUTTERLESS CAKE

1 c. water
1 c. brown sugar, firmly packed
2 c. raisins
¼ t. nutmeg
⅓ c. lard or shortening
¼ t. salt
1 t. cinnamon
½ t. cloves
2 c. flour
1 t. baking soda
½ t. baking powder

Put water, brown sugar, raisins, lard, salt and spices in a saucepan and mix. Bring to a boil. Cook for 3 minutes; cool. Sift together flour, soda and baking powder. Stir into cooled mixture, mixing well. Pour into a greased loaf tin. Bake in a 350° oven for 1 hour. Frost, if desired, or serve plain.

50

Pictured opposite
Puzzle Cake
(page 50)

CHOCOLATE GLAZE

1 1-oz. square unsweetened chocolate
1 T. butter
¾ c. confectioners' sugar
½ t. salt
2 T. hot milk (about)

Melt chocolate with butter over low heat. Stir in sugar and salt. Add milk, a small amount at a time, until mixture is of glaze consistency. While glaze is still warm, pour on cake, spreading with spatula. Makes ½ cup.

CHOCOLATE POUND CAKE

1 c. butter or margarine, softened
1 t. vanilla
2¾ c. sifted cake flour
1½ t. cream of tartar
¾ t. baking soda
½ t. salt
1¾ c. sugar
¾ c. milk
3 eggs
1 egg yolk
3 squares chocolate, melted
Chocolate glaze

Cream butter and vanilla. Sift together flour, cream of tartar, soda, salt and sugar. Add dry ingredients to butter, alternating with milk. Mix until all flour is moistened. Then beat for 2 minutes at medium speed of electric mixer or 300 vigorous strokes by hand, scraping the sides of bowl. Add eggs, egg yolk and melted chocolate. Beat 1 minute longer with mixer or 150 vigorous strokes by hand. Pour batter into a 10-inch tube pan which has been buttered and lined on the bottom with waxed paper. Grease paper. Bake in a 350° oven for 65 to 70 minutes or until cake springs back when lightly pressed. Cool cake in pan for 10 minutes. Remove from pan. Cool thoroughly on rack. Glaze, if desired.
Note: This cake may also be baked in a 9 x 4 x 2-inch loaf pan for 60 to 65 minutes. Cool in pan 10 minutes before turning out to cool.

TOMATO SOUP CAKE

½ c. butter
1 c. sugar
½ t. nutmeg
½ t. cloves
½ t. salt
½ t. cinnamon
2 c. flour
2 t. baking powder
1 t. baking soda
1 c. tomato soup
1 c. dates, cut up
1 c. chopped nuts

Melt butter. Add sugar and cream well. Add spices and salt. Sift flour and baking powder together. Dissolve soda in soup and add alternately with flour to sugar mixture. Beat well. Add dates and nuts, slightly floured. Bake in two 9-inch buttered layer cake pans in a 350° oven for 45 minutes or until the cakes test done. Cool on cake rack when turned out of pans. Spread with icing.

ICING FOR TOMATO SOUP CAKE

1 3-oz. pkg. cream cheese
1½ c. confectioners' sugar
1 t. vanilla or lemon juice

Mix thoroughly and spread on cake.

BOILED CHOCOLATE FROSTING

1 c. sugar
2 T. cocoa
½ c. cream *or* evaporated milk
1 t. vanilla

Mix all ingredients in a saucepan. Boil to the soft-ball stage (234°-238° on a candy thermometer). Remove from heat and beat until thick enough to spread on the cake.

MAGIC CHOCOLATE FROSTING

1⅓ c. sweetened condensed milk
2 1-oz. squares unsweetened chocolate
⅛ t. salt
1 T. water
½ t. vanilla

Cook milk and chocolate in double boiler stirring constantly until thick. Gradually add water and salt. Cool. Stir in vanilla. Spread on cooled cake.
Note: To make a chocolate sauce, add ½ to 1 cup hot water.

CHOCOLATE FROSTING

⅔ c. softened butter or margarine
½ t. salt
6 c. sifted confectioners' sugar
1 egg yolk
3 1-oz. squares melted chocolate
½ c. milk
1 t. vanilla

Beat butter with salt and 1 cup of the sugar. Stir in egg yolk and chocolate. Gradually beat in remaining 5 cups sugar. Add milk and vanilla, beating until smooth. Frost top and sides of cake.

BOILED WHITE FROSTING

⅓ c. water
1 c. sugar
1 t. vinegar
2 egg whites
¾ t. vanilla

Boil water, sugar and vinegar to 238° on a candy thermometer, or until syrup spins a long thread when dropped from tip of spoon. Beat egg whites stiff. Gradually add syrup to egg whites, beating constantly until frosting holds its shape. Add vanilla. Use to frost one 8-inch layer cake.

CONFECTIONERS' SUGAR FROSTING

¼ c. butter or margarine
2 c. confectioners' sugar
3 T. milk (about)
¼ t. salt
¾ t. vanilla

Cream butter or margarine. Sift sugar; add gradually until of creamy consistency. Add enough milk to make mixture of spreading consistency. Add salt and vanilla. Makes enough for 2 layer cakes or 12 medium-size cupcakes.

VARIATIONS

Chocolate frosting: Add 2 tablespoons cocoa or 1 1-oz. square melted chocolate.
Mocha frosting: Add 2 tablespoons cocoa and 3 tablespoons strong coffee.
Orange frosting: Add 3 tablespoons orange juice and 1 teaspoon grated orange rind.
Caramel frosting: Add 3 tablespoons brown sugar, moistened with 3 tablespoons milk. Add ¼ cup melted butter or margarine and ½ teaspoon maple flavoring. Add enough confectioners' sugar until of spreading consistency.

BROWN SUGAR BOILED FROSTING

1½ c. brown sugar, firmly packed
⅓ c. water
2 egg whites
¼ t. salt
1 t. vanilla

Boil sugar and water to 240° on candy thermometer or until a small quantity dropped in cold water forms a medium firm ball. Beat egg whites stiff. Gradually add syrup to egg whites, beating constantly until frosting holds its shape. Add salt and vanilla. Makes enough to fill and frost one 8-inch layer cake.

Pies and Piecrusts

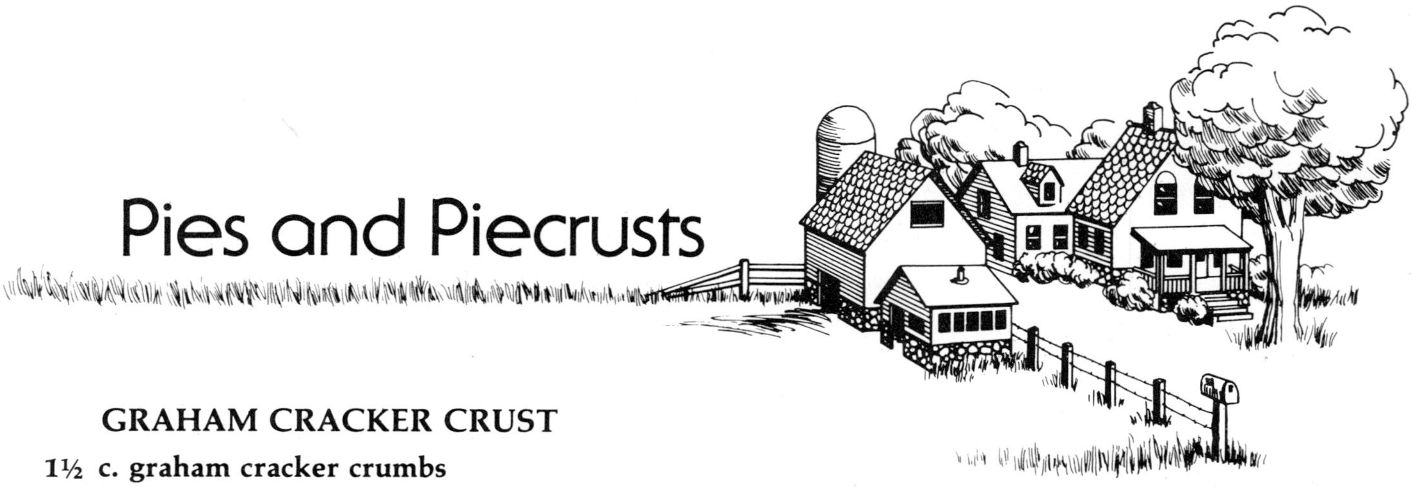

GRAHAM CRACKER CRUST

1½ c. graham cracker crumbs
2 T. sugar
¼ c. melted butter

Mix all ingredients and press in bottom and sides of a 9-inch pie pan. Can be baked 10 minutes in a 350° oven or placed in refrigerator for ½ hour to set.

PASTRY FOR TWO-CRUST PIE

1½ c. flour
½ c. shortening
½ t. salt
¼ c. water

Combine flour and salt. Cut in shortening until mixture resembles grains of rice. Add water, a little at a time, mixing to a workable dough. Use more water if needed. Divide dough in half; roll out top and bottom half of crust on a floured board.

MOLASSES PECAN PIE

3 eggs, slightly beaten
¾ c. unsulphured molasses
¾ c. light corn syrup
2 T. melted butter or margarine
⅛ t. salt
1 t. vanilla
1 T. flour
1 c. pecans
1 unbaked 8-inch pastry shell

Combine the eggs, molasses, corn syrup, butter, salt and vanilla; mix well. Mix the flour with a small amount of egg mixture. Stir into remaining egg mixture. Add pecans. Turn into pastry shell. Bake in a 325° oven for 60 minutes or until done. Serve cold.

PUMPKIN CHEESECAKE PIE

15 graham crackers
2 T. brown sugar
¼ c. melted butter or margarine
8 oz. cottage cheese
1 c. canned pumpkin
2 egg yolks
¾ c. sugar
½ t. nutmeg
3 T. cornstarch
¾ c. milk
1 T. grated lemon rind
2 T. lemon juice
1 t. lemon extract
2 egg whites

Roll graham crackers into fine crumbs. Combine with brown sugar and melted butter or margarine. Set aside ¼ cup of the crumb mixture. Press remaining crumb mixture into a deep 9-inch pie pan. Bake in a 350° oven for 9 minutes. Cool. Press cottage cheese through a fine sieve. Combine with pumpkin, egg yolks, sugar and nutmeg. Mix well. Combine cornstarch with some of the milk, blending to a thin paste. Add remaining milk. Combine with cheese mixture. Add lemon rind, juice and extract. Beat egg whites stiff and fold into the pumpkin mixture. Spoon into crust; sprinkle top with reserved crumbs. Bake in a 350° oven for 30 minutes, or until a knife inserted comes out clean. Allow pie to cool before serving. Serves 6 to 8.

Pictured opposite
Molasses Pecan Pie
(page 54)

GRASSHOPPER PIE

1½ c. chocolate wafer crumbs
¼ c. melted butter
25 large marshmallows
⅔ c. cream
1 c. heavy cream, whipped
4 T. green creme de menthe
4 T. white creme de cacao

Reserve 2 tablespoons crumbs for topping. Mix remaining crumbs and butter. Press evenly on bottom and sides of a 9-inch pie pan. Chill in refrigerator while preparing filling. Combine marshmallows and cream. Heat slowly until marshmallows have melted; cool. Fold in liqueurs and whipped cream. Pour into chilled crust. Sprinkle remaining crumbs over top. Freeze until firm. Makes 1 pie.

KEY LIME PIE

1 baked 9-inch pastry shell
1 T. unflavored gelatin
1 c. sugar
¼ t. salt
4 eggs, separated
½ c. water
1 T. grated lime peel
  Green food color
½ c. lime juice
1 c. heavy cream, whipped

Mix gelatin, ½ cup sugar and salt in a saucepan. Beat together egg yolks and water; stir into gelatin mixture. Cook over medium heat, stirring constantly, until mixture boils. Remove from heat and stir in grated peel and lime juice. Add enough food coloring to make a pale green color. Chill, stirring occasionally, until thick. Beat egg whites until stiff peaks form. Gradually add remaining sugar. Fold gelatin mixture into egg whites and fold in whipped cream. Spoon into pastry shell. Chill until firm. Spread with additional whipped cream and sprinkle additional grated lime peel around edge of pie. Serve cold.

DUTCH APPLE PIE

Pastry for single-crust, 9-inch pie
4 c. peeled, sliced tart apples
¾ c. sugar
½ t. cinnamon
¼ t. nutmeg
¾ c. flour
½ c. brown sugar, firmly packed
½ t. cinnamon
½ c. butter

Combine apples, sugar, ½ teaspoon cinnamon and nutmeg. Pour in a pastry-lined, 9-inch pie pan. Blend flour, brown sugar, cinnamon and butter by mixing with fingers to make coarse crumbs. Place on top of apple mixture in pie pan. Bake in a 425° oven for 45 minutes. Serve with whipped topping. Serves 6 to 8.

LEMON MERINGUE PIE

1 baked 9-inch pastry shell
1 c. sugar
¼ c. flour
⅛ t. salt
¼ c. water
3 egg yolks
¾ c. water
3 T. butter or margarine
¼ c. lemon juice
2 t. grated lemon rind
3 egg whites
½ t. salt
9 T. sugar

Mix sugar, flour, salt and ¼ cup water until smooth. Beat egg yolks, add with ¾ cup water. Cook over hot water, stirring constantly, until thick. Cover and cook for 10 minutes. Add butter or margarine, lemon juice and rind. Pour into pastry shell. Beat egg whites until stiff but not dry. Add salt. Gradually add sugar, beating constantly. Swirl on pie filling. Bake in a 325° oven for 20 minutes, until lightly browned.

MOTHER'S OLD-FASHIONED APPLE PIE

4 to 5 c. peeled and sliced tart apples
1½ c. sugar
⅓ c. flour
1 t. cinnamon
¼ c. water
1 T. butter
Pastry for double-crust, 9-inch pie

Prepare pastry. Roll out half and line pan. Combine sugar, flour and cinnamon in a bowl; stir in water. Add apples, mixing to coat thoroughly. Pour into pan and dot with butter. Roll out top crust; cut a design in the center to allow steam to escape. Place top crust on pie, pressing around the edge to seal. Brush pastry with milk and sprinkle with sugar. Bake in a 350° oven 45 to 60 minutes or until apples are tender and crust is browned.

CHESS PIE

½ c. butter
1½ c. sugar
3 eggs
1 t. vanilla
1 unbaked 9-inch pie shell

Cream together butter and sugar until mixture is light and fluffy. Add eggs, one at a time, beating well after each addition. Add vanilla and blend. Pour into unbaked pie shell. Bake in a 350° oven for 35 to 40 minutes or until filling has set. Remove from oven and cool on wire rack.

RHUBARB PIE

Pastry for 9-inch 2-crust pie
3 c. rhubarb, cut fine
1½ c. sugar
1 egg
¼ c. flour
½ t. cinnamon
1 T. butter

Place rhubarb in large bowl. Add sugar, egg, flour and cinnamon. Mix well. Spoon into pastry lined pie pan. Dot with butter. Place top crust on pie; crimp edges. Brush with milk and sprinkle with sugar. Bake in a 350° oven 45 to 50 minutes or until rhubarb is done and crust is brown. Makes 1 pie.

PUMPKIN PIE

1 c. canned pumpkin
1 c. brown sugar, firmly packed
2 eggs, beaten
¼ t. ginger
½ t. nutmeg
1 t. cinnamon
1 T. butter, melted
1 c. milk
1 unbaked 9-inch pie crust

Mix all ingredients until well blended. Pour into crust. Bake in a 350° oven for 60 minutes or until done in center. Serve with whipped cream or whipped topping mix.

HERSHEY PIE

1 10-inch graham cracker crust
20 marshmallows
6 small Hershey bars
½ c. milk
1 c. whipped cream

Combine marshmallows, Hershey bars, and milk in top of double boiler. Heat until chocolate and marshmallows melt. Cool, then fold in whipped cream. Pour mixture into pie crust; sprinkle a few graham cracker crumbs on top. Refrigerate. Serve cold.

Candies

CARAMEL CORN

- 1 c. butter
- ½ c. white corn syrup
- 2 c. brown sugar, firmly packed
- 1 t. salt
- 1 t. butter flavoring
- 1 t. burnt sugar flavoring
- ½ t. baking soda
- 8 qts. popped corn
- 2 c. peanuts

Melt butter, syrup, brown sugar and salt in a saucepan. Boil for 5 minutes. Add flavorings and soda. Put popped corn and peanuts in a large pan. Pour syrup over popcorn and nuts, stirring well to coat each kernel. Bake for 1 hour in a 250° oven. Stir every 10 or 15 minutes. Remove from oven and cool, stirring often.

DIVINITY

- 5 egg whites, at room temperature
- ¼ t. salt
- 5 c. sugar
- 1 c. white corn syrup
- 2 c. water

Add salt to egg whites and beat until stiff and dry. Set aside. Combine sugar, syrup and water. Cook until it forms a hard ball in cold water (265° to 270° on a candy thermometer). Slowly add syrup to egg whites, beating all the time. Do not scrape sides of pan when pouring. Beat until mixture holds its shape. Pour into a buttered 13 x 9 x 2-inch pan. After it cools, cut into squares; or drop by teaspoons onto waxed paper to cool. *Note:* One cup chopped nuts, chopped candied fruit or shredded coconut may be added just before beating.

MILLION-DOLLAR FUDGE

- 4½ c. sugar
- Pinch salt
- 2 T. butter
- 1 13-oz. can evaporated milk
- 1 12-oz. pkg. chocolate chips
- 1 12-oz. bar German sweet chocolate
- 2 8-oz. jars marshmallow creme
- 2 c. nut pieces

Combine sugar, salt, butter and milk. Boil for 6 minutes. Remove from heat and add chocolate chips, German chocolate, marshmallow creme and nuts. Beat until all chocolate is melted. Pour into a buttered 13 x 9 x 2-inch pan. Let stand a few hours before cutting. Store in a tin box with waxed paper between layers.

FAIRY FOOD

- 1 c. sugar
- 1 c. white corn syrup
- 1 T. vinegar
- 1½ T. baking soda
- 1 6-oz. pkg. semisweet chocolate chips

Combine sugar, syrup and vinegar in a 3-quart saucepan. Cook to a hard-crack stage (300°). Turn off heat and add soda, mixing quickly. Pour immediately into a greased 11 x 7 x 1½-inch pan. Cool. Then invert on a tray. Spread with melted chocolate. Break into chunks. Yields about 1 pound.

Pictured opposite
Divinity
(page 59)

Cookies

BANANA COOKIES

¾ c. shortening
1 c. sugar
1 egg
1 t. vanilla
1½ c. flour
½ t. baking soda
1 t. salt
¼ t. nutmeg
¾ t. cinnamon
1 c. mashed banana
1 c. rolled oats
½ c. chopped nuts

Cream shortening and sugar. Add egg and vanilla. Sift flour, soda, salt and spices. Stir into sugar mixture. Add banana, oats and nuts. Drop by teaspoons onto a greased cookie sheet. Bake in a 400° oven for 12 minutes. Yields 3½ dozen cookies.

WASHBOARD COOKIES

1 c. sugar
1 c. brown sugar, firmly packed
1 c. shortening
2 eggs, well beaten
3¼ c. flour, sifted
2 t. baking soda
2 t. cream of tartar
1 t. vanilla
1 t. lemon extract
1 c. coconut
1 c. raisins
½ c. chopped nuts

Cream together sugars and shortening until smooth. Add eggs and mix well. Sift together flour, soda and cream of tartar. Set aside a small part in which to dredge the raisins, nuts and coconut. Add dry ingredients to batter and mix. Add flavorings, raisins, nuts and coconut. Mix well. Shape dough into small balls. Place on a greased cookie sheet and press flat with a fork. Bake in a 350° oven about 12 minutes.

MARSHMALLOW FUDGE SQUARES

½ c. shortening
¾ c. sugar
¾ c. flour
¼ t. baking powder
¼ t. salt
2 T. cocoa
1 t. vanilla
½ c. chopped nuts, if desired
12 marshmallows, cut in halves

Cream shortening with sugar. Sift together flour, baking powder, salt and cocoa. Add to creamed mixture. Stir in vanilla and chopped nuts. Spread in a 13 x 9 x 2-inch greased pan. Bake in a 350° oven for 25 to 30 minutes. Remove from oven and arrange the marshmallow halves evenly over the top. Turn off oven; return pan to oven for 3 minutes. Make Topping and spread on top. Cool and cut into squares.

TOPPING

½ c. brown sugar, firmly packed
⅓ c. water
2 1-oz. squares chocolate
3 T. butter
1 t. vanilla
1½ c. confectioners' sugar

Boil brown sugar, water and chocolate for 3 minutes in a saucepan. Remove from heat and stir in butter, vanilla and sugar.

DROP DATE COOKIES

3 c. flour
1 t. salt
1 t. cinnamon
1 t. cloves
2 t. baking powder
¼ t. baking soda
1 c. lard or shortening
1½ c. brown sugar, firmly packed
3 eggs
1 T. cold water
1 c. dates, cut up

Sift together flour, salt, baking powder, cinnamon, cloves and baking soda. Set aside. Cream shortening and sugar. Beat in eggs and water. Gradually add dry ingredients, beating well after each addition. Stir in dates. Drop by teaspoonfuls onto greased baking sheets. Bake in a 350° oven for 20 minutes, or until done. Cool on a wire rack. Makes 6 dozen.

ICEBOX COOKIES

3 c. flour
½ t. salt
1½ t. baking soda
1½ t. cream of tartar
1½ c. brown sugar, firmly packed
½ c. sugar
½ c. lard or shortening
2 eggs
1½ t. vanilla
1 c. chopped nuts

Sift flour with salt, soda and cream of tartar. Set aside. Cream sugars and shortening; add eggs. Gradually add dry ingredients, beating well after each addition. Stir in vanilla and nuts; mixture will be stiff. Form into several rolls and wrap in waxed paper. Refrigerate overnight. Slice ½ inch thick and place on greased cookie sheets. Bake in a 350° oven for 10 minutes or until light brown around the edges.

CHRISTMAS COOKIES

1 c. butter
1 c. sugar
3 eggs
1 t. vanilla
3 c. flour
2 t. cream of tartar
1 t. baking soda
1 t. nutmeg
Colored sugar

Cream butter and sugar; mix well. Add beaten eggs and flavoring. Sift together flour, cream of tartar, soda and nutmeg. Mix with sugar mixture, stirring well. Roll out on floured board. Cut with assorted Christmas cookie cutters. Sprinkle with colored sugar. Bake in a 425° oven for 10 minutes.
Note: If dough is refrigerated overnight it is easier to handle and roll.

OLD-FASHIONED SUGAR COOKIES

½ c. butter or margarine
1 c. sugar
1 egg *or* 2 egg yolks, beaten
1 T. milk
½ t. vanilla
1½ c. sifted flour
1 t. baking powder
¼ t. salt

Cream butter or margarine. Beat in sugar, egg or egg yolks, milk and vanilla. Sift together flour, baking powder and salt; add to butter mixture. Mix well. Cover and refrigerate 3 to 4 hours or until dough is firm. Heat oven to 375°. Roll dough into small balls about ¾-inch in diameter. Place 2 inches apart on lightly greased cookie sheets. Lightly flatten tops with the bottom of a glass that has been dipped in sugar. Bake 8 to 10 minutes or until cookies are lightly browned around the edges. Transfer to wire racks. Cool. If desired, lightly brush warm cookies with melted butter or margarine and dust with confectioners' sugar. Makes 3 dozen.

Desserts

RHUBARB DESSERT

CRUST

2 c. flour
¼ t. salt
2 egg yolks
2 T. sugar
1 c. butter or margarine

Mix ingredients together and spread in a 13 x 9 x 2-inch pan. Bake in a 350° oven for 10 to 15 minutes.

FILLING

4 c. rhubarb, chopped
4 egg yolks, beaten
2 c. sugar
2 T. flour

Mix the above ingredients and spread over the crust. Bake in a 350° oven for 30 minutes.

TOPPING

6 egg whites
1 c. sugar
½ t. cinnamon

Beat egg whites until stiff. Gradually add sugar and cinnamon. Spread on top of rhubarb. Bake in a 350° oven for 30 minutes. Serves 8 to 10.

VANILLA SAUCE

1 c. milk
3 egg yolks, beaten
½ c. sugar
1 t. vanilla
3 egg whites, beaten stiff

Scald milk; remove from heat. Stir some of the milk into the egg yolks; add yolks to milk. Add sugar and cook until thick, stirring to melt. Remove from heat. Fold in beaten egg whites and vanilla. Serve, hot or cold, over pudding.

SUET PUDDING

1 lb. ground suet
4 c. flour
1 t. salt
1 c. water
2 lbs. ground beef
2 medium-size onions, chopped
1 c. finely chopped celery
1 t. salt
½ t. pepper
4 T. catsup
1 c. water

Mix suet, flour and salt in a large bowl. Mix in water to form a dough. Roll out with a rolling pin on a floured board. Place cloth on a large bowl. Put dough on top of the cloth. In a bowl mix the ground beef, onion, celery, seasonings, catsup and water. Put the mixture inside the dough. Tie up cloth and put in a kettle of water. Bring to a boil and boil for 2 hours.

APPLE BROWN BETTY

5 or 6 medium-size apples, peeled
½ c. flour
¼ c. brown sugar, firmly packed
¼ c. soft margarine or butter
½ t. cinnamon
¾ c. granola

Slice apples into 1½-quart greased casserole. In a bowl, mix flour, brown sugar, margarine or butter, cinnamon and granola. Spread the crumbs over the top of the apples. Bake in a 350° oven for 35 to 40 minutes. Serves 4.

Pictured opposite
Apple Brown Betty
(page 63)

63

Book III Index